Daniel Webster

BIOGRAPHIES IN AMERICAN FOREIGN POLICY

Series Editor: *Joseph A. Fry, University of Nevada, Las Vegas*

The Biographies in American Foreign Policy Series employs the enduring medium of biography to examine the major episodes and themes in the history of U.S. foreign relations. By viewing policy formation and implementation from the perspective of influential participants, the series humanizes and makes more accessible those decisions and events that sometimes appear abstract or distant. Particular attention is devoted to those aspects of the subject's background, personality, and intellect that most influenced his or her approach to U.S. foreign policy, and each individual's role is placed in a context that takes into account domestic affairs, national interests and policies, and international and strategic considerations.

Volumes Published

Lawrence S. Kaplan, *Thomas Jefferson: Westward the Course of Empire*
Richard H. Immerman, *John Foster Dulles: Piety, Pragmatism, and Power in U.S. Foreign Policy*
Thomas W. Zeiler, *Dean Rusk: Defending the American Mission Abroad*
Edward P. Crapol, *James G. Blaine: Architect of Empire*
David F. Schmitz, *Henry L. Stimson: The First Wise Man*
Thomas M. Leonard, *James K. Polk: A Clear and Unquestionable Destiny*
James E. Lewis, Jr., *John Quincy Adams: Policymaker for the Union*
Catherine Forslund, *Anna Chennault: Informal Diplomacy and Asian Relations*
Lawrence S. Kaplan, *Alexander Hamilton: Ambivalent Anglophile*
Andrew J. DeRoche, *Andrew Young: Civil Rights Ambassador*
Jeffrey J. Matthews, *Alanson B. Houghton: Ambassador of the New Era*
Clarence E. Wunderlin, Jr., *Robert A. Taft: Ideas, Tradition, and Party in U.S. Foreign Policy*
Howard Jablon, *David M. Shoup: A Warrior against War*
Jeff Woods, *Richard B. Russell: Southern Nationalism and American Foreign Policy*
Russell D. Buhite, *Douglas MacArthur: Statecraft and Stagecraft in America's East Asian Policy*
Christopher D. O'Sullivan, *Colin Powell: American Power and Intervention from Vietnam to Iraq*
David F. Schmitz, *Brent Scowcroft: Internationalism and Post–Vietnam War American Foreign Policy*
Christopher D. O'Sullivan, *Harry Hopkins: FDR's Envoy to Churchill and Stalin*
Donald A. Rakestraw, *Daniel Webster: Defender of Peace*

Daniel Webster

Defender of Peace

Donald A. Rakestraw

ROWMAN & LITTLEFIELD
Lanham • Boulder • New York • London

Published by Rowman & Littlefield
An imprint of The Rowman & Littlefield Publishing Group, Inc.
4501 Forbes Boulevard, Suite 200, Lanham, Maryland 20706
www.rowman.com

Unit A, Whitacre Mews, 26-34 Stannary Street, London SE11 4AB

Copyright © 2018 by The Rowman & Littlefield Publishing Group, Inc.

All rights reserved. No part of this book may be reproduced in any form or by any electronic or mechanical means, including information storage and retrieval systems, without written permission from the publisher, except by a reviewer who may quote passages in a review.

British Library Cataloguing in Publication Information Available

Library of Congress Cataloging-in-Publication Data
Names: Rakestraw, Donald A. (Donald Allen), 1952-
Title: Daniel Webster : Defender of Peace / Donald A. Rakestraw.
Description: Lanham : Rowman & Littlefield, 2018. | Series: Biographies in American foreign policy | Includes bibliographical references and index.
Identifiers: LCCN 2018016934 (print) | LCCN 2018024198 (ebook) | ISBN 9781442249950 (Electronic) | ISBN 9781442249943 (cloth : alk. paper)
Subjects: LCSH: Webster, Daniel, 1782-1852. | United States—Foreign relations—1815-1861. | United States—Politics and government—1815-1861. | Webster-Ashburton Treaty (1842 August 9) | Cabinet officers—United States—Biography. | Statesmen—United States—Biography. | Diplomats—United States—Biography. | Legislators—United States—Biography. | United States. Congress. Senate—Biography.
Classification: LCC E340.W4 (ebook) | LCC E340.W4 R25 2018 (print) | DDC 973.5092 [B]—dc23
LC record available at https://lccn.loc.gov/2018016934

∞™ The paper used in this publication meets the minimum requirements of American National Standard for Information Sciences—Permanence of Paper for Printed Library Materials, ANSI/NISO Z39.48-1992.

Printed in the United States of America

For Tom and Finlay

Contents

	Preface	ix
	Acknowledgments	xiii
Chapter 1	From the Valley to the Hill, 1782–1823	1
Chapter 2	Taking the National Stage, 1823–1839	25
Chapter 3	Taking the International Stage, 1839–1842	47
Chapter 4	From Webster-Ashburton to Wanghia, 1842–1843	75
Chapter 5	From State to the Senate and Back Again, 1843–1850	101
Chapter 6	Last Turn at the "Old High Table," 1850–1852	125
	Epilogue	155
	Chronology	161
	Notes	167
	Bibliographical Essay	191
	Index	197
	About the Author	209

Preface

> By the vigor, argumentation, and eloquence with which you uphold the Union, and that interpretation of the Constitution which makes us a Nation, you have justly earned the title of *Defender of the Constitution*. By masterly and successful negotiations, and by efforts to compose the strife concerning Oregon, you have earned another title—*Defender of Peace*.
>
> —Charles Sumner, September 1846

Few names in American history are more recognizable than that of Daniel Webster. In fact, students assigned the task of listing the prominent figures of nineteenth-century US history would most likely include Webster, although it is doubtful they could explain with any depth the reason for his appearance on such an elite list. Many students, as historian Robert Remini laments, would confuse him with Noah and credit him with the production of America's first comprehensive dictionary. Others, perhaps, would conjure an image of a fictional Daniel Webster who out-lawyered the devil before some mystical magistrate. More astute young scholars might remember him for his masterful performance in the debate with Senator Robert Y. Hayne, his pivotal role in the Bank War, his association with Henry Clay and John C. Calhoun in the so-called Great Triumvirate or for the enduring influence of his arguments before John Marshall's Supreme Court. Given a bit of prompting, a few might even remember that he was a powerful and influential Whig from Massachusetts—that he was a native son of New Hampshire notwithstanding—instrumental in reshaping the American political landscape. But the number of students to acknowledge Webster for his monumental contributions to US foreign relations as secretary of state under three presidents would be sadly wanting.

No one would deny that Webster's substantive domestic achievements assured his prominent place in American history and that his virtual embodiment of nation and union guaranteed his rank among the most significant personalities of the Jacksonian era. It can be argued, however, that his domestic résumé that garnered him the title "Defender of the Constitution" is rivaled by an equally impressive international one that yielded far-reaching results for a nation still struggling to find a respectable position among the Atlantic powers. Indeed, Webster's "masterly and successful negotiations" with Lord Ashburton justly earned him the additional title of "Defender of Peace"[1]—a title awarded for his cultivation of Anglo-American rapprochement in the 1840s but also descriptive of his general approach to US foreign relations. Webster's accomplishments in this area too often receive short shrift, falling victim to the textbook author's inclination to hold Webster to the dominant domestic narrative that ultimately saw the nation fractured. My object in the pages that follow is to shift the balance in favor of Webster's development in and impact on foreign policy and international relations.

It is common to read in introductions of books addressing iconic persons or subjects something to the effect that this topic is too complex to adequately address within the constraints of this project, leading one to wonder if the author is sincere in this assessment or conceding that he or she is unlikely to do the subject justice. On this occasion, I plead guilty to both. The more I studied Webster, the larger and more complicated he became. Most figures in American history are remembered for a singular and dominant attribute—Winfield Scott the general, Walt Whitman the poet, Thomas Edison the inventor, or Andrew Carnegie the industrialist. All may be complex in their own ways but can be identified concisely on the typical history timeline with a specific icon. Webster could elicit multiple competing icons, all accurate and each equally appropriate—Webster the constitutional and legal scholar, Webster the orator, Webster the political leader, and Webster the secretary of state. This makes Webster worthy of the level of attention he has received from previous biographers through this current study, but it also makes him unusually challenging.

Though the focus of my work is on his development as a diplomatist, it became apparent early on that the various components of Webster could not easily be segregated. His life in law, politics, the written and spoken word, and his commitment to the American experiment, all in varying degrees, informed his view on international affairs and the republic's expanding global engagement. I have, therefore, attempted to balance the essentials of his biography with an examination of his critical role in nineteenth-century American foreign relations. If I have been successful in this pursuit, I gladly share that success with the numerous Webster scholars who have supplied such a sound foundation.

Acknowledgments

The pages that follow reflect the support, engagement, and encouragement of a number of individuals, some of whom faithfully followed the Webster project from concept to completion. At Georgia Southern, frequent conversations with Johnathan O'Neill stimulated my examination of Webster the diplomatist. Longtime colleagues Anastatia Sims, Vernon Egger, Craig Roell, Chuck Thomas, and James Woods have continued to express interest in my work, as have former students turned professional peers Lisa Denmark and Cory Andrews. At Winthrop, history department colleagues and my family at University College offered encouragement throughout the process. My dear friend, fellow wordsmith, and dean, Gloria Jones, offered consistent and enthusiastic support, rarely allowing a week to pass without asking about Webster. Encouragement for this project likewise was provided by my good friend and provost, Debra Boyd, whose confidence in my scholarship is a reliable motivator. I am also grateful for the efforts of the folks associated with Rowman & Littlefield beginning with Vice President and Senior Executive Editor Jon Sisk, whose decision to include Daniel Webster in the series made the project possible. Series editor Andy Fry's much-appreciated patience as I worked to complete the manuscript joined his exhaustive review and rigorous editing to make both an enjoyable process and a vastly improved treatment of Webster. Production editor Elaine McGarraugh directed the crucial final phase of the project from fonts to figures to ensure that *Webster* emerged exactly as envisioned. For this, the "godlike" Daniel and I are exceedingly grateful.

For her skills at converting manuscript to book and for graciously entertaining my tiresome questions, I am indebted to Assistant Acquisitions Editor Kate Powers. The manuscript also benefited from the critical eye of my old friend and companion in all things historical, Paul R. Grass, who spent hours scrutinizing each page and provided numerous edits and insightful comments. Of course, I learned years ago to not send anything to press without the input of my mentor, coauthor, and dearest of friends Howard Jones. Despite a demanding schedule of his own and suffering a devastating personal tragedy, he remained a meticulous reader and faithful advisor on Webster. Both he and Mary Ann have provided a depth of support and friendship that is beyond measure.

I have become indebted over the years to so many individuals at libraries and repositories on both sides of the Atlantic that attempting to record names would be a futile exercise, but sincere gratitude is extended to the capable staffs of the British Library, the Library of Congress, the National Archives (US), the National Archives (UK), and numerous university libraries and document repositories. This effort also draws from almost three decades of engagement with promising young scholars, especially those who participated in my graduate seminars at Oxford. My Winthrop students now join them in keeping me engaged and my enthusiasm for history alive.

My daughters (and colleagues) Charity Wait Rakestraw and Foster Rakestraw Hays expressed sincere and persistent interest in the Webster book from the beginning, and Foster applied her remarkable editorial and technical skills to improve each chapter of the manuscript. Her husband, Phillip Hays proved an indispensable professeur de bibliothèque at Winthrop's Dacus Library, efficiently providing needed resources as I worked through the project. My best friend and life companion, Jennie, not only read every word of Webster but also posed discerning questions and astute recommendations that made the work more accessible to a broader audience. Her love, patience, and support through a lifetime have made this and all previous efforts possible. Finally, Tom, Finlay, and Maleigh provided much needed distractions. Maleigh, my old yellow dog, has been under foot for every word I have written or read for the last fourteen years. My wee grandchildren, Tom and Finlay, continue to warm my days with smiles and laughter.

CHAPTER ONE

From the Valley to the Hill, 1782–1823

> It seemed to me as if he was like the mount that might not be touched and that burned with fire. I was beside myself, and am so still.
>
> —George Ticknor, December 1820

Daniel Webster was born in Salisbury, New Hampshire, on January 18, 1782, four generations deep in the life and history of New England. It seems almost providential that his birth and life so precisely paralleled the birth and development of the nation to which he became so important. As Abigail Webster delivered Daniel, London faced the *fait accompli* of American independence, a second nation (Netherlands) stood ready to recognize the sovereign Thirteen United States of North America, and the American commissioners in France prepared to open talks with British envoys that would a year later "deliver" a new nation in North America. It is no wonder that Webster's early affection for George Washington and his reverence for the noble experiment of the American republic would lock him into a lifelong commitment to champion the ideals of liberty and union.[1]

Daniel's father, Ebenezer, was the single most important figure in his developmental years, and his investment in and commitment to the upward trajectory of his young son's life established him as a fundamental and enduring influence. A Federalist and a frontier fighter with Rogers' Rangers in the French and Indian War, Ebenezer's larger-than-life image was set early in his son's eyes as he learned of his father's heroics that included standing sentry outside the tent of General Washington himself in the aftermath of the Benedict Arnold betrayal during the American Revolution. When Daniel was two, Ebenezer moved the family a short distance to a farm in the Merrimack Valley. Here, at Elms Farm, Daniel grew to manhood and formed an attachment to "The Elms" that he and his older brother Ezekiel would nurture throughout their respective lifetimes.[2]

Nineteenth-century politicians often boasted that the farm "made them." For Daniel, it was perhaps his inability to farm that made him. A fragile child, he had to defer farm labor to the more able Zeke while he spent his time at the family mill at Punch Brook. There, he could set the milling process in motion and turn to reading whatever book happened to be within reach. His appetite for the printed word developed so early that it almost seemed that he exited the womb ready to read.[3]

The house at Elms Farm proved fortuitous in Daniel's early connection to the wider world. Ebenezer ran a tavern out of the house, which stood on the main road north of the political activism of Concord, future capital of New Hampshire. At the tavern, the young Daniel witnessed raucous political discourse and became instantly intrigued by developments not only in New England but also in the new nation and its interaction with the Atlantic world. After all, Daniel's youth coincided with European turmoil over revolutionary France and that republic's seismic tangles with Britain, all of which directly affected the United States. When Daniel was eleven, for example, Europe watched in horror as the Reign of Terror bled out of Paris across the French countryside.

Ebenezer tried to provide an adequate education for Daniel, but the boy quickly outpaced the mediocre teachers who passed through the area. All noted his exceptional ability, but none had a greater influence on expanding his opportunities to learn than a Harvard-educated lawyer who opened an office in the village. Thomas Thompson encouraged Ebenezer to send Daniel away to school. This he did, at considerable financial strain. In May 1796 he delivered Daniel to Phillips Academy in Exeter. Here Daniel's formal training began—but with an early and surprising setback. At Phillips Exeter, the boys were required to do routine declamations before students and instructors. When called upon, Daniel froze, later reflecting that "when my name was called, and I saw all eyes turned to my seat, I could not raise myself from it." This is a most astonishing start for someone who would become one of the finest and most effective orators the country has ever produced.[4]

After nine months at Exeter, he returned to Salisbury where he began teaching in a one-room schoolhouse. Soon, Dr. Samuel Wood, a minister from nearby Boscawan, convinced Ebenezer to send Daniel to college and offered to prepare him for admission. In 1797, again at considerable financial hardship, Ebenezer took the fifteen-year-old to Hanover where he enrolled him in the pastoral and unassuming Dartmouth College. Here Daniel found his voice, and by his junior year he was one of the most impressive orators on campus. His roommate prophetically declared that he had set his sights on becoming a "great man in public life."[5]

Daniel Webster delivered his first published oration at Hanover's celebration of the Declaration of Independence on July 4, 1800. Striking all the right chords of patriotism, from praise of the warriors for their gift of freedom to his adulation of Washington, he eventually moved to comparisons with Europe and its perennial threat to the American republic. "There is not a single government now existing in Europe," the youthful Webster declared, "which is not based in usurpation, and established, if established at all, by the sacrifice of thousands. But in the adoption of our present system of jurisprudence," he continued, "we see the powers necessary for government, voluntarily springing from the people, their only proper origin, and directed to the public good, their only proper object." Delivered in the context of the rise of Napoleon's France and the routine harassment of American commerce, he warned of the persistent French threat: "Our ancestors bravely snatched expiring liberty from the grasp of Britain, whose touch is poison; shall we now consign it to France, whose embrace is death?" The speech, while at times succumbing to the uncultivated skills of youth, nevertheless was well received and showed hints of the proud voice for American nationalism that Webster would in due course command.[6]

Later in the year he revealed a glimpse of his developing nationalism in an essay advocating the transfer of the Floridas from Spain to the United States. The essay, simply titled "Acquisition of the Floridas," acknowledged that the nation's growth would require outlets for the "superabundance" of the agricultural production of the western territories. "How shall the lumber, wheat, and cotton of this country be conveyed to a West India or European market?" They would depend on access to the "Mexican Gulf" along rivers controlled by "the king of Spain—a monarch, capricious as a child," who could at any time threaten the commerce and prosperity of the western states "whenever interest, ambition, or the whim of his fancy dictate." Since this would inevitably limit the United States to either conflict or capitulation, "it is respectfully submitted, whether it would not be proper for our government to enter into some convention with the king of Spain, by which the Floridas should be ceded to the United States."[7]

After graduation in August 1801 at the age of nineteen, he returned to Salisbury with little direction for his future and by default read law in Thompson's office. In 1802, he took a teaching position in Fryeburg, Maine, to assist with Zeke's expenses at Dartmouth. After eight months, he returned to Salisbury, again with no direction. By now Zeke had graduated, taken a teaching post in Boston, and invited his brother to join him there. The decision to accept Zeke's offer proved momentous. In Boston, fired with the confidence of youth, he walked unannounced into the law office of Christopher Gore and offered his services as a clerk. Gore, recently returned from eight years in London administering the terms of Jay's Treaty (1794), was instantly taken with Webster, setting him to work that same day and soon becoming an engaged and effective mentor. From his work in the law office, Webster not only studied the ample titles from Gore's library but also learned the style and methods of some of the best lawyers in New England. His association with Gore provided a path of opportunity on which he moved steadily forward toward national notoriety. Only once did he briefly contemplate retreat.[8]

At the end of 1804, Webster received a letter from his father informing him that he had arranged for a lucrative position for Daniel back home in New Hampshire. Since this seemingly positive prospect threatened to derail his Boston ambitions, Daniel approached his mentor for advice. Gore's instructions were swift and certain: decline the offer immediately. Gore viewed this opportunity from home as a potential anchor on Daniel's grander aspirations and wasted few words in conveying this opinion to his young clerk. Accepting Gore's reasoning, Daniel struggled to inform his generous father that he had greater ambitions than a clerkship in rural New Hampshire. Back in Salisbury, he broke the news to Ebenezer that he would decline the clerkship, preferring to "use my tongue in the courts, not my pen." Ebenezer's reaction was perhaps surprisingly resigned as he reminded his son that Abigail had early predicted that Daniel would "come to something or nothing, she was not sure which." It appeared to both that Daniel Webster was soon to demonstrate which.[9]

Increasingly interested in politics—not in small measure because of what both he and Zeke believed to be the growing virus of Jeffersonianism—Webster agreed to Thompson's request in early 1805 to write an essay in support of the struggling New Hampshire Federalists. In February he penned "An Appeal to the Old Whigs of New Hampshire," his first published political piece. In it, Webster attempted to saddle New Hampshire Republicans with the unsettling four years of the Jefferson administration, which he excoriated as undermining the constitutional legacy of Washington and the Founders. With this essay and his frequent orations, Webster began to make his way into the Federalist power circle.[10]

Admitted to the bar in March 1805, Webster established his first practice at Boscawen where he could remain close to his fading father, who died in spring 1806, sadly missing the opportunity to see what a mature communicator his son had become. In July, Daniel was asked to deliver the Independence Day address in Concord. In it he reprised some of the sentiments he had delivered in Hanover; but circumstances had changed, and Britain and France had now drawn much of Europe into war. After Napoleon overran Prussia and closed ports to British ships, London responded with a series of Orders in Council (OIC) declaring much of Europe under blockade. The British knew that international law defined such a broad blockade as mere paper, but they appeared less interested in its effectiveness than the cover it provided for harassing all neutral traffic—neutral traffic that included any American ship with cargo for France. London applied this outrageous practice with impunity, confirming the oft-noted dictum later ascribed to Britain that "she not only rules the waves, she waives the rules." Webster addressed these circumstances in what has been identified by some as his first major oration. He attacked both Britain and France for their abuse of American neutrality and romanticized (as he would for the rest of his career) the glories of the American model of a government rising from the people.[11]

After his father died, Daniel invited Zeke to take over his practice in Boscawen so he could advance his personal and professional agendas. Zeke agreed. Now, relieved of filial duties and with his practice and the family in Zeke's dependable hands, Daniel moved to Portsmouth where he hung his shingle in September 1807. The following May he married Grace Fletcher and focused his attention on building his practice and his family and engaging in the Federalist cause, a cause that became all the more critical as New England began to feel the onerous impact of Jefferson's Embargo Act.[12]

At the close of 1807, Jefferson had responded to the escalating assault on American commerce and neutral rights. Napoleon's arbitrary decrees joined with Britain's abusive Orders in Council to make American trade on the high seas, in the estimation of Jefferson, too hazardous to continue. When, on June 22, 1807, the British frigate *Leopard* fired on the American warship *Chesapeake* just off the coast of Virginia and left three Americans dead and eighteen wounded, action could no longer be delayed. The people called for war, but Jefferson chose an economic option instead. In the third week of December, he convinced a special congressional session to pass the Embargo Act. The legislation, in effect, quashed American oceangoing commerce by prohibiting merchant ships from clearing American harbors unless issued permission by the federal government. This act injured no section of the country more acutely than Webster's New England and, as expected, that region's voice rose in protest: "O Jefferson! with deep amaze, Thou'st overset our cargo; We've nought to do but stand and gaze At thy own curst embargo."[13]

The Federalists tapped the agitation over the embargo as an issue to exploit in upcoming elections and engaged Webster's pen in the cause. Soon he had a pamphlet, "Considerations on the Embargo Laws," circulating throughout New England. In it he attacked the embargo as both incompatible with the constitutional authority of the federal government and an assault on the liberties of the citizens. He also contended that the embargo's real intent was to oppose Britain and to surreptitiously aid France. He predicted that the embargo would likely lead to something far more nefarious than commercial distress—war with Britain. Webster's assessment reflected precisely the practical effect of the embargo. Since Britain was master of the seas, the impact would naturally be more detrimental to British concerns. It also seemed to favor France in another way. Napoleon's so-called Continental System was designed to threaten, if not destroy, Britain's oceangoing commerce. The Embargo Act would, in fact, complement that effort.[14]

Webster's essay bore limited political fruit. Although the Federalists were successful in sending their candidates to Congress, and New Hampshire, along with most of New England, supported the Federalist presidential contender, the rest of the country's support for James Madison ensured his elevation from the State Department to the executive mansion as Jefferson's successor. Before Madison was sworn in, Jefferson accepted the obvious ineffectiveness of the embargo and had it lifted and replaced with the equally anemic Non-Intercourse Act. Under the new policy, all ships could depart for international ports but were not permitted to trade with either of the belligerents. This, of course, was impossible to enforce, which meant that once ships cleared American jurisdiction, they could and would trade with the most lucrative clients and markets. The shift from Embargo to Non-Intercourse relieved New England commerce by allowing the resumption of international trade. It did not, however, redress the issue that the embargo had been designed to address. American ships were still subject to the whims of French decrees and British OICs.

To add insult to injury, Britain embarrassed Madison with the Erskine Agreement. David Erskine, British minister to America, disingenuously informed Madison that the British were willing to lift the OICs on American shipping and negotiate a new trade agreement. According to Erskine, the OICs would be lifted in June 1809. What appeared to be a simple concession on London's part was no more than a subterfuge perpetrated by the British minister. The London government attached conditions to the anticipated lifting of the OICs, conditions Erskine had withheld from Madison. The president, unaware that a British *quo* was dependent on an American *quid*, authorized American ships to clear for British trade. Approximately six hundred ships did just that and could not be recalled after the ruse was unmasked. And further, Non-Intercourse applied to Napoleon's France did little more than provoke the issuance of more decrees.[15]

President Madison subsequently conceded that he had been duped by Erskine and that Non-Intercourse was a failure; consequently, in 1810 he announced an attempt at another remedy, Macon's Bill No. 2. This arrangement permitted trade with all nations but promised to reimpose Non-Intercourse on the opponent of either belligerent who acknowledged respect for American neutrality. This course, Webster would admonish, invited manipulation; one nation might feign compliance by sending word to the Madison administration that it intended to respect American neutrality to prompt the application of Non-Intercourse on its enemy. After all, in the Erskine affair Madison had exposed a susceptibility to just such a manipulation.

In August, Napoleon's foreign minister informed America's minister to France that the offensive decrees would be revoked and respect for American maritime rights restored at the end of October. Similar to the Erskine Agreement, the French had added a critical qualifier; revocation of the decrees would only occur if the British followed suit by revoking the OICs and also agreeing to respect American neutrality. Taking the French at their word, Madison activated the rules of Macon's Bill No. 2 and reinstituted Non-Intercourse on Britain. But since Britain had refused to lift the OICs, Napoleon felt no obligation to follow through with the promise to respect American neutrality.[16]

Once again, it appeared that Madison had acted on limited knowledge, but the result this time was war with Britain. London had little tolerance for what appeared to be a policy harming them and helping France. American fever had continued to rise over London's general lack of respect and treatment of Americans as underlings. All this joined stirrings of nationalism to force a declaration of war against Britain in June 1812. While Webster could appreciate the appeal of nationalism, he could countenance neither the apparent bungling nor the machinations that took that cause to war.

Federalist suspicions of Madison's pro-French proclivities seemed validated, and Webster, when given a platform, gladly voiced those suspicions. Madison had maneuvered the nation into war with Britain, and, in the estimation of the Federalists, moved the nation in the direction of a de facto alliance with Napoleon. Within weeks Webster was offered a forum for an all-out assault on the questionable justifications for "Mr. Madison's War." He was asked, once again, to deliver an Independence Day address. This time it was for the Washington Benevolent Society in Portsmouth and, as before, Webster did not disappoint. Highlighting the wisdom and steady leadership of Washington, Webster portrayed Madison as lacking in the first president's attributes and exhibiting little beyond rash reaction. The only logical rationale for this war, Webster argued, was to assist the efforts of the French, a prospect that was completely unpalatable to New Englanders. "There is no common character, nor can there be a common interest," Webster asserted, "between the Protestants, the Dissenters, the Puritans of New England, and the Papists, the Infidels, the Atheists of France."[17]

The following month, Webster issued the Rockingham Memorial, a full broadside on the administration's reasons for taking the nation to war. The memorial provided the first comprehensive insight into Webster's opinion of the conflict. Addressed directly to "James Madison, Esquire, President of the United States," the message purported to speak for over fifteen hundred citizens of Rockingham County, New Hampshire. The memorial laid out a point-by-point refutation of the rationale for war. Webster opened with a challenge to the constitutional legitimacy of the conflict by reminding the president that the "inhabitants of the Atlantic coast" had signed on to the "National Constitution" as a benefit to all. The commercial states, however, had seen their interests routinely sacrificed from the Embargo forward to an unsubstantiated argument for war with Britain. Careful to avoid appearing unsupportive of a just cause, Webster admonished the president to "give us but to see, that this war hath clear justice, necessity, and expediency on its side, and we are ready to pour out our treasure, and our blood in its prosecution." But the case, Webster contended, had not been made on any of the points raised. While it was true, for example, that the British policy of impressment—the forceful conscripting of men into military service—had historically resulted in American sailors being plucked from American ships, close examination did not substantiate the magnitude of the problem alleged by the administration. Further, no evidence suggested that impressment was worse at this time than during either the Washington or the Adams administrations, neither of which found it worthy of a war. Besides, he continued, Britain had demonstrated a willingness to come to some amicable terms on the issue. Moreover, why was impressment suddenly so provocative when it had not merited any attention during the discussion leading to the Erskine Agreement?

Webster then raised an issue that he would later turn into his cause célèbre as a freshman congressman from Portsmouth. This involved the question of French duplicity over Macon's Bill. The chronology of events that led to a supposed French respect for American neutrality and hence reapplication of Non-Intercourse on Britain and subsequent war was flawed. The administration's position that France had repealed its decrees in November 1810 was betrayed by the French government's declaration that the decrees remained operational—as evidenced by losses suffered by Americans during the interim—as late as March 1812. Webster highlighted an April 28, 1811, French declaration that had retroactively placed revocation of the Berlin and Milan decrees at November 1810. "This proves beyond contradiction," he argued, "that those decrees were not repealed" when the Madison administration "adopted measures against England, founded on their supposed repeal."

In March 1811, the administration activated Non-Intercourse on Britain under the assumption that France had repealed the decrees. Only later did the French repeal the obnoxious decrees. And why, Webster wished to know, had the French finally made good on the promise? They did so only "because our government had actually taken measures against England." To add to the insult, Webster noted, the British had revoked its OICs in the interim between the promised repeal of the French decrees and their actual repeal. This prolonged shell game had thus led an unprepared United States to engage in war with Britain unnecessarily.

Webster then returned to an assault on the federal government's failure to satisfy the constitutional pledge to protect commerce and property; the Madison administration had, he contended, failed to produce a navy capable of fulfilling that pledge. Using Madison's own words from the early days of the constitutional government, he posed a series of rhetorical questions to show that the guarantees pledged by the federal government had not been honored. This failure of the national government to meet its obligations might lead states to consider separation from the Union, an admittedly lamentable prospect. Having raised the specter of secession, he lowered the temperature with the assurance "that the tie that binds us to the Union, will never be broken, by us." While Webster placed no stylistic emphasis on the last two words, the implication could not be missed. The ties presumably could be broken by the heavy hand of a forceful majority that threatened the interests of "a large and respectable minority."

Webster's closing remarks underscored the recurrent apprehension over an alliance with France. It seemed reasonable to assume that the threat of Britain, the common enemy of both, would lead the two nations into an arrangement. Webster found this prospect intolerable. "No pressure, domestic or foreign," he contended, "shall ever compel us to connect our interests with those of the house of Corsica; or to yoke ourselves, to the triumphal car of the conqueror and the tyrant of continental Europe."[18]

With the Rockingham Memorial, Webster had clearly established himself as the voice of his fellow Federalists, a voice soon to join them in carrying their views to the halls of Congress. In 1812, he was nominated as a Federalist candidate for Congress, won handily, and in spring entered the rather disappointing capital city. The unfinished nature of the city did not compare favorably to the historic vistas of Portsmouth and Boston. "Five miles of scattered shacks and houses interspersed," he lamented, "with woods and gravel pits, it looked more like Hampstead Heath than a city."[19]

Although the city did not impress him, the caliber of his colleagues soon would. He boarded in Georgetown with his mentor, now senator, Christopher Gore; Senator Rufus King from New York (senior leader of the party); and his old friend Jeremiah Mason, now senator from New Hampshire. Seated in Congress, he met for the first time two individuals with whom he would be closely connected for the rest of his life—Speaker of the House Henry Clay of Kentucky and Clay's fellow war hawk, Congressman John C. Calhoun of South Carolina. A number of powerful personalities populated this Congress, but none were bigger than these two who were destined to be joined by Webster as the third member of a "Great Triumvirate." Over the subsequent decades, these three voices would profoundly influence both the nature and the direction of the nation.[20]

Soon after taking his seat in Congress in May 1813, Webster was named to the Committee on Foreign Relations, chaired by Calhoun. From this seat, the new congressman from Portsmouth could build upon his Rockingham Memorial and press the president on having been duped into the war by French machinations. The vehicle for the attack was a French document from April 1811, verifying the alleged revocation of the offending French decrees. When the French foreign minister presented this document to the US legation in Paris in May 1812, the American envoy was astonished, especially when told that his predecessor, Jonathan Russell, had known of it a year before. When no one, including Secretary of State James Monroe, corroborated the French insistence that the American diplomats were told, a consensus developed that the French had backdated the document to perpetuate the ruse that they had complied with the promise to revoke the decrees. This alleged misdeed presented too much of a target against Madison for the Federalists to ignore. They disingenuously peddled an assumption that the document was legitimate and that the administration had known of French compliance over a year before the war declaration and kept it quiet. If the administration had made this public, the British would likely have responded by revoking the OICs, thereby eliminating the need for war.

In the House, Webster offered five resolutions on the matter, each posing a pointed question to the president. The first asked when exactly the administration had learned of France's April decree. This was key to the attack. If the administration had, in fact, known of the French move earlier than acknowledged, the chronology leading to war could not be defended. Second, what, if anything, had Russell said about the allegation that he had been informed of the April decree by the French foreign ministry? Third, had the French minister in Washington approached the administration about the decree? The fourth resolution was a general question soliciting any additional information the president held on the matter. Webster's final query sought to determine whether the French had been held accountable for the alleged delay in receiving the decree in timely fashion. The nation deserved the whole truth; the president, after all, had taken the country to war. Had he done so, Webster asked, under false pretenses?[21]

Several days of debate followed, as Federalist attacks drew a spirited response from Republican defenders of the administration. Webster sat back and watched as his colleagues in the minority contended that the evidence supported only two possibilities: Madison was either duplicitous and had conspired to deceive the people into war, or Madison was a dupe who Napoleon had manipulated into war. The charges were harsh, with some contending that the president had bowed to reelection pressure from hawks in his party to seek a war declaration. A number of Republicans countered the Federalist charges, but none was more effective than Felix Grundy of Tennessee. Grundy pointed out that the timing of French revocation of the decrees would have had no effect on the determination to go to war with Britain. He noted that Britain's requirement for a reciprocal arrangement hinged on France lifting its restrictions on "all" neutral commerce, not just American. The April declaration only addressed the restrictions on the United States. Having established to his own satisfaction that the cause and effect suggested by the Federalists was errant, he recalibrated to attack the motives of the Federalists as unpatriotic. "To my mind," Grundy declared, "it is impossible to draw a line of distinction between adding to the strength of the enemy and taking from the strength of his own country."[22]

As the debates drew to a close on June 21, Webster looked forward to taking the stage to defend his resolutions; but Calhoun felt that an extended debate would serve no purpose beyond encouraging the antiwar voices. The chairman thus reported Webster's resolutions out of committee with no changes. The House approved the resolutions, and Webster and a colleague were dispatched to the White House to deliver the unsavory package. Now the waiting began. Webster vacillated between retreating from the humidity of Washington for the comfort of New England and continuing to wait for the president's response. Duty won out, and he remained in Washington until July 12 when an unsatisfying response finally appeared.[23]

Secretary of State Monroe's response simply stated that no one in the administration had prior knowledge of the alleged French revocation of the decrees. Monroe echoed general Republican arguments that the entire affair had been concocted by the French via a contrived document with a falsified date. Webster and his fellow Federalists were not impressed with the response and did not let the issue long sleep. While Webster made no secret of his contempt for Madison and the president's apparent preference for the French, his sincere aim was to see the nation extricated from a needless and debilitating war.[24]

Webster's initial foray into foreign relations produced disappointing results, but by the time he escaped Washington in mid-July he had signaled that a new and effective Federalist voice had arrived on the national scene. He returned to Portsmouth to praise from his supporters and equally appreciated scorn from his detractors. Meanwhile, British forces validated his assessment of the ruinous nature of the war by turning back a bungling American attempt to attack Montreal and setting fire to Buffalo.

Sadly for Webster, fire was in his future as well. Returning to Portsmouth in time for the birth of his first son, he spent the remainder of the year attending to his family in their comfortable and stately residence in Portsmouth only to receive word after his return to Washington at the end of December that a fire had swept through his section of Portsmouth and consumed his home. The bad news was tempered by word that Grace and the children—baby Fletcher and three-year-old Grace—had escaped injury and were taken in by their friends, the Jeremiah Masons. Webster stayed on in Washington, satisfied that Grace and the children were in good hands in Portsmouth, and was even more reassured when he learned that she had taken the children to Boscawen to winter with Zeke's family.[25]

In Washington, Webster continued his assault on the president, initially hoping to resume deconstruction of the French deception, but soon training his fire on other war issues. While Webster was still in New Hampshire, Madison had implemented another embargo, shutting down all exports; early in the second congressional session, he submitted a request for more troops. Webster responded on the first day of debate in mid-January 1814, with an attack on both the troop request and the new embargo. He castigated the

Enlistment Bill, contending that a troop buildup signaled another foolish attempt to invade Canada. If, Webster argued, the purpose of the military was to defend US territory, no additional troops should be required. But the administration seemed determined to make the strategy about conquest, which in Webster's estimation, was "a wild one, commenced without means, prosecuted without plan or concern and ending in disgrace." It seemed, Webster chided, that Madison was caught "between rash counsels and feeble execution."[26]

And rash indeed had been the return to the failed notion of an embargo. Webster's attack on it echoed his belief that the embargo was contrary to the spirit and letter of the compact that had brought the republic into existence. Similar to the ham-handed policies of the British ministry of Lord North that led to the American Revolution, this policy did not regulate but destroyed commerce, especially in New England. With his now customary flare, Webster challenged the administration to unshackle the very commerce that the war promised to protect, for in "the commerce of the country the Constitution had its growth; in the extinction of that commerce it will find its grave."[27]

American commerce would soon be unshackled, but not by the force of Webster's rhetoric. It would be freed by circumstances flowing from the power of British forces that liberated the European continent with the defeat of Napoleon at Leipzig in October 1813. In early 1814, Madison realized that the embargo no longer injured Britain as much as the United States and moved to have it repealed and Non-Intercourse modified. Perhaps this gesture would encourage peace negotiations in Belgium where Madison had dispatched commissioners, including former Speaker Clay, to pursue direct talks in the wake of Britain's rejection of a Russian mediation proposal. With Napoleon subdued, Britain could now turn its attention to North America, and Webster did not see how these circumstances were likely to produce peace. He did, however, enjoy Madison's vacillation in surrendering the embargo. In fact, the young congressman could not resist gloating over the corpse of the dead policy as he offered a cynical sorry-for-your-loss to his Republican colleagues.[28]

In the spring, Webster used the congressional recess to sort out his family's accommodations in Portsmouth and to secure his and his Federalist cohort's reelection to the next Congress. In the August 1814 elections, Webster joined in victory with much of the so-called Peace Ticket. Despite the success of Federalists in New England, the rest of the country ensured increased majorities for Republicans. Webster postponed his return to Washington to head Portmouth's committee for defense as the British appeared poised to add the city to their trophy case. In the second week of September, he issued an appeal for the men of Portsmouth to muster with arms at the parade grounds. There was no attack, but Webster now could add a moment of *ad hoc* military service to his résumé.

Meanwhile, Washington had not fared so well. In late August, British forces raided the capital, forcing the president—like "a faint-hearted, lily-livered runaway," Webster mused—to evacuate the city before torching almost all government buildings. The president's residence was not destroyed but would require considerable work before the first couple could move back in. The only government building spared was the Patent Office, which became the temporary home of the US government.[29]

When Webster rode back into the city in October for an emergency session, he was distressed by both the magnitude of the destruction and the ease with which it had been accomplished. It was apparent to all that Britain, having now available troops steeled by battles with Napoleon's forces, could inflict immeasurable pain on the United States. In fact, peace talks at Ghent might soon turn into concession talks, forfeiting US territory to a victorious Britain. Offensive operations from Canada to New Orleans threatened to achieve whatever ends Britain chose to pursue.

Under these circumstances, it is not surprising that Webster's return to Congress coincided with presidential requests for more troops and additional funds. Monroe, now serving as both secretary of state and interim war secretary, laid the detailed options before Congress. These options ranged from a complicated selective service scheme, to recruitment from state militias, and doubling land bounties for service. The addition of troops would not, Webster believed, turn the war from defeat to victory; it was "the cause of a party" and not "the cause of the people." He had made this argument earlier in the war and continued to believe that the nature of the war remained the biggest impediment to victory.[30]

Of these options, only the one involving the state militias gained enough support to move forward. To validate this plan under the Constitution, supporters relied simply on the government's authority to field an army. On December 9, Webster rose to challenge this assumption. The militia language in the Constitution clearly intended a defensive force. Madison meant *to invade* Canada. How could this be reconciled with the clear intent of a constitution that the president had helped author? "Where is it written in the Constitution, in what article or section is it contained," Webster demanded to know, "that you may take children from their parents, and parents from their children, and compel them to fight the battles of any war in which the folly or the wickedness of government may engage it?" Before concluding his remarks, he posed a potential remedy whereby the states might be forced to "interpose between their citizens and arbitrary power" in order to safeguard "their own rights and the liberties of their people." Although Webster failed to block the measure when the bill moved between houses of Congress, the legislation, nevertheless, found no consensus.[31]

Meanwhile, Federalists in New England engaged in a plan to formalize their opposition to the war in what culminated between mid-December and the first week of January 1815 in the Hartford Convention. Webster's comments about interposition clearly anticipated the sentiments discussed at Hartford, and he was generally supportive of the delegates' mission. He nevertheless took care to issue a disclaimer in Congress that attaching the threat of secession to the convention was "unfounded." The Hartford Convention included proposals for self-serving constitutional amendments, all arriving in Washington in early January around the same time as news of Andrew Jackson's epic victory in New Orleans and the Christmas Eve peace treaty at Ghent, Belgium. The Hartford delegates' timing could not have been worse; their missive appeared foolish if not treasonous. Webster wisely held his speech to Congress off the record and unpublished. His association with the sentiments of Hartford—never mind its kinship with Jeffersonian states' rights—would not have aided his stature as a rising figure in the promotion of nationalism.[32]

Webster returned to Portsmouth before the treaty vote, determined to advance his law practice and to ponder relocating his family offices to a more dynamic venue. He contemplated New York City but settled on a return to familiar Boston, a decision that set his path toward a permanent affiliation with Massachusetts. He had, of course, to satisfy first his commitment to the remainder of his term as New Hampshire congressman. On his return to Washington in mid-February 1816, he found that the "victorious" mood of nationalism had overwhelmed the country and its representatives. Proposed legislation reflected this. For example, during the last weeks of the session, Webster joined with Calhoun in structuring a sound national bank and, somewhat tacitly, a modest but stable tariff. For the United States to sever the last tentacles of British control, it must develop a thriving, independent economic system. Webster's support was more for modifications of the bank and tariff than for their contribution to nationalism. At the moment, the champions of nationalism were the other two members of the triumvirate—Clay from the Speaker's chair and Calhoun from the floor.[33]

At the close of the congressional session Webster returned home, and in August he moved to Boston with Grace and the children to focus on his legal practice and the promotion of his traditional New England conservatism.

Figure 1.1. Daniel Webster, lawyer and lawmaker. Courtesy of the Library of Congress Prints and Photographs Division, LC-DIG-pga-11871.

At thirty-five, he was already widely known in Boston circles and seemed perfectly compatible with the elite Boston social structure. Before he could fully test the waters of the bay culture, he was obliged to finish his work for New Hampshire. Following the illness and untimely death of his daughter in January 1817, Webster's sad departure for Washington was, truly, only to fulfill the obligation to his Portsmouth constituents. His attendance was sparse, and he left Washington for Grace, family, and his legal practice the day before James Monroe's inauguration the first week of March.

As it happened, Webster did not need a political post for the development of his bona fides in American nationalism; he could do so under the shingle of a law office. Boston had been his crossroads when Gore advised him to decline a position back home and his father had identified the decision as Webster's moment to "come to something." Now, from that city, he seized opportunity after opportunity to insert himself into the national dialogue as he stood regularly before John Marshall's Supreme Court. He had already caught the notice of the Chief Justice as an effective speaker from the floor of Congress. He would now have the chance to impress him again below the floor of Congress in the old Supreme Court chamber.

His earliest moment of note before the high court concerned a New Hampshire squabble over the status of his alma mater—a private institution by its original charter, or a public institution by state government fiat. On March 10, 1818, Webster opened before the Marshall Court in what has been described as one of the strongest arguments ever made before that body. In *Trustees of Dartmouth College v. William H. Woodward* (1819), Webster argued for the constitutional protection of contract. Dartmouth College originated as a charter and thus could not be arbitrarily reconstituted on the whim of the state without violating the US Constitution. If this New Hampshire action were allowed to stand, every institution in the United States would be vulnerable. Indeed, no contract would be safe. Marshall agreed, and early the following year he issued the majority opinion, a landmark in constitutional jurisprudence. Webster knew that he had struck judicial gold and reported to an associate, "Our College cause will be known to our children's children."[34]

The two most conspicuous examples of Webster's growing nationalism would be likewise "known to our children's children." In both *McCulloch v. Maryland* (1819) and *Gibbons v. Ogden* (1824), the authority of the federal government—derived not from a compact of the states, Webster reasoned, but from the people directly—prevailed over that of the state. In *McCulloch*, Marshall's majority opinion not only accepted Webster's argument but also adopted much of his language. In *Gibbons*, the so-called steamboat case, the Court ruling against a transportation monopoly sanctioned by the state of New York relied on and expanded the commerce clause of the Constitution. This effort put Webster's mark on one of the most powerful devices of the federal government, one that would eventually come to control everything from industry and labor to civil liberties. "The power of Congress to regulate commerce," Webster argued, "is complete and entire, and to a certain extent, necessarily exclusive."[35]

Although Webster took a hiatus from politics for a season, he continued to move in political circles both when in Washington arguing before the Court and at home in New England. As a result, he was expected to stake a public position on all important state and national issues. Even when he opted to stay on the periphery of the Missouri statehood debate, his political enemies assigned nefarious motives to him, going so far as to blame him for plotting to fracture the Union. The shadow of his affiliation with the Hartford Convention made this a recurring issue for Webster. He did participate in a meeting concerning Missouri at the Massachusetts State House in December 1819, where he was asked to lead a committee in drafting a message to Congress opposing the extension of slavery.

The document, as was Webster's practice, contained a healthy dose of history and a hearty portion of constitutional reasoning. Now, Webster declared, was the time to end the evil of slavery; the fate of "unborn millions" depended on it. It was within the constitutional purview of Congress to set requirements for admission into the Union and had been since the implementation of the Northwest Ordinance of 1787. Echoing Rufus King in the Senate, Webster noted that, since the Constitution expressly authorized Congress to admit new states, it was only reasonable that Congress should set the qualifications for that admission. Webster also advanced the commerce clause to bolster his argument for congressional discretion over the disposition of slaves in the new territories. It is noteworthy that, while Webster identified slavery as "evil," he neither at this time nor later focused his attack on moral grounds. He seemed satisfied to base his opposition exclusively on the constitutional and political issues slavery evoked.[36]

Congress issued the final compromise for Missouri's admission in 1822, a compromise that included the simultaneous admission of Maine to maintain the congressional balance between slave and nonslave states. Since Maine had been part of Massachusetts, the reconfiguration necessitated a reapportionment of Massachusetts' congressional districts. State politicos seized on the event as an excuse to rewrite the state constitution. This presented Webster an opportunity to actively engage in state politics and increase his visibility for the future.

As if to prepare the stage, he agreed to deliver in October what would be his first of many speeches in Boston's historic Faneuil Hall. He spoke on tariffs and clearly came down as an opponent of protectionism. His concern with the protective tariff centered on the dependency engendered by government intervention. Once industry became accustomed to government largesse, it would struggle when under duress and expect government to step in with a bailout.[37]

The convention to rewrite the constitution opened on November 15, 1820, with Webster emerging as a leading conservative advocating the importance of "property" as a central component for apportioning representation. Although his assignment focused on representation in the state senate, he took the opportunity to make a broader philosophical defense of property's essential relationship to government. Property remained at the core of government institutions, he contended, and government, therefore, "should look to those who hold property for its protection." Property should thus "have its due weight and consideration in political arrangements." Although Webster had limited success at the convention, the power of his presence alerted his colleagues that his political fortunes were just beginning to gather.[38]

The following month, while the convention was still in session, he delivered an address at the old First Church in Plymouth commemorating the two hundredth anniversary of the Pilgrim settlement, an address that, in the thinking of former president John Adams, distinguished Webster as "the most consummate orator of modern times." The address, Adams continued, "ought to be read at the end of every century, and indeed at the end of every year, for ever and ever." The presentation has been described by Webster biographer Robert Remini as "the first of his mature orations." Webster friend and admirer George Ticknor felt more than he heard the address: "Three or four times I thought my temples would burst with the gush of blood." On this occasion, Ticknor described Webster as "godlike," a descriptor that resurfaced on occasion for the remainder of his days. Ticknor's Harvard colleague Edward Everett later designated it "in some respects the most remarkable of his performances." At thirty-eight, Webster's light was shining with blinding intensity. Many began to wonder if this light would not be better suited to the nation's capital than the old First Church. Webster's days of daily dedication to his legal practice were fleeting. The next election, in 1822, would see to it.[39]

Before again dividing time between his practice and Congress, Webster engaged in two cases that both contributed to his foundation in international jurisprudence (especially the law of the sea) and prepared him for his future as a diplomatist. The first resulted from Andrew Jackson's Florida incursion in 1818 that Secretary of State John Quincy Adams parlayed into a treaty with Spanish minister to the United States Don Luis de Onís in 1819. Under Pinckney's Treaty of 1795, Spain was obligated to control its Florida subjects. Routine raids by Seminoles across the border into Georgia proved

Spain incapable of meeting that obligation. In late 1817, President Monroe deployed General Jackson to secure the border and authorized him, if necessary, to pursue the troublesome Seminoles into Spanish Florida. Jackson did so in March 1818 with a force of some three thousand, seizing the fort and town of St. Marks in East Florida; Pensacola, the capital of West Florida; and two ill-fated British subjects in the process. Although Jackson had gone well beyond his authority, Adams persuaded the president to give the State Department time to leverage Jackson's success at the bargaining table with Onís. On February 22, 1819, Adams and Onís completed the treaty that bears their names. While deliberating, Adams shrewdly added to the talks the question of the western boundary of the Louisiana Territory. Since the territory sold by Napoleon to the United States in 1803 had previously belonged to Spain, Adams wished to have a definite line drawn. Onís agreed and traced a line westward until it struck the Pacific Ocean. Consequently, the Adams-Onís Treaty validated a transcontinental claim for the United States. Both the Floridas and the western components of the treaty would play a role in Webster's diplomatic future, the former almost immediately, the latter twenty years hence.[40]

In this brilliant treaty by all measures, the only compensation committed by the Monroe administration was the assumption of $5,000,000 in American claims against Spain. The claims issue ran deeper than the immediate negotiations and had roots in the early republic. A previous attempt in 1802 to address mounting claims against Spain remained unratified by Spain until Adams began discussions with Onís and then deferred to the new arrangements under the 1819 treaty. As a result, the claims, which had begun to accrue in 1796, continued to build throughout the Napoleonic Wars. Their resolution involved a three-member American commission appointed by the president and directed "to receive, examine, and decide upon the amount and validity of all the claims."[41]

Boston merchants and Philadelphia insurance groups retained Webster to represent their interests, and over the next three years, he either filed or joined over two hundred cases. As he engaged in this work, he must have reflected on that of his mentor, Christopher Gore, who had dealt with similar claims issues in London under the terms of Jay's Treaty (1794).

As soon as the Senate took up the Adams-Onís Treaty, Webster, knowing that claimants would require legal representation, seized the opportunity for his law office. He and Alexander Bliss, his former student and junior partner, focused their attention on New England merchants and, at the suggestion of a colleague, Philadelphia insurance groups. On February 24, 1819, Webster wrote Peter Chardon Brooks—president of the New England Insurance

Company and soon to be a fellow delegate at the Massachusetts constitutional convention—offering his services. If the amount of the claims was as substantial as Webster predicted and his services should prove useful, he informed Brooks, "it would suit my objects entirely to be employed in it." As he concluded his letter to Brooks, he noted the significant boundary terms in the treaty and highlighted the expansive western line. For Brooks, he traced that line from the Sabine River stair-stepping north and westward until it followed "the Arkansaw [sic] to the 42nd de. Of N. Latitude, & thence West to the Pacific—giving us about 7 Degs of Latitude on the Pacific—& the mouth of Columbia River." This line on the Pacific that involved the mouth of the Columbia would return to his desk later as secretary of state. Almost as an afterthought, he mentioned the acquisition of the Floridas "in cons[ideration] of the 5 millions paid to our own citizens." Despite his interest in the transcontinental character of the treaty, it was, of course, the "5 millions" that prompted the letter to Brooks.[42]

At the end of July, Brooks, along with about two dozen representatives of claimants, met with Webster to retain his services before the Commission. The arrangement called for expenses and a 5 percent commission at final settlement. Webster made it clear that he would only support legitimate claims, especially those from residents of Massachusetts, New Hampshire, and Maine. To be precise, he noted which claims he considered illegitimate: those that "happened from smuggling, illicit trade, the Slave trade, the occlusion of New Orleans, or any offence against the law of Nations, and, generally, for none whose claim is, in his judgment, inadmissible under the Treaty."[43]

Agreeing to the terms, Webster and Bliss set about collecting evidence and preparing memorials for the Commission. Webster worked out of the office gathering memorials and transmitting them with directions to Bliss in Washington. It was an onerous task at times, considering that some of the claims were almost twenty-five years old. Webster was committed to arguing the cases and would, when needed, swap locations with Bliss. As it happened, the Commission called for written arguments to expedite the cumbersome process.

In the end, the firm represented almost two hundred clients made up of New England merchants and Philadelphia underwriters. Chief among the latter was the Insurance Company of North America. All were powerful names in American commerce, most qualifying as part of the "who's who of the early nineteenth-century commercial elite of New England." For this group, Webster, with his able assistant Bliss, won over a third of the entire treaty allocation of $5 million and drew approximately $70,000 in compensation. Webster's work on the claims greatly expanded his network of friends and associates, including power brokers among the Eastern commercial elite.[44]

The work on the claims was among the most tedious of Webster's career, requiring him and the office to pore over mountains of documents, many of which had atrophied with time. The multinational nature of the claims compounded the difficulties. Some documents were in foreign repositories/collections, and some terminology differed by nation. For example, when dealing with underwriters, American companies covered a "voyage" as "out and home" together. The British, on the other hand, only covered either "out" or "home" as a voyage. Before the Commission concluded its three-year appointment, matters were complicated for Webster by an election in 1822 and his return to Congress. By then, he had proven the depth of his attachment to section, insisting that the commissioners be reminded in what part of the country most of the damage had been done.[45]

His impressive level of work was reflected in his effort to not only prepare and present cases but also to keep his clients informed. It is not surprising that Webster would on occasion close his note to Bliss, "Yours, in fatigue." Bliss must have taken this with a chuckle considering Webster's habit of leaving to him the more tiresome tasks. After winning the awards, Webster turned his influence in Congress toward securing the allocation of funds to satisfy those awards. "My great business of the Session remains yet undone; that is, to get thro [sic] the law for paying the Spanish claims."[46]

Webster's other legal work while transitioning back to Congress likewise provided useful experience for his diplomatic portfolio. This involved a ship under French colors accused of violating the slave trade prohibition. Arguing before Joseph Story's First Circuit Court in Boston in late 1821, Webster and George Blake defended the actions of Lt. Robert Stockton who, as captain of the US armed schooner *Alligator*, had seized the French ship *La Jeune Eugenie* off the coast of Africa for allegedly engaging in the illicit slave trade. Stockton had determined that the ship was a slaver, not by observing any slaves on board but by noting the nature, appearance, and location of the vessel. On the basis of this somewhat questionable evidence, he seized the vessel and brought it to Boston for adjudication. Stockton's impulsive actions created tension between Paris and Washington that President Monroe hoped could be relieved with a prompt ruling by the First Circuit Court.

The president's hopes for a quick disposition by the court, however, fell victim to the complications of origination, ownership, and evolving American legislation targeting the slave trade. The French owners (the claimants) filed for the restoration of their vessel, but by the time the court met, it had been determined that the ship was built in America for American owners and some question remained about the authenticity of the French papers. If this were the case, American ownership meant American violation of the slave trade prohibition, a serious offense stemming not only from the 1807 law but also from several recent amendments to that law. An 1818 act had placed the burden of proof on any American accused of importing African-born slaves instead of on the prosecution. The following year, Congress directed US vessels to seize any ship of an American citizen engaged in the slave trade and treat it and its cargo as a war prize. Further, in May 1820, precisely one year before Stockton took his action, Congress had enacted additional legislation stating that any American under any circumstance found to be engaged in any way in slaving should be brought in as a pirate, and "on conviction shall suffer death."[47]

In the climate and context of the slavery debate and the government's renewed dedication to combatting the trade, Webster clearly sympathized with Stockton's actions; after all, the very reason for his deployment to African waters was to apprehend violators. Perhaps Stockton garnered Webster's sympathy all the more from his apparent desire to address the immorality of the slave trade. So, while Webster and Blake argued the case on legal grounds, they also elevated the argument to an attack on the depravity of trading in bound humans. Not only was the trade contrary to the laws of nations generally, it was also contrary to the laws of nature. "This traffic preyed upon the *innocent* and the *free* to make them slaves for no *crime* or *offence*." It was therefore nothing more than "a barbarous, unauthorized, private, piratical, warfare carried on against *Africans* to make them *slaves*."[48]

On the strict legal argument, Webster consulted all laws, domestic and international, that governed both the slave trade and the disposition of seized vessels and cargo. The court should appreciate, he argued, that they had at the very least proved the vessel guilty of violating the laws of France, and the claimant should be denied recovery. Although sympathetic to Webster and Blake's arguments, Justice Story, for a reason not clearly explained, determined to defer a ruling and transfer the ship to the French Crown for dispensation. Webster could hardly claim victory, but he nonetheless concluded his respite from Congress with a résumé that added experience in international law to his impressive credentials as a constitutional scholar. He could not have imagined at the time just how critical this developing international experience would be for his future success at the helm of US foreign relations.[49]

CHAPTER TWO

Taking the National Stage, 1823–1839

> We covet no provinces; we desire no conquests; we entertain no ambitious projects of aggrandizement by war. This is our policy.
>
> —Daniel Webster, April 1826

Webster's return to Congress resulted from incumbent Benjamin Gorham's ill health and decision to surrender his seat as representative of the Boston district. New England Federalists responded to Gorham's decision by dispatching a number of party loyalists to encourage Webster to take his place and run for the 1822 election. Hesitating to set aside his successful practice and feigning hard to get, Webster nevertheless agreed and won handily. Ironically, he acknowledged his victory with the pronouncement that he would be in Washington for the two-year term and no more. He might have been sincere when he made this promise, but fate conspired to assure that he would seldom be without a Washington address for the remainder of his life.[1]

He arrived at the Capitol in early December 1823 to see a familiar face in the Speaker's chair; Henry Clay had returned after a brief hiatus and assumed the perch overlooking the floor from which he dispensed committee appointments. He quite logically offered Webster the chairmanship of the Judiciary Committee. Webster, of course, accepted the appointment, but had already intended to mark his reentry to the "Hall of Representatives" with an issue that reached beyond America's shores.

The Greeks were engaged in a bloody independence struggle against Turkey that would continue for the better part of a decade. The conflict had already awakened a sympathetic American public, keen to link it with their own history, the defense of Christianity, and the romantic appeal of defending the cradle of democracy. President Monroe addressed the conflict in his annual address to Congress in December 1823, but his remarks were tempered by Secretary of State John Quincy Adams's reminder that his recently constructed Monroe Doctrine did not merely exclude Europeans from further adventure in the Western Hemisphere, it also promised American restraint in European affairs. As a result, Monroe limited his remarks on Greece to a simple offering of "strong hope" and "ardent wishes" that its people would be victorious and "that Greece will become again an independent nation."[2]

By the time Webster took his seat in the newly renovated House chamber, he had settled on the Greek issue for his reintroduction to Congress. As was his practice, he set out to learn as much as possible about the subject. For this he had an able source, his friend Edward Everett, whom Webster had tutored at the Short Street School in Boston. Everett, now a Harvard professor of Greek literature, had traveled and studied in Europe for over four years and had just returned from a visit to Greece and written a piece on the revolution for the *North American Review*. Between Webster's commitment to the topic while in Boston and his reorientation to Washington in the last weeks of 1823, he had continued to probe Everett for information and encouraged Everett to join him at the capital. These exchanges with Everett and the public mood had so ignited his passion that by the time he settled in Washington he had digested two Everett manuscripts and reported back to his former student that he had "mastered the campaigns of 1821–1822, historically and topographically."[3]

Webster hoped to secure something more than congressional endorsement of Monroe's tepid encouragement of the Greeks. He wanted to facilitate the dispatch of an official envoy to Greece to demonstrate American support for its fight for independence. Everett should be that envoy. After all, the professor had established his knowledge of the subject in print, scholarship, and as a witness to the conflict. Webster's opening remarks to the House, therefore, took the form of a resolution to appropriate funds to advance the appointment of a diplomat (presumably Everett) to Athens.[4]

During the two weeks between Webster's introduction of the resolution and the opening debate, a number of challenges stalled the proposal and prevented it from gaining traction. One challenge took the form of a resolution asking the president to make pertinent diplomatic documents available to Congress. The administration complied, and the correspondence included an exchange between the Greek envoy in London, Andreas Luriottis, and Secretary of State Adams that exposed the latter's lack of enthusiasm for the Greek cause. Adams told Luriottis that the United States had adopted a policy of nonintervention in European affairs. Certainly the administration, as well as congressional leaders, should take care to consider the broader impact of raising the ante. Greece was not the only affected party. How would the appearance of an official diplomatic legation affect US commerce with Turkey? There was little doubt that commercial centers such as Webster's own Boston had lucrative trade ties with Turkey that might be disrupted. In fact, at that moment, the United States had a trade representative in Constantinople working to flesh out commercial arrangements.[5]

On January 19, despite the unexpected opposition, Webster rose to perform before an anticipatory crowd packing the gallery. Everett was among them. He was in Washington not just to see Webster hold forth but also hoping that Webster's success would lead to his appointment to Athens. Early in his address, Webster took care to state that it was not his intention to intrude on the president's "unlimited exercise" of judgment over foreign policy; it was rather an attempt to "adopt some resolution reciprocating" the administration's "sentiments." Having voiced this disclaimer, he launched into an exposition of the threat to democratic principles posed by the machinations of the Holy Alliance. This post-Napoleonic association of Russia, Prussia, and Austria advanced two sentiments that were incompatible with the enlightened doctrines of liberty and freedom championed by the United States, the "leading republic of the world." The monarchists believed that the rights of the people were merely "favors" to be "dispensed by the sovereign power" and, further, that nations had the "right of forcible interference in the affairs of other states." This was, by Webster's reckoning, archaic thinking that, left unchecked, would devolve Europe back "into the middle of the Dark Ages." America, he believed, should promote the "cause of civil and religious liberty" maintained by "the principle of lawful resistance" and governance emanating from the people. This, and not a descent into the autocratic past, should command the present and guard the future. Webster's praise for the American example reflected, as Webster biographer Claude Fuess suggested, "a missionary zeal for guiding the world towards democracy," and in it the man from Salisbury "glowed with romantic idealism." He did not, however, glow with interventionism. Webster pressed for a diplomatic, not a military, posture for the United States in both Latin America and Greece.[6]

Colleagues debated the resolution over the next week. Joel Poinsett, a member of the Foreign Relations Committee, expressed concern for the suffering of the Greeks but noted that "the duty of a statesman is a stern duty," and so policy cannot be swayed by emotions. He thus sounded the administration's cautious position—encouraging words for the rebels but no envoy whose presence might be seen as provocative. Some who opposed the resolution took a personal swipe at Webster. For example, John Randolph dismissed Webster's hapless move to "open Pandora's box of political evils" as mere attention seeking; and Ichabod Bartlett suggested that, like Don Quixote, Webster would take a tilt at whatever windmill presented itself. The measure, Bartlett concluded, should "pass into forgetfulness, with the momentary excitement, that may have given it rise." But Webster was not without support. Speaker Clay directed a withering volley at Webster's critics, especially Bartlett, but even this support could not secure adoption of the resolution.[7]

Of the motives ascribed to Webster, Randolph's observations perhaps came closest to the mark. It is also possible that Webster was motivated by both high principles *and* political opportunism—seizing on the American mood for support of the Greek revolution as a dynamic platform from which he could announce his return to the ranks of congressional leadership. If these tandem motives were his aim, he certainly hit the target. The revised published speech appeared in multiple languages throughout the Atlantic world, and one admirer described it as "the foot of Hercules." Following the Greek printing of the speech, he was heralded as "the Demosthenes of America."[8]

Webster's harmony with Clay was short-lived; the return of the tariff to the congressional calendar placed the two at odds once again. Protectionism remained central to Clay's American System but was antithetical to Webster's current commitment to free trade. The tariff to Webster was "a tedious and disagreeable subject" that he, nonetheless, was compelled to address in early April. Clay delivered a rousing speech at the end of March and Webster responded immediately. Surprisingly adept in the economics of protectionism, Webster supplied not only a philosophical opposition to Clay's resolution but concrete data as well. Webster noted that the proposed tariff would move the United States in the opposite direction from that of the Europeans, who were trending increasingly toward free trade. The tariff, Webster chided, would have Americans expressing "affection for what others have discarded" as they chose "to ornament" themselves "with cast-off apparel." Moreover, the economic crisis the tariff was meant to relieve had passed. To adopt protectionism when America's trading partners advanced unfettered commerce, Webster warned, would harm American producers. Although a detailed and laudatory performance, his effort to block the tariff proved unsuccessful. It achieved little more than to narrow Clay's margin of victory and to establish Webster as a free trade advocate, a profile that soon became politically awkward.[9]

Webster's most satisfying spring accomplishment came in his successful shepherding of a bill through the House to arrange payment of the Spanish claims in fulfillment of the Adams-Onís Treaty of 1819. Having won substantial awards for his clients and a healthy commission for his law office from those claims, Webster made this piece of legislation a personal priority for the Eighteenth Congress. Despite opposition by Clay and Randolph and some effort to delay the bill to clarify the funding method, it passed. On June 12, 1824, a draft was issued to Webster, as attorney representing over forty claimants, in the amount of $777,426.29. The percentage of the awards that accrued to Webster's account expanded his coffers to respectable levels—enough to make most men financially secure. But this was the Daniel Webster who had developed a skill for mishandling money in his youth that famously persisted throughout his life. To say he was not good with money would be to understate the truth since money passed out of his hands as quickly as it came in. Perhaps the real value of his work on Spanish claims, however, had less to do with its immediate financial benefits than with the additional expertise it attached to his growing résumé in transnational matters.[10]

When Webster finally made it home to Boston in early summer, the historically dysfunctional presidential campaign of 1824 was well underway. Of the candidates, Webster should, it would seem, choose fellow New Englander, John Quincy Adams. Adams, however, had abandoned Federalist orthodoxy when he supported Jefferson's embargo, the residue of which produced the current dilemma for Webster. To support Adams would require him to set aside his pique over recent circumstances, but failing to back a Massachusetts Adams might harm his own political future. After none of the four presidential contenders received a majority of electoral votes, the decision moved to the House of Representatives where Webster, not surprisingly, had been returned by his constituents without a whimper of opposition.

Webster arrived in Washington in early December and soon settled into congressional business. The immediate task at hand was the selection of the president. In early February 1825, a few days before balloting began, Webster extracted a tacit commitment from Adams that old Federalists would have a role in his administration; personally, Webster hoped to receive a diplomatic appointment to the Court of St. James's as US minister to Great Britain. Somewhat reconciled, Webster came out for Adams. This decision, although failing in the end to secure him a post in London, placed him in good stead with the new administration. The second week of February, the House by roll call gave Adams the presidency with thirteen states in support. Andrew Jackson won seven states, and four went for Treasury Secretary William Crawford.

The House cleared the impasse and made Adams president, but at a price that all but ensured him a rocky single term. When Henry Clay was named secretary of state, charges of a corrupt bargain issued from administration opponents. Clay, they howled, had traded his supporters to Adams for the top cabinet post, a post that historically served as a springboard to the presidency. Administration opponents picked at this sore for the next four years.[11]

Back in Boston after the session ended in March, Webster was asked to deliver a speech commemorating the fiftieth anniversary of the Battle of Bunker Hill. The June 17, 1825, address would take its place among his growing list of historic orations. An enormous crowd attended the outdoor event. Special guests included veterans of the Revolution joined by their French comrade-in-arms, Marquis de Lafayette. The large gathering, animated with excitement, caused a section of seats to collapse. The chaos that followed seemed certain to derail the event until Webster's booming voice demanded order, and order came. His command of the day continued as he spoke in his fashion of grand images of the American experiment brought forth from "the great event in the history of the continent . . . that prodigy of modern times . . . the wonder and the blessing of the world . . . the American Revolution." Turning his eyes on the veterans seated before him, he addressed them directly with words rehearsed in waders while fishing with his son Fletcher: "Venerable men!," God "has allowed us, your sons and countrymen, to meet you here, and in the name of the present generation, in the name of your country, in the name of liberty, to thank you!" He closed his remarks to the emotional attendees with the admonition to "Let our object be, our country, our whole country, and nothing but our country . . . a vast and splendid monument . . . of Wisdom, of Peace, and of Liberty, upon which the world may gaze with admiration for ever!" Seemingly endless notes of approval followed when he retired from the platform; but one reporter's subsequent reflection, borrowing from poet Thomas Gray, captured the impact of Webster's delivery best with "thoughts that breathe, and words that burn."[12]

In the Nineteenth Congress, Webster took a leading role for the Adams administration on a foreign policy matter. Leaders of several Central American countries had called for a conference of all nations in the hemisphere. Panama would host. Once the invitation to participate in the Panama Congress arrived in Washington, Secretary of State Henry Clay grasped the chance to expand US contact with and influence in the Americas and encouraged Adams to appoint delegates. This, Clay felt, could lead to an alliance structure in the Americas to counter European influence. The day after Christmas 1825, Adams submitted his nominees to the Senate and seemed to expect not only their confirmation but also approval of the mission to be *pro forma*. Webster knew this would not be the case. "An opposition is evidently brewing," he wrote to Associate Justice Joseph Story of the Supreme Court, and "will show itself on the Panama question." The atmosphere has been colorfully described by Claude Fuess as a "smoldering flame of animosity between the Jacksonians and the President" that the Panama issue "fanned into a conflagration by what at first seemed a gentle breeze from the South." The faithful followers of the failed presidential contenders rallied against the Panama plan more over the alleged deal that had gotten Adams to the White House than in response to the substance of the proposed mission.[13]

Webster pursued a strategy in the House to move the Panama mission forward for the president by routing it through the appropriations process. In February, he piloted a resolution through the chamber to *ask* the president for reasonable details concerning the mission to Panama that would inform the funding process. This required some effort on his part to constrain his colleagues to a simple request for information; a number of Adams's opponents demanded a role in defining the mission and directing the delegates. George McDuffie of South Carolina called for the president to outline for Congress his precise intentions. Webster curtly replied that McDuffie "was leaping before he got to the stile." In other words, the House should not get ahead of its constitutional role. The president, Webster pointed out, had articulated the purpose of the mission in his December message; this purpose was his alone to determine.[14]

Webster's success in producing the narrowly worded resolution requesting information did not translate into immediate approval of the funding appropriation. Prolonged debates followed, with some continuing to press for congressionally established parameters for the Panama mission. The arguments, whether sincere or political, drew from concerns that American participation in the conference would imply a US commitment to the welfare of the hemisphere and risk entangling the United States in the affairs of Latin America. In the first two days of February 1826, Congressman (and future secretary of state) Louis McLane from Delaware reminded his colleagues that the nation's longstanding policy had been to restrict US engagement with other nations to commerce and to avoid "political connections." The delegates to Panama, he suggested, should be instructed to behave solely as diplomats and be forbidden "to discuss, consider, or consult, upon any proposition of alliance, offensive or defensive, between this country and any of the Spanish American governments."[15]

McLane's amendment was a clear encroachment on executive purview, provoking Webster, on April 14, to tutor his colleagues on the delineation of authority set out by the Constitution. This matter should remain with "executive discretion and executive responsibility," where the Constitution had clearly placed it. Congressional involvement in foreign policy was limited to dispersing the necessary funds, a minor role that certainly did not extend to instructing diplomats. Webster worried that McLane's stricture would hamstring *all* diplomatic engagement, not simply the matter at hand. Perhaps, Webster suggested, McLane had been "surprised into an expression which does not convey his meaning." Surely he did not intend to suggest that the House might attach conditions to funding that prevented Executive-appointed and Senate-confirmed envoys from discussing, considering, or consulting. If so, no diplomat would have any role to play at all, and hence the national interest could not be engaged with any foreign party over any issue. Webster's thoughtful and exhaustive defense of the very nature of diplomacy indicated a sound understanding of both methods and constitutional structure.[16]

Webster's speech intimated—and in the conclusion pronounced unequivocally—President Adams's paternalistic attitude toward Latin America. Considerable attention centered on Cuba, "the hinge," Webster felt, "on which interesting events may possibly turn." Adams, while secretary of state, had famously stated that if Cuba detached from Spain, "laws of physical gravitation" would naturally have it fall into the "North American Union, which by the same law of nature cannot cast her off from its bosom." Some congressional leaders disagreed; if Madrid determined to transfer Cuba to another European power, Spain would be fully justified in doing so. At the moment of the pending resolution to fund the Panama mission, this seemed imminent. Spain's control over the island was tenuous at best. In fact, Mexico and Columbia contemplated intervention and a French fleet maneuvered nearby, ready to move on the island should the current upheaval force a Spanish withdrawal. Webster rejected the notion that the United States had no business in blocking a transfer of the island to another European power. American commerce with Cuba and its proximity to the "mouth of the Mississippi" made the disposition of the island a vital American interest. While Webster defended American interest in the disposition of Cuba based on practical considerations, implicit in his remarks was a sense that America had both a right and responsibility to the weaker parties in the Americas. Leaving no doubt of this general sentiment, he closed his speech by admonishing his colleagues to not "shut up our senses and smother our faculties" to the fact that Latin America "looked steadily, in every adversity, to the great Northern light."[17]

Webster's words, though resonant, neither ended the debate nor persuaded the committee to reject McLane's amendment. As a result, after suffering through seemingly endless diatribes, McLane's measure carried. Webster held to his objections and stiffened with those of like mind to vote down the amended resolution. Funding for the mission did not find adequate support until a bare-bones appropriations bill was introduced in the third week of April. The stale victory for Adams ultimately proved inconsequential to anything beyond damage to his political agenda. By the time the delegates departed for the conference, one had fallen ill and died en route, and the other arrived after the meeting had adjourned.[18]

Webster, while keeping party affiliation at arm's length, had now established himself as part of Adams's loyal coterie and a voice for the administration in the legislature. He retained the core position of his Federalist youth that parties were anathema to sound government. Party lines in America, he argued, had been the product of contrary positions taken during the upheaval in Europe from the 1790s to Ghent in 1815. Since Monroe ushered in an "Era of Good Feelings," the attraction of faction had dissipated. It is difficult to accept that the brilliant Webster honestly believed this, especially when Adams's opponents had no doubt that Clay assured Adams's selection as president by bartering his own supporters for an appointment as secretary of state. This machination reflected political division and guaranteed a fracture that would produce a new party system. But for the near term, Clay noted that there was only one party, the "Republican party. Names may be gotten up or kept up . . . for local or personal purposes, but at this time" there is only "that of the Administration and the Opposition."[19]

Webster ran under the Republican banner for reelection to Congress in 1826 and did so with overwhelming success. But the victory that sent him back to the House did not keep him there. Effective though he was in the House—even in this short session, he began his shift toward protectionism and helped steer a bill for woolen interests through the body—the decision of incumbent Senator Elijah Mills not to stand for reelection in 1828 opened the possibility for Webster to apply his skills in the upper chamber. Wrangling among Massachusetts politicos over who would best represent the state in the Senate produced an invitation to Webster. Although he enjoyed seniority and power in the lower chamber, the allure of the prestige and stature of the Senate convinced him to accept.[20]

Webster's first action in the Senate addressed a new tariff proposal and reflected an "evolution" in his thinking from free trade to protectionism. Having suffered the death of Grace between his introduction to the chamber at the end of 1827 and the close of January, he buried his beloved wife and despondently returned to Washington in February. There, as if responding to the advice of his friend Justice Story "that the great secret of comfort must be sought, so far as human aid can go, in employment," he turned to his work in the Senate. The burning subject now was the tariff bill introduced in the House and passed by that body in early spring. The bill, as it arrived in the Senate, was unfavorable to New England manufacturers, so it required Webster's attention. Martin Van Buren eventually guided amendments in the Senate that raised certain tariffs friendly to New England, and Webster's constituents (no longer simply the commercial interests of Boston) pressed him to approve. The second week of May, Webster rose to speak and, by supporting the amended bill, revealed a major change in his attitude toward the tariff. His position had evolved, as he conceded, because the economic landscape had changed for both his constituents and the national mood for protectionism. The early iterations in 1816 and 1824 would have created a dependency among manufacturers on tariff protection—protection that might vanish as quickly as it had appeared, with debilitating losses for dependent producers. It now appeared, he contended, that the government had committed to protectionism on principle, thus eliminating the *ad hoc* nature of the previous tariffs that had made them objectionable. Although the current bill did not include a number of Webster amendments, he voted yes, the bill passed, and he moved closer to becoming an outright champion of protectionism.[21]

Meanwhile, distraught at Grace's death, Webster considered resigning from the Senate to focus on his personal affairs, the welfare of the children, and new professional pursuits. He envisioned a departure from the Senate followed by the realization of a long-held aspiration to represent the United States as minister to Britain. His plan hinged on Adams winning a second term in the fall. But continuing intraparty intrigue and maneuvering made it impossible for Adams to appoint Webster *and* win a second term. In the end, the question was rendered moot by Andrew Jackson's victory. There would be no second term for Adams and no London mission for Webster. Jackson won decisively and ushered in a new era of rigid party alignment to which Webster, in countering the Jacksonian impulse, would make a significant contribution.

In 1829, Webster resumed his new role in Congress, but did so with little enthusiasm and without his characteristic fire. The year had begun with the sad anniversary of Grace's death, sadness that was soon compounded by the equally devastating loss of his brother. In April, a late-night courier appeared at the Webster home in Boston delivering the somber news that Zeke had dropped dead of a heart attack while arguing before a Concord court. Webster had lost his two most intimate confidants in just over a year. It would be difficult enough for him to bear the added burden of Zeke's death, but the children had been over a year without a mother. The future was, in a word, unsettling. Then, in December, a brief and improvised search for a new wife ended with the exchange of vows with Caroline LeRoy, the daughter of a New York merchant. While his marriage to Caroline could not fill the gulf left by his dear Grace, it did relieve his need for a companion who could attend to him and the needs of his household. His domestic situation settled, perhaps the proper spark might reignite the Webster fire and draw him back into the arena as champion of union and liberty.[22]

What began as an innocuous resolution by Senator Samuel Foot of Connecticut at the end of 1829 concerning the disposition of public lands morphed into a heated debate in January over the fundamental nature of the federal Union. Sectional lines emerged between the South and West on the one side and the "elitist" Northeast on the other. The debate moved from ordinary to extraordinary when South Carolina's Robert Hayne shifted the discussion to the damage done to the South by the tariff and by federal favoritism extended to the North for internal improvements. This bullying of the South, he charged, threatened the constitutional rights of southerners. To Hayne, Webster was the embodiment of the Northeastern political class. The South Carolinian charted Webster's record, from his "unpatriotic" opposition to the War of 1812 and affiliation with the Hartford Convention to inconsistencies on his tariff position(s). Finally, Hayne turned to the very structure of the republic, a voluntary association of sovereign states that retained autonomy and gave each, he argued, the right of interposition when the national government threatened its interests. In fact, the interposition by his own state "has kept steadily in view the preservation of the Union, by the only means by which she [South Carolina] believes it can be preserved—a firm, manly, and steady resistance against usurpation."[23]

When Hayne finished his speech the next week, few members of Webster's cohort felt that the masterful performance of the junior senator from South Carolina could be successfully assailed. Story feared that Webster would not be adequately prepared with counterpoints and so offered his help. The son of Ebenezer, though grateful for the offer, assured the judge that he would "grind him [Hayne] as fine as a pinch of snuff!"[24]

Webster's now-famous "second reply to Hayne" packed the Senate gallery in anticipation. Even congressmen abandoned their stations to crowd into the other wing of the Capitol building to hear Webster's rejoinder. He did not disappoint. After drawing in the audience with anticipated remarks targeting Hayne for both his flawed positions and his improper air of "taunt and disparagement," he offered a patriotic flourish on behalf of his adopted state of Massachusetts, which was "too near the north star to be reached by the honorable gentleman's telescope." By the time he turned to schooling the hall on the structure of the republic, he held fast the attention of all present. The Constitution, he proclaimed, is not about northern states or southern states; in fact, it is not a product of the states at all, but of the people. "It is, Sir, the people's Constitution, the people's government, made for the people, made by the people, and answerable to the people." To have states assert that they, as creator of the Union, might arbitrarily disregard laws passed down from the national government would certainly invite civil war. There must not be "Liberty first and Union afterwards." This would, in effect, undermine the noble project embodied by the United States. He then delivered the line that would become immortalized, the line that impressed even Hayne to emotion: "Liberty and Union, now and forever, one and inseparable!"[25]

The hall froze in place as if the words had at that moment transcended the present. Webster's start with sheepish silence as a boy when called on to speak in front of peers and faculty at Phillips Exeter seemed a distant and implausible illusion. His stature was set at this moment, and his words would find their way into the declamations of countless schoolchildren for the remainder of the century. After this, the debate limped along unnoticed until it closed with a sigh the third week of May.

Webster's popularity naturally ranked him high—in both his own mind and those of others—as a possible nominee for the presidency. Nevertheless, Webster knew that Clay, his senior, was a certainty for the National Republican nomination in 1832. The Anti-Masons invited Webster to run under their party banner, and, although he gave it passing consideration, it was more important to preserve his standing with his own party, "a Union party." This, it should be noted, was not the end of Webster's presidential aspirations. Every four years for the remainder of his life, he wondered if he would get the call, but the call never came. Ironically, on two occasions he was offered the vice-presidential nomination but declined, thinking it a career ender. On both occasions the ticket won (Harrison in 1840 and Taylor in 1850), and the president died in office.[26]

Webster continued to wield influence in the Senate for the remainder of the decade with most of his attention devoted to recurrent debates over the National Bank and tariffs, both of which threatened to undermine the Union. Webster knew that Jackson's reelection assured an all-out assault on the National Bank. The president had consistently reminded Americans of his opposition to the bank and routinely vented his disapproval in his annual messages to Congress. Webster, Clay, and supporters initiated a scheme to bring the bank up for renewal approximately four years before the current charter expired. They hoped to make the bank an issue for 1832 that might increase the election chances of presidential nominee Clay and his fellow National Republicans. During the third week of May, Webster initiated the debate over the recharter. In early summer the bill passed both houses and was forwarded to the president for a promised veto, which he issued on July 10. Jackson's veto ignored Webster's rationale for the bank and instead characterized the bank as an elitist institution that did nothing for the common man while making "the rich richer and the potent more powerful." Irrespective of what the Supreme Court may have ruled, Jackson held that the bank was, in fact, unconstitutional.[27]

Webster replied immediately to the "extraordinary grounds of reasoning" in the veto message. The president, Webster charged, proposed to elevate the executive's opinion on the Constitution to that of the Court by suggesting that its opinion was just that, an opinion. This attitude that assumed the executive's power to annul any law that did not suit him threatened the constitutional system itself. Webster was alarmed at the instability implied by Jackson's statement, as well as the president's appeal to class warfare. The veto message "manifestly seeks to influence the poor against the rich; it wantonly attacks whole classes of people, for the purpose of turning against them the prejudices and the resentment of other classes." Webster's rebuttal failed to rally a veto override. The scheme to use the bank for campaign advantage likewise failed. Jackson, the champion of the common man, demonstrated his popularity with a lopsided election victory—219 electoral votes for the president and a disappointing 49 for Clay. But the bank issue was not dead. Jackson's second term ignited an epic struggle over the institution that contributed considerably to a realignment of parties in the wake of the so-called Bank War.[28]

After Jackson's reelection, Webster soon found himself in the awkward position of aligning with Jackson at the cost of aloofness from his normal political allies. The senator first joined with his colleagues in opposing Jackson's appointment of Martin Van Buren to the Court of St. James's, a post that Van Buren had already occupied, but he then backed the president on the resurgent tariff issue. Within weeks of Jackson's reelection, a called convention in Columbia, South Carolina, voted overwhelmingly for a state Ordinance of Nullification, rejecting both the 1828 tariff and the compromise tariff of 1832. The South Carolinians threatened secession and the formation of a sovereign government should Washington resort to force to execute the nullified tariffs. Calhoun, the architect of nullification, resigned as vice president, knowing that he could not remain in the executive branch while opposing his own president. When Hayne resigned his senate seat to become governor of South Carolina, Calhoun returned to the upper chamber, where he expected to reassert his dominance and carry his attack to the Senate floor.[29]

Figure 2.1. John C. Calhoun. Courtesy of the Library of Congress Prints and Photographs Division, LC-DIG-ppmsca-19251.

Jackson did not dawdle but sent word the second week of December that the people of South Carolina flirted with treason and should consider the consequences of pursuing that course. Webster, from Faneuil Hall in Boston, voiced his agreement with Jackson's determination to enforce the law and signaled an alliance against Calhoun. While Clay worked on a compromise that protectionist convert Webster opposed, Jackson asked Congress in mid-January for a Force Bill that, among other things, called on the legislators to offer adequate latitude to the executive for deployment of arms in the event South Carolina animated its belligerent threats.[30]

In mid-February 1833, the tension escalated as Calhoun launched into his defense of nullification and Webster responded. Once again, South Carolina and Massachusetts tangled over the nature of the Union. Calhoun described his state as a victim of federal abuse. As to the Force Bill, South Carolinians stood ready to bleed, if needed, to guard their state's sovereignty. Calhoun then pushed the constitutional interpretation that would essentially give a state or states veto power over federal legislation.[31]

Webster responded by revisiting many of his central points from the Hayne debate. Patronizingly lamenting Calhoun's position, Webster described it as "a strong man struggling in a morass; every effort to extract himself only sinks him deeper and deeper . . . into the bottomless depths of the Serbonian bog." Webster then expounded on the nature of the republic, arising from the people and not from the states. It was no accident, Webster noted, that the Constitution opens with "We, the people of the United States . . . do ordain and establish this Constitution," not we the sovereign states. In the end, nullification was no more than subversion of the people's creation, and secession was nothing short of revolution. The debate continued, with other voices joining for several days, until a vote was called on February 20. With a handful, including Calhoun, withdrawing from the chamber, the Senate voted to approve the Force Bill thirty-two to one.[32]

About a week later, Clay's compromise tariff reappeared as the House completed its appropriations task and sent it to the other wing of the Capitol for Senate consideration. Again, Webster argued the protectionist position and fought Clay's tariff reduction. In the climate of crisis produced by South Carolina, many who ordinarily would have sided with Webster now joined Clay; the bill passed on the first of March by a vote of twenty-nine to sixteen. Webster held to his opposition and voted no. Fittingly, the tariff compromise accompanied the Force Bill to the White House where the president affixed his name to both. South Carolina had two options: (1) continue to resist and force the hand of an agitated

Jackson, or (2) accept Clay's compromise and come down from the ledge before Jackson pushed. They chose the latter. As the crisis subsided, so did the brief rapprochement between Webster and Jackson when the focus returned to the National Bank.[33]

Although Webster continued to entertain hope that he could work with the Democratic president, Jackson's determination to slay the bank in his second term made it impossible. The battle over the bank began when Jackson had his treasury secretary, Roger Taney, redirect federal deposits to select state banks. A financial panic in the winter of 1833 to 1834 drew allegations of fault from both sides—Jackson for the erosion of confidence and bank president Nicholas Biddle for squeezing credit. Though Webster and Clay proposed remedies, the president's power was too great and his plan to bring down the bank prevailed. Clay's final resort was to censure Jackson and Taney. The resolutions carried against both, but even that symbolic gesture was short-lived.[34]

The censure of Jackson and Taney stood no longer than the National Republican majority in the Senate. When the Democrats gained the upper hand in the next election, they proceeded to undo the censure and expunge it from the records. As Webster watched this play out in the winter of 1836 to 1837, he commented to his colleagues on the surreal moment: "We collect ourselves to look on, in silence, while a scene is exhibited, which, if we did not regard it as a ruthless violation of a sacred instrument, would appear to us to be little elevated above the character of a contemptible farce." Farce or not, Missouri senator Thomas Hart Benton, who had orchestrated this moment, must have felt supreme satisfaction as he watched "a square of broad black lines" drawn "around the sentence condemning Jackson" with the explanatory notation that the censure was "expunged by order of the Senate, this 16th day of January, 1837."[35]

Meanwhile, the 1836 election had witnessed disparate political factions converge to form an anti-Jackson coalition adopting the British title "Whigs" to indicate their opposition to "King Andrew I." Webster quickly rose in the leadership of the new party and was promoted by some adoring fans to run as the first Whig presidential nominee in 1836: "Why then may we not unite, in support of a man like Webster, the full strength of the friends of the Constitution? It is time that the Whig candidate should take the field. Why should the friends of Mr. Webster throughout the country delay any longer to present his claims to his fellow citizens?" But as logical as a Webster run seemed, he had amassed a substantial negative account, and the Democratic press was certain to open wide the ledger.[36]

In addition to the routine reminder of Webster's association with the Hartford Convention, the press exposed the unseemly exploitation of his position for personal gain. As for Hartford, Webster continued to insist that he had been about his work in Washington at the time and took no part in the meeting, a fact he was willing to document if necessary. He dismissed threats from his opponents to publish private letters exposing his collusion with Hartford as a "stale device." The accusation of fiscal mischief proved more difficult to rebut. For example, Webster had not only engaged his law offices in litigating the Spanish claims, he led the charge in the House to see to the appropriation of funds for the payout, much of which passed through his firm and left behind a handsome commission. More recently, when a claims treaty with Denmark—negotiations for which he and legal associate Henry Wheaton opened in 1827—came before the Senate in 1830, he immediately approached insurers to make his offices available for representation.[37]

Likewise, when Jackson became impatient with the French failure to honor an 1831 convention committing to compensate American claimants for damages during the Napoleonic Wars, Webster seemed unconcerned about a conflict of interest. An anonymous letter (presumably from Webster foe, Missouri senator Thomas Hart Benton) to the press alleged that Webster had cleared $20,000 for his work on French claims while the issue was pending before the Senate. Granted, the president had asked Congress to step up pressure on Paris to fund the promised compensation, but Webster's fees were not *directly* associated with that *particular* measure. His fees, he contended, were issued on claims prior to 1800, clearly predating the current business. This was little more than subterfuge. Webster had, as chairman of the Senate Finance Committee, noted a substantial profit to be made off of the pre-1800 claims when they appeared before his committee as "French spoliations prior to 1800." He likewise sought to benefit from a settlement in October 1832 with the Kingdom of the Two Sicilies, writing to Thomas Wren Ward of the British financial house, Baring Brothers, that he would "be glad to take charge of any such claim [emanating from the Naples agreement], if agreeable to you to place it in my hands." Finally, thanks to his sleight of hand with French claims, Webster secured approximately $5,000 from those claimants as well. The opposition press exploited these issues to draw an image of Webster as a money grubber who had little concern for the average man beyond his potential vote.[38]

The Democratic assault on Webster's reputation, however, did not undercut his political ambitions nearly as much as the credentials of one of the other Whig contenders. In the age of affection for the war horse, the

Whigs found theirs in William Henry Harrison. Webster's accomplishments and "godlike" presence lost to the broader popularity of an unpretentious general. While Webster continued to mine his legal fortunes, his political ones had taken a number of hard blows. It is no surprise that the senator not only considered abstaining from the presidential race but also resigning from Congress. He left Washington long before the session closed, and when he contemplated his return to the capital in the first week of April, he confided to fellow Massachusetts senator John Davis, "I have had more than half a mind not to return at all, I see no good to be done, & there is little, either in or out of Congress, to encourage effort."[39]

But return he did, and to a sensitive international issue regarding a new republic adjacent to Louisiana. The month before his return to Washington in April 1836, Texas had declared its independence from Mexico and, by the third week of April, made good on its declaration by defeating and taking captive the Mexican leader Antonio López de Santa Anna at the Battle of San Jacinto. Before Webster left for Washington, a Texas official had already sent him a letter seeking his help in securing US recognition of the Lone Star Republic. Texas secretary of state Samuel P. Carson knew how to appeal to Webster's ego and, in his request to "invoke Your [Webster's] aid in obtaining an immediate recognition of our Independence," he stroked the senator, "What may not be doen [sic] for 'millions Yet unborn' by the voice, Yes Sir the mighty voice of Daniel Webster? And who can estimate the loss, if that voice is withheld?"[40]

Webster was sympathetic to the Texans, but "that voice" expressed little enthusiasm for rallying the hoped-for support for Texas recognition. Several factors contributed to Webster's hesitation, foremost of which was slavery— a blight that he described the following year as "a great moral, social, and political evil." Although, as a perennial presidential candidate, he hoped to avoid alienating any potential supporter over the issue, he simply could not palate the massive expansion of the peculiar institution, especially when recognition of Texas independence anticipated a request to join the United States. Granted, Webster did not qualify as an abolitionist, but he did detest slavery. While he believed that the Constitution prevented action against existing slaveholders in the South, he did not feel compelled to support any action adding to their numbers by the annexation of Texas.[41]

In early May, Webster cautioned Congress to go no further than neutrality on the Texas question; the existing conditions of "peace and amity" with Mexico, he contended, must be maintained. After all, the Senate, in fulfillment of its shared duties with the president, had recently approved a treaty with Santa Anna's government. As he prepared these remarks to the Senate, he wrote Everett that this Texas issue with Mexico was extremely sensitive and capable, he feared, of provoking war.[42]

Toward the end of the month, Webster noted that circumstances had changed and, sensitivity or not, America must take action on the Texas matter. It appeared that the Texans had gone well beyond a rebellion against Mexican rule by establishing de facto viability as an independent government and would soon seek recognition from other countries. Webster volunteered that he "would be one of the first to acknowledge the independence of Texas, on reasonable proof that she had established a Government."[43]

Webster's conversion, while still calling for discretion, resulted from broader geopolitical concerns. His rationale at this point was less about Mexico and Texas directly and more about his fear that a detached Texas, not embraced by Washington, would prove too tempting to the Europeans. Mexico might be persuaded to transfer control to Britain, granting the Crown a position from which Britain could exert influence over all of Mexico. Webster managed to help spark enthusiasm for recognition among the American people but did not persuade Jackson to intervene—at least not in an election year when the impact might jeopardize his hand-picked successor's electoral prospects. In July, responding to pressure from increasing calls from constituents, both houses of Congress voted for recognition. Again, Jackson delayed. The president would not extend recognition to the Republic of Texas until the day before turning over the keys to the executive mansion to Martin Van Buren on March 3, 1837.[44]

Although Webster had succeeded in raising public awareness of the disposition of Texas during the recognition debate, he failed to arouse the public profile of another issue that appeared before the Senate that May. Jackson had forced a treaty with the Cherokee Nation at the end of 1835 in New Echota, Georgia, by which their claims to lands east of the Mississippi would be transferred to the United States in return for $5,000,000 and a new home in the Arkansas Territory (Oklahoma). In opposition to Jackson's treaty, Webster aligned with Adams as part of a congressional contingent challenging the legitimacy of this "base fraud" of a treaty. The fraud perpetrated on the Cherokee Nation resulted from a treaty negotiated by a select coterie of the tribe and opposed by the Cherokee National Council and its leader, John Ross. In other words, the legitimate representatives of the Cherokee rejected the treaty.[45]

Despite speeches by Webster and Clay in the Senate and Adams and others in the House, defenders of justice for the Indians had become, according to Webster, beaten down, "worn out and exhausted." Webster's ultimate frustration carried the name Robert Goldsborough, Whig senator

Figure 2.2. Henry Clay. Courtesy of the Library of Congress Prints and Photographs Division, LC-USZ 62-53083.

from Maryland. Having secured a promise from Goldsborough that he would vote in opposition to the treaty, Webster was furious at the betrayal when Goldsborough voted yea. "We relied on him," Webster fumed, "as a man of honor and religion; but he voted for the treaty, and turned the scale—mortified some of his friends severely." On May 18, 1836, the treaty cleared the two-thirds Senate threshold by one vote, with all three of the Great Triumvirate among the no votes. Despite continued efforts to nullify the treaty, the plans went forward—plans that would leave a nasty stain on Winfield Scott's résumé after he drew the assignment of removing the Cherokee from the Southeastern United States along the "Trail of Tears" to Oklahoma.[46]

The year 1836 was not a good year for Webster, and it increasingly worsened as he saw his candidacy for president virtually ignored outside of New England. The Massachusetts legislature had nominated him at the beginning of 1835, but the Ohio legislature selected its own native son, Supreme Court Justice John McKean, to carry the Whig banner. Whigs in the South selected a states' rights candidate, Hugh Lawson White of Alabama. But in the end, all three were outdistanced by a fourth Whig candidate, the famed victor of the Battle of Tippecanoe, General William Henry Harrison. While Webster might have hoped for a union of the party faithful behind a single candidate, the party chose instead to crowd the field: if no candidate received a majority, the decision would once again be left to the House of Representatives, giving the Whigs their best chance for victory. By the time election season arrived, the press and most of the nation saw it as a two-man race between Jacksonian Democrat Martin Van Buren and Harrison, "Old Tippecanoe." Surprisingly, when votes were counted, the Whig plan had almost worked. Although Van Buren won a majority with 170 electoral votes, a swing of just over two thousand ballots in Pennsylvania to Harrison would have sent the election to the House. Webster's performance did not equal that of the party; he trailed the presidential pack with only fourteen electoral votes. This setback did not dull the shine of the golden chalice; he instantly laid plans for 1840.[47]

During Van Buren's administration, Webster focused his opposition on Democrat culpability in a financial panic that started soon after the New Yorker's inauguration. Jackson's disastrous decision to divert federal deposits from the fading National Bank to various state banks had been compounded by his issuance of an executive order for the Specie Circular. This order required that all purchases of land from the federal government be made with specie (gold and silver) rather than paper. The net effect had been to throw the entire monetary system into disarray. While making a western tour to build support for his future presidential aspirations, Webster condensed his sentiments about the nation's economic woes to a rhetorical question: "Is there an intelligent man in the community, at this moment, who believes that, if the Bank of the United States had been continued, if the deposits had not been removed, if the specie circular had not been issued, the financial affairs of the country would have been in as bad a state as they now are?"[48]

When the Panic of 1837 descended on the Van Buren administration, the "Little Magician" proposed a new plan, one that would completely divest federal deposits from all banks by creating what became known as an Independent Treasury. Webster now had a clear target, and he worked for the next two years to block the Independent Treasury and to undo the Specie

Circular. Consistently arguing for the importance of a stable money supply, he joined opponents of Van Buren's Independent Treasury in both the Senate and the House to frustrate the president's plans. Van Buren's proposal was not approved until 1840. By then, Webster had helped Clay force the administration to rescind the Specie Circular. As important as this victory was, Webster felt that the only long-range remedy would come from a revitalized banking system, a central component of the economy that, through expansion of credit, would crank the economic engine.

While opposing Van Buren and massaging his potential presidential run for 1840, Webster worked to secure funding for his first and only trip to Europe. To many, his financial straits made such a journey seem impossible. During the recent boom Webster had overspeculated in western land and had to call on patrons with increasing desperation just to maintain his standard of living. In fact, one of his purposes in making the trip to Europe was to attract buyers for some of his land. Despite discouraging reports that the prospects of finding buyers were not good, he pressed forward with plans for an Atlantic crossing. He had long desired to make a trip to Europe and, in the midst of recent professional struggles, felt the time propitious. Not only could he enjoy a lengthy holiday with family, he could also mix in a bit of business, and perhaps even parlay the trip into a diplomatic mission. He had been disappointed when Adams did not select him as US minister to London in the 1820s. Perhaps now was the moment to secure a role for himself in US foreign relations. Either through an official appointment, or the largesse of his deep-pocketed friends and supporters, Webster was determined to see Europe. As it happened, a strain in Anglo-American relations at the end of the decade made the prospects of the "official capacity" look most promising.[49]

CHAPTER THREE

Taking the International Stage, 1839–1842

> The time has come when, if the controversy cannot be terminated by some sort of negotiations; it must be settled otherwise. . . . Delay, while it can benefit neither party, everyday endangers the peace of both.
>
> —Daniel Webster, February 1839

As Webster made his plans for the long-awaited visit to Europe, he was well aware of the rising tension between the United States and Britain over a number of issues, the most incendiary of which involved the controversial northeastern boundary between the United States and Canada and the recent inflammatory activities between Americans and British Canadians on that border. He could not have known that his career trajectory was about to shift decisively toward foreign policy, which for the remainder of his days would demand more of his attention than "independent treasuries" and court briefs. Before he decreed his last breath (and he practically did), he would become intimately familiar with the US-Canadian boundary controversy, the maps that lined and misaligned it, and the host of Anglo-American irritants that came to be associated with it.

The boundary issue had roots in the very beginning of the republic and the Treaty of Paris that codified its birth. The negotiators in Paris had relied on a 1775 edition of John Mitchell's map of the continent that placed topography and general features of the area at odds with the verbal description rendered in the treaty. For example, the northeastern segment in the treaty seemingly laid out a definite border "From the North West Angle of

Nova Scotia, viz. That Angle which is formed by a Line drawn due North from the Source of Saint Croix River to the Highlands" and then "along said Highlands which divide those Rivers that empty themselves into the Atlantic Ocean, to the northwestern-most Head of the Connecticut River." This description, however, could not be reconciled with features on the ground. The entire boundary delineation was flawed from the Atlantic Ocean to the Lake of the Woods (in present-day Minnesota)—in other words, the entire northern boundary of the new American nation. From that moment in Paris, the question of where British North America, especially eastern Canada, stopped and the United States started provoked a running dispute between London and first Philadelphia, then Washington. The river described as the St. Croix in the treaty simply could not be found. The Schoodic River might be it, as the British claimed, or maybe it was the Magaguadavic River as the Americans contended. Even if this river could be located, no one could sort out what exactly Mitchell meant by highlands.[1]

This troublesome question routinely surfaced over the next six decades before it found its way to Webster's desk in the early 1840s. During the War of 1812, for example, the British forces, after taking northern Massachusetts, arbitrarily rerouted the border to the middle of present-day Maine for military and commercial purposes and to make it possible to connect the British maritime provinces of Nova Scotia and New Brunswick with the rest of Canada. Of course, this was unacceptable to Americans in the area who hoped that the peace commission at Ghent, Belgium, would make a satisfactory adjustment. Setting the border back to an equally vague and arbitrary position, however, would have achieved little more than temporary pacification.

At issue were both trade and security. Thousands of acres of timber and access to important fisheries became increasingly important to American citizens and British subjects in the disputed area. Besides the value of the land, London refused to accept the strategic problem presented by a piece of the United States jutting northward between Quebec and New Brunswick, making direct access between the two impossible and presenting an unacceptable logistical impediment to the security of the Canadian provinces. Likewise, Americans coveted the Aroostook Valley as well as Rouses Point on the British side of Lake Champlain. During the War of 1812 they errantly constructed a fort at Rouses Point that, in admission of the error, later drew the name "Fort Blunder." This area continued to hold strategic importance for the United States as a defensive position to secure northern New York and found its way into all future border discussions. Negotiators at Ghent in

1814 proposed a commission to study these matters and to settle the entire boundary to the Lake of the Woods, but the commission's efforts ultimately proved ineffective.[2]

After Maine followed its separation from Massachusetts with admission as a state in 1820, the boundary became an obvious concern for the new state. The following year, Secretary of State John Quincy Adams broached the issue with Britain, but since the disputed area around the St. John River basin included few Americans, the boundary issue languished with little demand for immediate attention. Still, by mid-decade, agents from both Maine and Massachusetts appeared in the area to issue grants to Americans to counter the encroachment of Canadian lumberjacks. Occasional incidents, such as the arrest by British authorities of an American in the area, provoked threats by Maine to take action to protect its citizens if Washington failed in its responsibility.[3]

The parties at Ghent had put in place an arbitration remedy should the commission plan fail—as it did—to settle the boundary. Given the increased agitation in the region, the Adams administration conceded to the remedy in 1827 and joined Britain in submitting the problem to King William I of the Netherlands to examine the border question and propose a compromise. In 1831, his proposal to split the territory was considered by all concerned parties. Since London stood to gain the essential military route, it agreed. Maine, however, did not. President Jackson referred the matter to the Senate while dangling before Maine an incentive of a million acres of land in Michigan (valued at over $1 million) in return for the state's acquiescence to the Dutch king's plan. It did not help Jackson's scheme that the US minister to The Hague, William Pitt Preble, was a Maine man who operated under the suspicion that King William would do London's bidding in return for support in the ongoing Belgium attempt to break away from his country. By early summer of 1832, both Maine and the Senate had rejected the award. In the years that followed, the embers of failed compromise continued to smolder as lumberjacks from Maine and New Brunswick steadily logged deeper and deeper into the disputed territory. An explosion over the unsettled border was certain, and it came as Webster's dream of his transatlantic crossing moved closer to reality.[4]

It must have seemed to Webster that timing, if not fate, had presented the potential for a diplomatic mission just as plans came together for his grand European tour. Two recent flare-ups along the northeastern border called for direct Anglo-American diplomacy. The first involved American support, encouragement, and finally intervention by New Yorkers (self-described "Patriots") in a Canadian rebellion against British rule. South of the Canadian border, Americans idle from the economic panic were ripe for an adventure against the still-despised British. By the end of 1837 more than a thousand gathered in Buffalo, New York, all prepared to assist their Canadian brothers in throwing off the bonds of the British Crown. President Van Buren warned that if the impetuous New Yorkers violated the 1818 Neutrality Act, the US government would disavow them and leave them to their own devices. This caution must have seemed empty considering the limited muscle available to a commander in chief whose army had over half its forces scattered from Florida to the Western frontier.

Meanwhile, the Canadian rebels, who had mustered at Montgomery's Tavern near Toronto before a botched attempt to take the city, fell back to Navy Island across the Niagara River from Buffalo and formed a provisional government under William Lyon Mackenzie. Exuberant Americans, joined by Colonel Van Rensselaer from Albany, eventually made up the majority of Mackenzie's force. The situation soon became a tinderbox that Canadian officials feared would ignite into an Anglo-American war.[5]

Soon an American steamboat, the *Caroline*, entered the turbulent waters and the equally turbulent history of the northern border. Had the steamer remained true to her license to ferry passengers and cargo between the American ports of Buffalo and Fort Schlosser, the story would have ended here. But in addition to transporting passengers, it conveyed at least one six-pound cannon to Navy Island on the Canadian side of the river. According to Canadian authorities, the steamboat was aiding the insurrection and thus became a legitimate target. Unfortunately, acting on this knowledge became problematic when the target returned to Fort Schlosser on the American side of the river where it was presumably safe. The hotheaded leader of the Canadian contingent, Royal Navy captain Andrew Drew, ignored the technical detail of safe harbor and declared, "The steamboat is our object—follow me!" He and his men crossed the river to the American bank, boarded the vessel, killed at least one passenger, Amos Durfee of Buffalo, removed the rest to the docks, and towed the boat into the river current. To punctuate their success, they set the boat ablaze and watched with satisfaction as its smoldering carcass went down in the river and fragments spilled over the falls. In their moment of apparent triumph, they were oblivious to the international crisis they had unwittingly provoked. In the wake of the incident, the New York *Herald* reported from Buffalo that "war with England was unavoidable."[6]

Indiscreet celebrations occurred on one side of the river and fiery agitation on the other. Those involved in ordering the attack as well as Drew, who carried it out, were praised by the Canadian government and awarded ceremonial swords. Citizens of Buffalo marched up and down the street with muskets locked and loaded as they paraded Durfee's sad remains from the steps of the Eagle Hotel to the city hall with wounds exposed so all could see the "locks" of his hair "matted with his blood!" The Canadian press conceded that war could not be avoided. The Quebec *Mercury*, for example, reported a general feeling among officials that hostilities were inevitable and noted that the Parisian press feared an Anglo-American conflict would escalate into a general war.[7]

President Van Buren ordered General Winfield Scott "with all speed to the Niagara frontier." Van Buren then called for Congress to support war preparations. The legislators responded with an appropriation of over a half-million dollars to defend the border. This did not mean that Washington wanted war, but more than a steamboat had suffered. American honor had fallen victim to the attack on the *Caroline* and only restitution or retribution could set things right. Congressional leaders rhetorically elevated the incident to a "massacre" perpetrated by an invading force that, "with fiendish atrocity," murdered "our sleeping and unoffending citizens."[8]

An outraged secretary of state, John Forsyth, lodged an official complaint with Henry Fox, the British minister to Washington, over the destruction of life and property "on the soil of New York" and demanded redress. Fox argued that the *Caroline* was engaged in piracy, a legitimate assessment considering that the *Caroline* indeed carried war materiel. This position, however, was not competently argued. A less than satisfied Forsyth directed the US minster in London to demand reparations.[9]

Sadly, the slow boil in Anglo-American relations over the incident might have been avoided had Fox followed his instructions from the Foreign Office. The first step in the diplomatic process should have included an attempt by London to legitimize Drew's attack on the *Caroline* as a "public" act, meaning one undertaken by the authority of the British government. The ineffective Fox was directed to communicate as much to the government in Washington in early November 1838, but he failed to do so for two years. Scott calmed the border and convinced the Americans to withdraw from Navy Island to American soil, but the heat had only lowered, not cooled. The *Caroline* affair continued to simmer when New York authorities arrested a British subject and charged him with the *Caroline* incident and Durfee's murder shortly before Webster took the reins of US diplomacy in 1841.[10]

Agitation over the *Caroline* had been pacified *only* outside of the Niagara area. As the British government's representative dawdled in establishing that the attack on the steamer was a public act, emotions remained raw over the incident in New York where arrests routinely excited local passions but produced no evidence and, hence, no justice. Then, in November 1840,

Figure 3.1. Daniel Webster, statesman and diplomatist. Courtesy of the Library of Congress Prints and Photographs Division, LC-USZ62-11135.

Alexander McLeod, a deputy sheriff from Niagara, Ontario, was arrested in Lewiston, New York, and charged with murder and arson. This time justice seemed certain. McLeod, according to witnesses, had actually boasted in a Buffalo tavern of having done the deed. At first it seemed that, despite his barroom confession, lack of evidence would also allow him to go free. In fact, he was released twice before witnesses, who had heard him boast of having killed at least one American (presumably Durfee), assured his indictment for the infamous *Caroline* atrocity.

His incarceration and the move to prosecute a British subject in a New York court not only reawakened the unsettled *Caroline* affair but also added the new and more volatile element of an Anglo-American confrontation. A month after McLeod's arrest, Fox issued an appeal to President Van Buren to order his release, finally arguing that a British subject could not be held responsible for a public act in the service of the Crown. President Van Buren, now a lame duck, acted as one and kept his head down while politicians argued over state versus national sovereignty and as his successor, William Henry Harrison, prepared to assume office. The following March, when Harrison offered Webster the State Department, the McLeod and *Caroline* problems awaited the new secretary as matters of urgent concern. One of the first official communiqués to appear on his desk was another from Fox, this time *demanding* "from the government of the United States, formally in the name of the British government, the immediate release of Mr. Alexander McLeod."[11]

In the meantime, yet another issue in Anglo-American relations had surfaced on the northeastern border, this time involving citizens of Maine and Canadian subjects of Britain in the so-called Aroostook War. A brief eruption occurred on the Maine-New Brunswick border in early 1837 when New Brunswick, agitated by Maine's attempt to take a census in the disputed area, arrested Maine's land surveyor for trespassing. Two years later, after watching New Brunswick loggers extract thousands of dollars in timber from the Aroostook Valley, the Maine government funded the defense of the area with an appropriation of $10,000. In February 1839, Maine dispatched a land agent, Rufus McIntire, with two hundred volunteers to the area, and the lieutenant governor of New Brunswick responded by sending in his own force. Both sides made arrests: Maine took several British subjects, including a New Brunswick official, Warden James MacLauchlan, and New Brunswick took McIntire. Hostilities seemed imminent. Maine increased the initial defense appropriation by 80 percent and, within a week, had ten thousand militia deployed to the region. Despite the reciprocal release of prisoners, passions fueled by decades of indecision over the boundary called for settlement on the battlefield if necessary. The men of Maine were feeling the Anglophobic spirit of their revolutionary forbears and were pleased to exhibit it against the pompous British. And now that the national press had picked up the sensational story, sympathetic passions led to displays of support for Maine. In Boston, for example, men "curled their whiskers and sported mustaches as licenses to hold forth the honorable word, 'War! War!'"[12]

In Washington, Van Buren promised support for Maine should events escalate into hostilities. At the same time, he pressed Fox to have the New Brunswick armed contingent withdraw from the area. In Congress there were calls for war for honor, and Senator Webster proposed a deadline of July 4, 1839, for London and Washington to come to terms on the boundary line. If this deadline passed with no settlement, the United States should occupy the disputed area. Ironically, within two years Webster, as secretary of state, would find that settlement of the boundary line would require more than a tepid ultimatum. Over the next few days, Congress authorized the president to use force, if necessary, to secure the claim and appropriated $10 million to support a volunteer force of fifty thousand should the commander in chief find it necessary to call them up.[13]

Conventional diplomacy in the form of a memorandum between Fox and Secretary of State Forsyth joined the informal diplomacy of Winfield Scott who, once again, had been dispatched to the northern border. Fox and Forsyth pushed for more time to resolve the border issue by agreeing to have their respective constituents stand down. In the calm climates of London and Washington, officials found it easy to agree to the memorandum, but Scott was placed in the delicate position of convincing the impatient forces on the ground. This he masterfully accomplished by meeting Maine officials in Augusta and the Canadian lieutenant governor in Fredericton, not as a soldier but as a diplomat. The accepted terms orchestrated by Scott in March left New Brunswick in control of the upper St. John Valley and Maine in exclusive occupation of the Aroostook Valley. War, for the moment, was averted. The altercation had lasted little more than a month and resulted in only two fatalities, one from measles and the other from an errant celebratory bullet. Nevertheless, patience was in short supply on both sides of the border, and the two governments would prolong this boundary dispute at great peril. Scott knew and intimated in his memoirs that the time for diplomacy was fleeting.[14]

Webster weighed in on the Maine debate with two speeches before packing for his European trip. The first was in the heat of the Aroostook conflict on February 27, 1839, when he called on the president to inform Congress "why this negotiation has not been pressed to some practical result," or terminated. "Sir," Webster addressed the chamber, "I think this matter must be settled, and that it will not permit delay. . . . I believe our right is clear; and although I am willing to concede much for peace and good neighborhood, I am not willing to delay a final adjustment indefinitely, or at the hazard or in the face of the certainty of border conflicts." Maine "ought not to be kept" in a "state of dissatisfaction and neglect." It was at the conclusion of this speech that he proposed the ultimatum July Fourth.

The senator continued his defense of Maine the following month, calling for a change in the language of the Committee on Foreign Relations's resolution implying that the state might be expected to defend its own territory. Webster was tapping, not his developing diplomatic skills, but his established credentials as a constitutional authority. His point was simple and persuasive:

Any communication issued by Congress should clearly state the hierarchy of responsibility within the republic. Under no circumstances could a state engage in direct conflict with a foreign nation. "This cannot be. We must prevent war, or carry it on ourselves. . . . Maine is not our ally; she is part of ourselves." With this, Webster returned his focus to his customary concerns with sound money and the nation's financial stability and setting his plans for a six-month European adventure, little knowing how deeply he would soon plunge into the politics, diplomacy, and cartography of the northeastern boundary.[15]

Preparations for Webster's trip to Europe hinged on sorting out his finances. Overspeculation in western lands and his chronic difficulties with money combined to make it impossible to fund the trip without sponsors. Maybe the alarming events that threatened Anglo-American harmony and consequently essential trade would make it possible to underwrite the trip with a diplomatic appointment. He had been disappointed once when he thought Adams, with whom his relationship was cordial, might send him as minister to Great Britain. It is difficult to understand why he thought he had a chance at an appointment by the Democrat Van Buren, for whom he had exhibited such disdain and whose policies he had opposed. Making his proposition all the more unlikely was his role in sinking Van Buren's own appointment to London during Jackson's administration earlier in the decade. Van Buren not only lost the post, he suffered the embarrassment of being recalled from London after introductions.[16]

Nevertheless, Webster arranged a meeting with Secretary of War Joel Poinsett, who was rumored to be amenable to his London appointment. Webster arrived at the meeting with a memorandum he had drawn up for the president that outlined his boundary proposal in fourteen detailed points. He followed up with a visit to Van Buren, who graciously asked for a copy and then shelved the idea of a special mission entirely. Webster was too astute to have been overly disappointed with the president's decision. In fact, he noted in a letter to Samuel Jaudon, an American friend and business associate living in England, that "party considerations" would "doubtless have much influence" over the matter, and he was not optimistic about the mission prospects. He did volunteer that the "Maine business is now all quiet. Nothing of a disturbing character will take place in that quarter, until the two governments shall have had ample time and opportunity for bringing the pending negotiation to a close." This was certainly at odds with his public statement of imminent doom a month before![17]

Jaudon was one of several people Webster approached as he schemed to finance his trip. In January he had contacted Jaudon concerning the prospects of locating buyers for his western lands, but the reply offered little optimism. As a result, Webster plied his customary patrons such as banker Samuel Ruggles in New York, who extended funds against his western lands but fell considerably short of the requested $50,000. When Webster talked of selling his Boston residence, his local friends contributed to his travel fund, determining that his public service should not only be rewarded but perhaps might extend to produce some value in England. Well acquainted with the British banking house Baring Brothers, Webster hoped to secure some support through their American agent, Thomas Wren Ward. Ward, citing Webster's propensity to confuse the concept "borrowed" with "given," nonetheless forwarded the message to the firm with his own observation that it might prove useful to contribute to Webster's private mission. By spring Webster had cobbled together the necessary funds to underwrite his entire entourage.[18]

Accompanied by several family members, Webster left New York for Liverpool on May 18, 1839, and docked at the Mersey River port on June 2. Since Webster's profile as one of America's finest statesmen, legal minds, and orators was well established in the Atlantic community, it was no surprise that the London press acknowledged his arrival. The *Times* opined that among his professional peers he had "few rivals and no superiors." For half a year, the New Englander born to a meager station on the New Hampshire frontier was quite literally wined and dined by a who's who of British lights. The circles within which the senator hobnobbed included Lord Palmerston, Sir Robert Peel, Benjamin Disraeli, William Gladstone, Charles Dickens, and the Duke of Wellington. Shortly after their arrival in London, the young Queen Victoria welcomed the Webster party with an invitation to a ball at Buckingham Palace. While all these experiences proved memorable, for Webster's future the most significant visit arose from a dinner invitation from Alexander Baring, Lord Ashburton, primary of the Baring Brothers financial firm and soon to be Webster's partner in his most important diplomatic achievement. At the dinner, Webster met Lord Chancellor Henry Brougham, one of several men "in high places" with whom Webster had the opportunity to engage "on the subjects of common interests to the two countries." Perhaps he might satisfy his sense of service after all, even if in an unofficial capacity.[19]

Webster maintained the posture of a touring guest and avoided being drawn too deeply into the present controversies between the two nations. In September, he wrote to his friend, New York attorney Hiram Ketchum, that he had intentionally avoided topics that might cause angst with his hosts and at home. Webster was too busy being admired to risk raising the topic of Canada and accepted only one speaking invitation. On July 18, he addressed the Royal Agricultural Society at University College, Oxford. In this uncharacteristically brief address, Webster, after commenting on the English skills in agriculture and husbandry, mentioned the current strain between the two nations. But connecting with a sentiment expressed in Lord Spencer's introduction that Americans were "brethren in blood," Webster proudly acknowledged that shared blood and felt that all difficulties should soon find an "amicable" remedy. This was, perhaps, an early hint of the Anglophile from New England's determination to develop and maintain cordial relations between Britain and the United States.[20]

Webster's hope to free himself from his western lands and his economic straits were dashed by the equally dismal financial circumstances he found in Britain. He did little more than cover expenses, "so as to go home no poorer than I came." He did find satisfaction in intervening with British creditors on behalf of American debts and paper. For example, at Jaudon's request, he volunteered his influence with the British bankers in support of Bank of the United States paper. He honored another inquiry from Baring Brothers, who sought some assurance that the American states had the constitutional latitude to deal with foreign lenders. Webster provided that assurance to the firm along with an explanation of the federal system. The "several states," he explained, "possess the power of borrowing money for their own internal occasions of expenditure," and they could be counted on to satisfy those debts because the American people expect the state to honor "her pecuniary engagements."[21]

Before returning home, Webster made a brief visit to France, expanding his European connections and relationships. He arrived in Paris in mid-October in the company of Colonel James Pinkney Henderson, former governor and secretary of state of the Republic of Texas, then serving as the republic's minister to both Britain and France. Henderson's acquaintance, though minor, added a potentially useful contact for the future, and at times rocky, American relationship with the Lone Star Republic. As in London, the French also proved gracious with a tour of Versailles and a meal with King Louis Philippe and Queen Maria. This was no doubt the highlight of the Websters' cross-channel trip, unencumbered by formal commitments and substantive interaction with policymakers.[22]

In early November, the Websters were back in London and making plans for the voyage to America. Before departing, Webster met with the Duke of Rutland, who raised the topic of current difficulties between the two nations. Webster wrote the duke in mid-November to offer assurances that there would be no "interruption of the harmony existing between the two countries" that might "derange the general prosperous course of trade and business in England." After noting the interdependent nature of the two economies, he offered an expression of hope "that between two Christian nations speaking the same language, having the same origin, enjoying the same literature, and connected by these mutual ties of interest, nothing may ever exist but peace and harmony, and the noble rivalship [sic] of accomplishing most for the general improvement and happiness of mankind." These positive and reassuring words were, perhaps, less than totally honest. In truth, Webster felt genuine concern over Anglo-American tension. Precisely one month before his comments to Rutland, he had written his close friend Edward Everett "quite in confidence about the troubles on the northern frontier" concerning the Aroostook Valley incident. Webster volunteered that Foreign Secretary Lord Palmerston was rumored to have told U.S. minister Andrew Stevenson that "if the American government does not repress or punish these outrages, the British government will." Further, Webster added, the foreign secretary sardonically read "us a lecture on the right of pursuing such marauders into their own country, out of Mr. Monroe's message," referring to "General Jackson's Florida Campaign, &c.!"[23]

Anyone who cared to consider the humor occasioned by serendipity might have betrayed a smile at the embossed golden letters on the stern of the vessel booked by Webster for the passage home: *Mediator*. Rather than returning to the bar for litigation, Webster was destined for mediation, first by the hapless though successful Whig political fortunes, then by a rising stack of grievances in Anglo-American relations. *Mediator* deposited the family in New York just after Christmas, and they were back home in Boston on the second day of January 1840.

Webster's return from Europe presaged a more stark transition than simply from Old England to New; the current campaign season soon sent him from palace to log cabin and from high tea to hard cider. The Democrats, hoping to see Van Buren serve a second term, had inadvertently yielded their "common man" class advantage to the Whigs by deriding the aging General William Henry Harrison as a hard-cider-drinking pensioner, content to swing on the porch of a log cabin with cider flowing and pensions collected. Rather than rejecting this incredulous image, the Whigs embraced it and adopted the cabin and the cider as campaign symbols. One might expect a refined, and now cosmopolitan, Webster to balk at this campaign style, but a politician he was, and a politician pleased to exploit a path to victory in whatever form it took. Webster lowered his lofty rhetoric to the level of every man and even romanticized on occasion about his birth in a log cabin that his father had built with his own hands. While technically accurate, Webster could not have remembered life in a log cabin; the family moved to Elms Farm when he was an infant. Moreover, his father had suffered much to see that Daniel rose far above those New Hampshire farm roots. But again, politics demands only tenuous ties to truth. Harrison himself, after all, was born in Virginia in the stately Georgian mansion at Berkeley Plantation, one of the finest homes in America.

In late March 1840, Webster wrote to Joshua Bates in London expressing optimism that the "popular outbreak for Genl. Harrison" placed him in strong contention for the election. The senator's commitment to Harrison and his hope for economic stability and sound money clearly yielded exceptional fruit: Harrison won in November with almost 53 percent of the popular vote to Van Buren's 47 percent with an electoral vote margin of 234 to 60. Soon Harrison asked Webster to advise him on cabinet appointments and offered him first choice of Treasury or State. Webster chose State but assured Harrison that he would take Treasury if the president-elect had someone else in mind for State. Fortunately for American foreign policy and, especially, for Anglo-American harmony, Harrison gave Webster his first choice, and on March 5, 1841, the Senate confirmed his appointment as secretary of state with not a single dissenting voice. He began his duties the following day.[24]

Webster, as a National Republican turned Whig, was highly critical of the Jacksonian "spoils system" that made government appointments prizes to be doled out to loyal partisans. As a victor, however, the spoils were now his to dole out, and dole he did to both his personal and public satisfaction. While he selected competent and qualified men for State Department posts, scruples did not prevent him from also allowing those competent individuals to conveniently supply some personal financial relief in the process. He named Washington Irving minister to Spain, for example, while Irving's brother-in-law's financial firm canceled the mortgages on some of Webster's burdensome real estate. Isaac Jackson secured a chargé d'affaires post in Denmark while extending credit to Webster for a Washington residence. He also rewarded friends and family on what, to critics, appeared to be solely nepotistic credentials; in practice, however, they justified their selection with a high level of competency in their respective positions. For example, Webster appointed his old and close friend, Everett, to represent the United States in London, an appointment that, by all measures, placed a highly experienced and capable diplomat in the nation's service. For his State Department clerk, Webster chose his son Fletcher, who proved an invaluable asset in the management of the office.[25]

Webster's appointment to State coincided with rising tension in Washington's relationship with London, which quickly consumed his time and attention. After the short-lived administration of Harrison, who died after only a month in office, Webster might have avoided what would surely be a difficult task of sorting out Anglo-American difficulties. He and his Whig cabinet colleagues had signed on to a Harrison administration; now they were asked to serve under Vice President John Tyler of Virginia—derisively dubbed "His Accidency." Tyler, until recently a Democrat, seemed to many Whigs still tainted with that pedigree and could not be counted among legitimate Whigs. After the president refused to submit to Clay's control and rejected Whig orthodoxy reflected by his September veto of the Bank bill, Harrison's cabinet resigned and the Whig leadership read Tyler out of the party.

Only Webster, in large measure because of his commitment to resolving matters with Britain, stayed with Tyler despite the cost to his party standing. This decision not only guaranteed his diplomatic stature in American history to rival that of orator, legislator, and lawyer but also set his nation on a path to an epic partnership with Great Britain. The tension he soon faced in Anglo-American relations resulted from three sources, one with a stale past and two fairly fresh. The old and neglected issue that tended to foul relations almost on schedule was, of course, the still unsettled northeastern boundary. The second item resulted from New York's determination to prosecute Alexander McLeod for his complicity in the *Caroline* incident. Finally, a maritime matter of visit and search arrived on Webster's desk late in the year and must have immediately taken him back to his participation in the *La Juene Eugenie* case of the early 1820s.

The first issue demanding Webster's attention was the disposition of Alexander McLeod. The behavior of the boisterous Canadian deputy sheriff had all but ensured his arrest by Anglophobic New Yorkers. On more than one occasion he taunted them with his alleged role in the *Caroline* incident. In November he had been arrested in Lewiston before leaving for Canada, was transferred to jail at Lockport, and remained behind bars when Webster sorted through his desk at Pennsylvania Avenue and 15th Street. The new secretary faced a triangular dilemma. This case involved three parties: New York, the United States, and Great Britain. New York governor, Whig William Seward, claimed jurisdiction to prosecute the British subject in the state system. But since the accused was a British subject, the issue was international and, Webster argued, should fall within the purview of Washington. London, not surprising, had no appetite for a replay of General Jackson's Florida performance that resulted in the trial, conviction, and summary execution of two British subjects. An already untidy problem with three

Figure 3.2. John Tyler. Courtesy of the Library of Congress Prints and Photographs Division, LC-USZ62-13010.

competing parties now appeared poised to add an even more sensitive fourth element—honor. This affair was not about the importance of an obnoxious and by all accounts shady Alexander McLeod. It was about honor and respect. For New York, it involved respect for the rights of the state to pursue justice over an egregious affront to its citizens. For Washington, British bullying continued to raise hackles even after two wars. For London, the idea of a British subject processed through the American system was intolerable. The honor of the Crown demanded a favorable settlement.[26]

By the time Webster unpacked his State Department office, two of the three sides had established inflexible positions, and the third, it seemed, could easily be goaded into an equally provocative reaction. Lord John Russell at the British Colonial Office joined with Palmerston, Fox, and the British press to send a clear message that the execution of McLeod would result in a third Anglo-American war. The London *Times* doubted that it would be difficult to find "three Englishmen living" who would not demand war. Americans, many of whom were members of the Hunters' Lodge from the volatile Maine frontier, converged on the jail where McLeod was held determined to provoke another tangle with their former colonial masters. When their mob behavior made it impossible for McLeod to meet bail as directed by two different judges, London chastised the rabble as "hot-brained democracy." Harrison had Webster inform the British that the onus was on them to admit that the attack on the *Caroline* was a sanctioned (public) act, thereby making it a matter of international concern. Under these conditions, all parties should understand that, should the case proceed to trial, the proper venue was the US Supreme Court.[27]

On March 12, 1841, Fox belatedly made the first move and acknowledged that the attack on the *Caroline* was a public act and McLeod could not be held personally accountable. He should be released. Not surprisingly, New York refused and Seward reiterated that the state had jurisdiction. In this climate any flash could ignite violence. Once again, Washington directed General Winfield Scott to maintain order and to inform Seward that Joshua Spencer would lead McLeod's defense. The addition of Spencer heightened Seward's consternation when he learned that Spencer also had been appointed US district attorney for the northern district of New York. This created the awkward situation of a federal attorney defending a British subject in a state court. Missouri senator Thomas Hart Benton sarcastically noted the absurdity of a New York attorney general prosecuting McLeod while a US district attorney defended him. Despite the obvious conflict of interest, McLeod's trial remained in New York. All of Webster's maneuvering to get the trial moved to the Supreme Court ended abruptly when McLeod announced that he would rather have a finding from a New York jury than suffer months of confinement before the case made it to the high court.[28]

Meanwhile, changed circumstances in London opened new hope for a peaceful settlement when old actors left the stage and those more amenable to compromise took their place. Sir Robert Peel became prime minister and chose Lord Aberdeen to replace the sardonic Palmerston at the Foreign Office. Also, the US minister in London, Andrew Stevenson, who had been an ill fit for proper English habits, was replaced by Everett, Webster's longtime friend. If the climate in New York would not be tempered, perhaps that in London could. The fencing that had characterized the American legation's interaction with Lord Melbourne's government was replaced by a more cordial and hopeful rapport. But regardless of conditions in London, if the trial went poorly, the impact on Anglo-American relations might be devastating.[29]

The trial finally opened on October 4, as the first of a long line of colorful witnesses testified before the New York jury—a jury entrusted with more than the fate of one Canadian. The prosecution was far more dramatic with its presentation of blood-stained swords and alleged public outbursts in which the defendant admitted to the crime. The defense featured a credible family, each member of which took the stand to report that on the night in question McLeod had been at their home and nowhere near the *Caroline*. All the drama of the lead-up to the trial and the courtroom performances faded to a less than dramatic climax: the jury delivered an acquittal after less than thirty minutes of deliberation. New Yorkers, perhaps surprisingly, accepted the verdict with a sense of triumph simply for having defied both Washington and London on the matter of jurisdiction.[30]

There must have been a nearly audible sigh of relief in both national capitals having survived the McLeod ordeal with relations intact. It should be added, however, that had the trial gone badly, Webster would have sought a way, with Seward's likely collusion, for the administration's intervention to prevent war. Despite the perception of a rogue governor cultivated by some in Washington, there is ample evidence that Seward would have pardoned McLeod before permitting his execution to provoke an Anglo-American altercation. To ensure against such an episode in the future, Congress, at Webster's direction, promptly passed the Remedial Justice Act, sanctioning federal removal from state jurisdiction of cases involving foreign relations.[31]

Before the trial ended, other troublesome Anglo-American issues had already summoned Webster's attention, one resulting from a new incident awakening old problems of neutral rights on the high seas. In November 1841, slaves revolted on the *Creole*, an American brig conducting legitimate trade within the territorial jurisdiction of the United States. The slaves seized their freedom, navigated to the Bahamas, and—with the exception of a small number who participated in the bloody takeover of the vessel—were reclassified as "free" by British authorities in Nassau. Southerners called for Washington to intervene and demand reparations. This demand might have seemed straightforward enough to those determined to quickly dispose of any issue raising the specter of slavery—Jefferson's "firebell in the night"—but this was far from a simple matter. It involved decades of squabbles and international vagaries concerning maritime law and American complaints of Britain's persistent transgressions ranging from impressment to illegal searches. These issues, like those of the northeastern boundary, desperately needed resolution.[32]

Concern over policing the illegal African slave trade had resurfaced in 1840 as Britain attempted to align the United States and other nations with the Crown's enforcement agenda. Although Congress had unilaterally outlawed the trade two decades before and made it a capital offense, the United States remained the only major nation to resist codifying its policy by treaty with Britain or other nations. Lord Palmerston attempted to bring the Americans on board by casting a distinction between what constituted a search as opposed to a visit; stopping and boarding a vessel to inspect papers but not cargo, in Palmerston's thinking, was merely a visit and not a search. Stevenson, speaking for the American government, dismissed this as a difference without a distinction. Since the United States abstained from any British multilateral attempt to stifle the trade—and all knew of Americans' sensitivity to British harassment—the American flag became the primary device employed by slavers to frustrate British efforts to suppress the trade. Under these conditions, Britain could either concede to an ineffective plan or risk having American ships caught in the nets.[33]

The new British government under Sir Robert Peel continued to test ways to make their efforts to stymie the African trade both more effective and more palatable to Americans. Perhaps Washington could be assuaged by the promise of reparations for any inadvertent harassment of ships legitimately flying American colors. Before the end of 1841, London pursued a multilateral agreement that would, it was hoped, include the United States. After Austria, France, Prussia, and Russia signed onto the multilateral Quintuple Treaty, Britain extended the invitation to Washington. Everett persuaded Lord Aberdeen to sweeten the offer with a promise of compensation for earlier violations of America's maritime rights. Although Secretary of State Webster found merit in the concept, Tyler rejected it. It was apparent that sectional interests would dictate opinion on anything touching slavery.

Tyler, a Virginia slaveholder, was not immune. The unresolved question remained an irritant when the *Creole* incident occurred.[34]

When the *Creole* limped into New Orleans in early December, the entire nation, especially southerners, vented their anger over yet another example of British high-handed treatment of the United States. It might have been about slavery in the South, but *all* Americans felt the slight to national honor. A generation of Americans who remembered British abuse during the Napoleonic years saw this as yet more victimization by John Bull. The *Creole* was not unique. There had been several incidents of British authorities in Nassau liberating slaves from American ships that arrived in their harbors. The *Creole* not only involved loss of life but also occurred after Britain had implemented the Emancipation Act outlawing slavery. This controversy would not be easily remedied, especially when American abolitionists adopted it as a cause célèbre, applauding the British while agitating southerners.[35]

Webster wrote to Everett in London at the end of January 1842, insisting that the British had erred in their handling of the *Creole* and owed reparations for the loss of American property. British law that banned slavery should not have been applied to Americans who, in the course of conducting lawful trade (by their nation's standards), were forced into British waters. The brig and cargo should have received assistance in completing the journey. The response from London went well beyond a simple dismissal of Webster's position. The British felt no obligation to compensate for allowing people who arrived in their jurisdiction as free people to remain free. As for the nineteen blacks accused of leading the rebellion, London determined that any alleged crimes had occurred in American jurisdiction, so the British courts had no grounds for prosecution. Further rankling the Tyler administration, the British noted that, since there was no extradition treaty with the United States, the blacks would not be returned for trial in American courts either. Hence, in mid-April the British authorities on the island released the nineteen rebels to join their compatriots from the *Creole* as free blacks registered as guests of British Nassau. Despite Webster's identification of these blacks as lost property, no compensation would be forthcoming. Southerners were livid. The intangible element of honor joined the tangible loss of property to promote agitation with Britain among southerners who soon found sympathy with their brothers in Maine as heat returned to the boundary dispute.[36]

The Canadian-American boundary issue fell only one year short of being as old as Webster. Failed and frustrating attempts over six decades had made it one of the most vexing problems between the two nations. The triage administered by General Scott after the bloodless Aroostook War had not held. The November before Webster came to State, Americans in the disputed area north of the Aroostook River and a contingent of French-speaking Canadians *all* voted in the US presidential election! New Brunswick officials on the scene naturally objected and an altercation developed that drew a response from both London and Washington. London proclaimed British rights to the area, while Maine—soon to be supported by states as far removed from the border in question as Alabama—defiantly did the same. London, Washington asserted, should remove all troops from the area. The kettle, left earlier to simmer, threatened to return to a boil.[37]

The two governments could pursue any number of avenues to lower the heat, but until the people in the disputed territory conceded to compromise, it would be a temporary fix at best. In the summer of 1842, complaints of heavy British military traffic crossing "their state" emanated from the American side of the border. Britain held firm to claims on the Madawaska River. Maine did likewise. An impasse resulted from a Tyler appeal to allow federal troops to relieve state forces at the mouth of the Fish River while British troops withdrew to the northern bank of the St. John. Neither side was cooperative. The British would not relinquish their position on the southern bank of the river. This cumbersome triangulation of players had to be addressed. Somehow the locals, Webster believed, should be persuaded to defer the disposition of the area to the two national governments.

Webster's potential remedy came in two disparate parts, both odd on the surface, but typical fare in the climate of nineteenth-century diplomacy. In 1841, shortly after Webster had assumed his duties at State, Francis O. J. (Fog) Smith approached him with a propaganda plan designed to move Maine to compromise by exploiting his connections to the state media. In what today is generally referred to as "spin," Smith offered to use his financial interests in several Maine newspapers to orchestrate a press campaign to convince the state's leaders that war loomed on the horizon if they held to their entrenched position. They must, Smith argued, yield authority to Washington to negotiate the border. If war came, no likely scenario would produce a favorable outcome for the state. Smith knew that if the press and politicos understood that continued unrest and conflict would be detrimental to all involved, they would agree to compromise. Webster quietly contracted with Smith to pursue his plan, arranging for compensation and expenses to be drawn from the president's discretionary secret service fund.[38]

By fall, Smith's scheme was well underway. Webster supplied him with a compromise proposal, and he placed the information in various papers such as Portland's *Christian Mirror*, a rag with wide distribution, and the more important *Eastern Argus* (also Portland). Articles in the *Eastern Argus* favoring Webster's compromise position began to show a clear shift from opposition to support for a settlement. Articles posing the headline question "NORTH-EASTERN BOUNDARY—WHY NOT SETTLE IT?" appeared over the name *Agricola* and anonymously sketched Webster's tantalizing answer: Britain would receive land for the required military access to the Canadian hinterland. Maine would secure title to the disputed territory, navigation rights for fifty years on the St. John, as well as compensation from Washington and indemnity from London. As more and more papers expressed support for the plan, it began to appear in early 1842 that the old sore might be healed.[39]

This sentiment heightened with news from Everett that the less acrimonious Peel government had elected to send a special envoy to Washington "clothed with full powers" to address all outstanding differences between the countries. Fox, Britain's resident minister in Washington, had worn out his welcome and would be a poor choice for sifting through the pile of issues that had accumulated between the two countries. A prominent statesman dispatched on a singular mission to mend Anglo-American relations would not only meet the primary motive but would also signal to France, Britain's perpetual irritant, that the English-speaking nations were on friendly terms. Aberdeen received the queen's approval for the special mission on Christmas Eve. The Peel government assigned the mission to Alexander Baring, Lord Ashburton.[40]

Optimism from either nation over Peel's decision to send a special envoy to America derived more from the "special" individual selected than in the decision itself. Attitudes were mixed initially. On the one hand, Americans still struggled for respect, and not a few feared that London would send a bully to remind them of their inferior station and to take their territory as well. The Richmond *Enquirer*, a voice of the Democratic Party, expressed doubt over the likelihood that the envoy's goals would seek anything less than exploitation of the moment to Britain's advantage. The governor of Massachusetts echoed this doubt, convinced that Britain was less inclined toward compromise than dominance. On the other hand, some saw the appointment of so prominent a person to negotiate nation to nation as a sign of respect for the sovereignty of the republic. The latter attitude drew affirmation from the stature of Lord Ashburton—former member of Parliament and retired head of Baring Brothers, one of the world's most powerful financial houses and underwriter of Jefferson's purchase of Louisiana.

Ashburton had solid credentials, not only as a leading figure and elder statesman in British society, economy, and government but also as a Yankeephile. His choice of a wife had, in his youth, confirmed an affinity for

Figure 3.3. Alexander Baring, Lord Ashburton. From Howard Jones and Donald A. Rakestraw, *Prologue to Manifest Destiny: Anglo-American Relations in the 1840s* (1997). Courtesy of Library of Congress.

America; at the age of twenty he married the daughter of US Senator William Bingham of Philadelphia, from whom he had purchased an enormous tract of land in Maine (far removed from the area in dispute). Before Ashburton's arrival, Webster, who had advised Baring Brothers throughout the past decade, received a note from Lady Ashburton assuring him of her husband's desire for an amicable settlement and asserting that he was the best hope to accomplish it. The government appointed him to this mission, "as the person most zealous in the cause of America, & most sanguine as to the possibility of settling the long pending differences between the two countries" and, she stressed, "if you don't like him, we can send you nothing better."[41]

Ashburton's directive to negotiate with Webster—a business acquaintance turned friend during Webster's England sojourn—carried surprisingly generous concessions from the Peel government. The Foreign Office instructed Ashburton to be prepared to relinquish land on the northern rim of Lake Champlain at Rouses Point, a portion of the Madawaska settlements, and navigation privileges on the St. John River. Despite vocal opposition from cabinet members, Peel and Aberdeen felt the retention of a corridor for the essential military road connecting Montreal to the sea would adequately balance the ledger. Aberdeen further permitted Ashburton to yield St. George's Island between Lake Superior and Lake Huron as a gesture toward clearing the unresolved western piece of the Canadian-American boundary disagreement.[42]

As Ashburton prepared for his mission, the second part of Webster's strategy for bringing Maine to heel on compromise appeared at his desk in a letter from Jared Sparks, McLean Professor of History at Harvard. Sparks's recent work in the French archives had, by happenstance, unearthed a letter from Benjamin Franklin to Comte de Vergennes, the French foreign minister at the time of Franklin's negotiations with Britain to end the American Revolution. The letter referred to a map on which Franklin had drawn a red line showing the boundary between the new republic and British Canada. Sparks set out to locate the map and, in fact, found a map with a red line marking the boundary. This, he elatedly presumed, must be the map. His elation soon turned to consternation when he realized that the red line conformed to the British rather than the American version of the boundary. Sparks struggled between his obligations as a good scholar that would have him make public his findings and those of a loyal American that would have him bury the map. Choosing a middle ground, he passed the map to Webster on his return to the States and left it with him to decide. As it happened, the map Sparks saw at the archives, despite the marked red line, could not have been Franklin's. The Paris negotiators used an edition of John Mitchell's map. The map that Sparks discovered was a map by French cartographer Jean-Baptiste Bourguignon d'Anville. Nevertheless, Sparks's find inadvertently contributed to Webster's diplomacy.[43]

The map that Sparks delivered to Webster did more than support the British position on the boundary; it set a line that pushed Maine off the

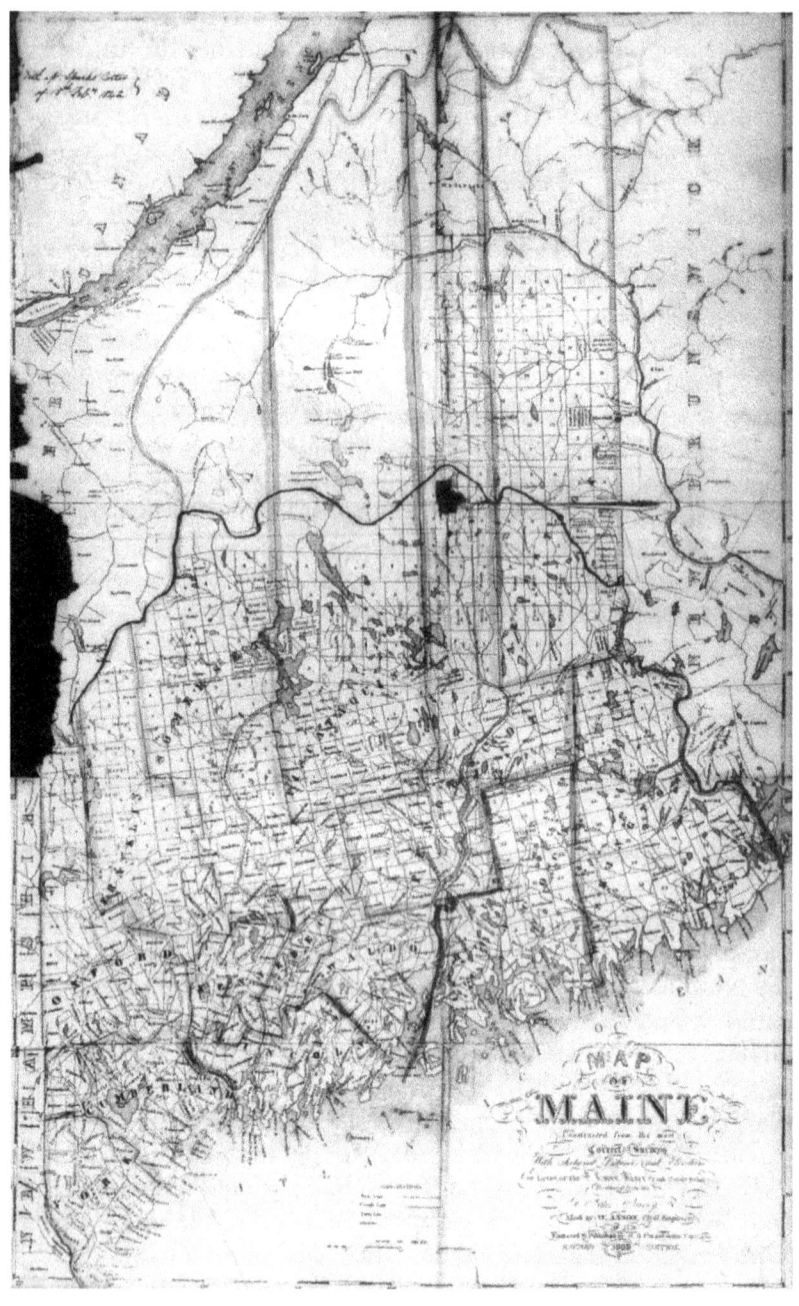

Figure 3.4. Jared Spark's map of Maine. From Howard Jones and Donald A. Rakestraw, *Prologue to Manifest Destiny: Anglo-American Relations in the 1840s* (1997). Courtesy of National Archives.

southern bank of the St. John and completely out of the Aroostook Valley. Webster was not surprised by the so-called red-line map; he had purchased a Mitchell map from the estate of Revolutionary War general Baron Friedrich von Steuben a few years before with almost exactly the same marking. Steuben had left the map to his secretary, John Mulligan, who offered it for sale to the British consul in New York who, fortuitously, could elicit no interest from Lord Palmerston and so let it go to Webster for $200. Webster subsequently resold the map to John Davies of Maine, presumably to soften the state's demands with evidence supporting a British claim to considerably more territory than London (or the Dutch king's earlier arbitration proposal) had envisioned.[44]

In the meantime, another act in the maps drama played out on the other side of the Atlantic. Everett suspected that the Foreign Office held in the public archives a Mitchell map that he believed would bolster the American claims. Aberdeen admitted that he had "heard that they had found an old map," but, he deflected, it was not the map at issue. Everett, undeterred, doggedly pressed his search. Perhaps, thought Everett, it was in the papers of Lord Shelburne, who had been prime minister at the time of the Paris peace negotiations. Sparks knew this to be a dead end and conveyed as much to Everett. Still, the map had to be somewhere; surely, the State Paper Office (present-day British National Archives) was the likely location. Unknown to Everett, in early summer of 1842 several government staffers had spent weeks searching the archives for such a map and had found one. In June, Aberdeen held a Mitchell map in his hands with what appeared to be Franklin's red line, a line that also substantiated the British claim. He did not share this information with Everett. Now, both London and Washington had the evidence required to resolve the boundary issue. How they would use it remained uncertain.[45]

While Everett worked to unearth evidence in London, Webster invited Maine and Massachusetts into the settlement process in Washington, hoping either to squelch their suspicions or to pacify their angst. In the first half of 1842, he engaged two Maine political leaders with ties both to the state and the federal governments. Peleg Sprague had represented Maine in the Senate and now held a seat on the federal district court in Boston. Albert Smith, formerly a federal marshal, was currently completing a term in Congress representing Maine. In February, Sprague reported from Boston that both political parties now favored a compromise boundary, "and the public mind generally in Maine are more disposed to an adjustment of this controversy now than at any time heretofore." The politicians, nonetheless, remained hesitant to come out publicly and give their political opponents an issue. Sprague's contribution was as "a medium of communication between" public figures in the state and Webster. Sprague sent Webster a potential compromise line he had received from Maine's land agent: Maine would yield territory north of the St. John in return for navigation of the river and some compensatory land, perhaps "the narrow strip of land on the West side" of the river. The following day Webster replied to a skeptical letter from Maine senator Reuel Williams in an attempt to calm his suspicion of the Ashburton mission and to prod him to consider compromise. The generally favorable reports from both Sprague and Smith satisfied Webster that the naysayers were in the minority and that state representatives might provide at least a guarded endorsement of the proceedings in Washington. Despite threats posed by abstractions such as national honor and Anglophobia, Webster had employed Fog Smith's propaganda campaign, Peleg Sprague and Albert Smith's political efforts, and soon deployed a "grand stroke" in map manipulation to set the negotiating table for the best opportunity in decades to resolve the border dispute.[46]

When the British naval vessel *Warspite* delivered Ashburton to America in early April 1842, the welcome was both warm and hopeful. Even contrarians like Senator Thomas Hart Benton of Missouri found the elder British statesman impressive. *Niles' Register* predicted a fair negotiation and reasonable settlement, believing Ashburton's mission to be "conciliatory, and sincere in its professions of pacific design." Those closer to the dispute remained guarded. Voices from Maine worried that Ashburton had come with a more traditional British approach: both the carrot and the stick, with the latter poised for implementation should talks not go favorably for the Crown. This suspicion could only be eased, Webster felt, by inviting Maine and Massachusetts to join the negotiations. Although Ashburton, with some reservation, acquiesced to this unorthodox arrangement, there was no guarantee that Maine and Massachusetts would actually send commissioners. After all, they would be sending them, in essence, to surrender territory to Britain. Massachusetts was a softer nut to crack and quickly agreed to supply commissioners, but only on condition that Maine followed suit.[47]

Webster knew that failure to secure Maine's cooperation meant failure to secure that of Massachusetts, which, in turn, meant failure to produce a treaty. At this juncture, Webster determined to use the maps. He bought back the Steuben map and had Sparks take it along with his own map from his research in Paris to Augusta to show Maine governor John Fairfield the evidence supporting Britain's claim—evidence that would undoubtedly surface should negotiations be delayed. There was no question that this would amount to an ace card for London should the Crown choose to play it. Sparks wrote to Webster in mid-May that Fairfield "saw at once their [maps'] bearing," considered them "as worthy of deep consideration," and believed that "now is the time to settle the dispute." Not surprising, Fairfield shortly recommended that his state select commissioners to the boundary talks in Washington. Just over a week later the legislature agreed with fewer than 10 percent of the legislators opposing. It appeared that Webster had played his own ace card to perfection; his shrewd use of the maps had removed a major obstacle to compromise.[48]

The only matter remaining for the states' participation in the compromise boundary was the selection of the commissioners and the drafting of their directives. Of four commissioners selected, William Pitt Preble, former minister to The Hague and vocal opponent of earlier compromise proposals, was most likely to foul the waters. The delegation carried fairly straightforward terms. To begin, honor precluded the acceptance of money in return for land. The introduction of money into the process would create the appearance of a crass real estate transaction. The terms instead should pivot on the exchange of equivalents—either land for land or land for navigation rights on the St. John. The only acceptable monetary remuneration would come from US coffers to reimburse Maine for expenses incurred in defending the territory.[49]

Armed with these directives, Maine's representatives met with Webster and Sparks in Boston in early June, where they were joined by the commissioners from Massachusetts. In Boston, the commissioners conferred with British consul Thomas Grattan, who, like Preble, had firsthand knowledge of the Dutch arbitration over a decade before. The Maine contingent, in a serious breach of protocol, asked the British consul to join their effort as an adviser. After meeting in New York briefly with the head of the American team surveying the land in dispute, the delegation joined Webster at the State Department in the second week of June 1842. So far, Webster's clever use of operatives and maps (subsidized by the president's secret service fund) had successfully queued the boundary dispute for settlement. But this only represented the American components of the negotiation. Webster had worked under the assumption that there were only three parties to coordinate—Washington, London, and Maine. Had he neglected the Canadians? Perhaps he worked under the assumption that they would simply fall in line with London's prescription.[50]

While Webster minded the American case, Ashburton, without consulting either his government in London or Webster, invited the lieutenant governor of New Brunswick, Sir William Colbrooke, to join the discussion. Although a reasonable move in light of Webster's inclusion of Maine and Massachusetts, it dangerously complicated matters by raising the number of interested parties to four, all pressing potentially irreconcilable agendas.

Colbrooke, at Ashburton's suggestion, sent three representatives from New Brunswick to Washington; the delegation included a warden and a land owner, both with direct ties to the disputed area. While willing to concede navigation rights on the St. John to the Americans, the delegates held firm against releasing *any* of the Madawaska settlements and, further, were determined to purge the St. John Valley of all Americans. Ashburton's instructions included forfeiting part of Madawaska. His courteous gesture to New Brunswick had, perhaps, removed that concession from consideration.

Before Webster sat down with Ashburton, two additional complications surfaced. In London, the military pressed Aberdeen to restrict Ashburton's concession's further. The baseline of the Dutch arbitration in his original instructions now shifted the minimum acceptable border beyond the upper St. John and St. Lawrence rivers, thus creating a security zone for the projected military road connecting Quebec with Halifax. This contraction of Ashburton's negotiating room was bound to make his job more difficult.[51]

Finally, one more potential impediment threatened to undermine Webster's success with Maine by introducing the exchange of money into the negotiations. Aberdeen wrote Ashburton that if adjustments of territory did not prove effective, he should propose monetary compensation for Maine's territorial concessions. This suggestion opened a proverbial can of worms whose contents, when out and circulating among the players, invited risky speculation. Once Ashburton had suggested the possibility of a cash disbursement (a figure of a half-million dollars was allegedly floated by Aberdeen at a dinner party attended by President Tyler's friend, James Hamilton) to Webster and dollars entered the broader conversation, there was no way to pull it back. Maine's leaders had attached honor to cash and instructed the commissioners to reject any hint of a British purchase of Maine real estate. Nevertheless, monetary considerations had invaded the boundary dispute to add yet another complication to the coming talks. Fortunately, the two primary individuals responsible for sorting it were up to the task. Ashburton and Webster would open formal discussions in early summer.[52]

CHAPTER FOUR

From Webster-Ashburton to Wanghia, 1842–1843

> It was an object of the highest national importance, no doubt, to disperse the clouds which threatened a storm between England and America.
>
> —Daniel Webster, September 1842

Above the swirl of intrigue about secret maps and closely held cards stood two very powerful and dominating personalities, Daniel Webster and Lord Ashburton. Their path was not clear, but their abilities to clear it stood second to few, if any, statesmen in the Atlantic world. When they finally sat across from one another to open official negotiations on June 18, 1842, they did so in an atmosphere of mutual respect, congeniality, and a determination to dispose of decades of discord in Anglo-American relations. Ashburton prefaced his opening gambit on the twenty-first with assurances that he came out of retirement only from "an earnest persevering desire to maintain peace and to promote harmony between our two countries," and, he continued, "I approach my duties generally without any of those devices and manoeuvres [sic] which are supposed, I believe ignorantly, to be the useful tools of ordinary diplomacy." The two would carry on their talks discreetly, with no records kept and with the state commissioners left to communicate outside of the primary meetings, and then only with Webster. Ashburton chose to have no formal contact with any of the seven commissioners. When agreements were reached and decisions were made, President Tyler alone would be informed through written reports that he would then make public at his discretion.[1]

Diplomacy is often characterized as the card game poker, gambling with high stakes in an atmosphere of bluff and bluster. If the nature of Webster's relationship with Ashburton suggested that their behavior would be otherwise, the realities of national honor and states' rights bet against it. By the time they approached the table, cards had been marked and slipped up each sleeve: Webster had colluded covertly with Sparks and the "maps" while Ashburton managed to ferret out little more than unsubstantiated suspicions of some ace that Webster held. He had written to Aberdeen a few days before the meetings began, "I have some reason to suspect that Webster has discovered some evidence, known at present to nobody, but favorable to our claim. . . . I have some clue to this fact and hope to get at it." All must be fair in love and diplomacy, for the British emissary in similar fashion conveyed to Webster a desire to be open while concealing revised, inflexible instructions from London and uncompromising terms from New Brunswick. Thus, the game began with both negotiators soon mired in the duplicity of "ordinary diplomacy."[2]

Ashburton's opening proposal did not follow his original instructions from the Foreign Office as much as it did the boundary terms he had unwisely solicited from New Brunswick. British subjects living in the Madawaska Valley on both sides of the St. John River, he informed Webster, had lived as British and all intended to remain under the queen's flag. This statement undercut Aberdeen's compromise by eliminating any of the Madawaska Valley from the discussion. Besides, the British envoy noted, the land could not be bargained acre for acre; the southern part that would go to Maine would be far more valuable compared to the northern portion, which was "waste and barren." If it were just about territory he would accept the "miserable" land for the sake of compromise, but duty would not permit him to "abandon the obvious interests of these people." To secure the Madawaska for them, Ashburton offered what he considered an equivalent that would similarly avoid the disruption of American citizens settled on a strip of land at the head of the Connecticut River, land that included the valuable American position at Rouses Point. In addition, he offered citizens of Maine duty-free navigation privileges on the St. John River. The "chief guide," Ashburton wrote, was for the "convenience and happiness of the people to be governed." In this, he expressed equal objection to the displacement of the Americans and the British.[3]

Despite Ashburton's seemingly generous concessions, Maine found the proposed sacrifice of all Madawaska so offensive that negotiations slowed to a standstill. On June 29, the Maine delegation wrote Webster that any attempt to proceed on the basis of Ashburton's proposal "would be entirely fruitless," and they were "surprized [sic], and pained to be repelled, as it were, in the outset, by such a proposition." Webster penned a lengthy reply on July 8, opening with a testy jab at Ashburton's doublespeak. On the one hand, the British envoy proposed to start fresh and not revisit the tiresome arguments on both sides that had cycled and recycled throughout the controversy. On the other hand, he cycled and recycled tedious, and to those familiar with the affair, stale arguments. Thus, "following your Lordship's example," Webster teased, "I must be permitted to say, that few questions have ever arisen under this Government, in regard to which a stronger or more general conviction was felt that the country was in the right, than this question of the Northeastern Boundary." He followed with "a very condensed view of the reason" for this conviction before pressing the rhetorical question: Can the current "desire to preserve harmony" escape the trap of rearguing what has been exhaustively argued and "incite us to come together and to unite on a line of agreement?" Sadly, the answer was no. What followed was a back and forth of stating and restating claims by all parties as both the heat of argument and that of the Washington summer rose.[4]

Ironically, after a frustrating month of impasse, Ashburton blamed the lack of progress on Webster for being cowed by the state commissioners. In truth, the British Lord's own determination to defer to New Brunswick (with no official standing in the negotiations) had set the talks on a potential path to failure. Having left an ailing wife in England and desperate to extricate himself from the humidity of the Potomac Basin, Ashburton appeared willing to throw up the sponge and return home empty-handed. The elderly envoy lamented to Webster that he was reduced to crawling "about in this heat by day" and spending his "nights in a sleepless fever" while fearing that he "would not outlive this affair if it" were "much prolonged." Had it not been for Tyler's application of southern charm to Ashburton's ego—the only Englishman, Tyler wheedled, capable of saving Anglo-American amity—the matter may have died there and presaged the deaths of future sons of both nations. But Tyler's intervention elicited a "Well! Well! Mr. President, we must try again."[5]

Ashburton's frustration was soon compounded by Aberdeen's intrusion into the process that solicited the aid of British consul Thomas Grattan. Aberdeen inserted a new aggravation by having Grattan, in clear violation of protocol, consult with William Preble, the most intransigent of the Maine commissioners as well as the target of much of Ashburton's ire. On the Preble problem, as it happens, Ashburton and Grattan soon arrived at the same assessment. Grattan wrote to Aberdeen that the troublesome commissioner had turned his rooms into an untidy archive of materials in search of any fragment that might bolster Maine's claims to the disputed territory. Preble, to no one's surprise, meant to cling to the extreme American position to the bitter end. All these complications conspired to extend Ashburton's mission intolerably longer than planned.[6]

In mid-July the wilting Ashburton surrendered any hope of exposing Webster's secret pro-British evidence or of backing Maine out of the Madawaska Valley, and he joined Webster in a compromise settlement. To advance the process and avoid catastrophic consequences for the future of the two nations, Ashburton returned to his original instructions formulated around the Dutch arbitration line. His compromise appeared fair to Webster and, even though the United States would be left with less territory than the arbitration award had proposed (7,015 opposed to 7,908 square miles), the secretary quickly assured the state commissioners that the land awarded constituted almost all of the valuable land in the disputed territory. Britain's aim continued to be a military artery connecting coast to hinterland; exploitation of the land for farming was of little concern. The compromise increased the land for London's primary goal of the Dutch arbitration from 4,119 to 5,012 square miles. The United States would receive clear claim to the strategic position of Rouses Point, and Maine would enjoy free navigation of the St. John for moving timber. To sweeten the deal for the states, Washington would transfer $250,000 to Maine and Massachusetts to be equally divided between the two. Additionally, Maine would receive an amount equal to its costs incurred over time for defending and surveying the border region.[7]

Webster's presentation gained approval from the states' commissioners, but only after they had dutifully complained and proffered counter conditions. Maine objected to the prescriptive nature of the navigation clause and proposed that it be expanded from timber to include grain as well. Further, it seemed that $300,000 from Washington might make the compromise go down easier than $250,000. There also remained an outstanding issue with New Brunswick over fines collected from Maine for cutting timber in the disputed area. Webster agreed to the additional $50,000 compensation for the two states, and Ashburton consented to the adjustment for grain transport in the navigation clause as well as reimbursement of the timber fines. A few days later, the British emissary wrote Aberdeen that the boundary had been settled but with very little thanks to the Maine contingent. The obstinate Preble had merely succumbed rather than agreed to the compromise and departed the proceedings, Ashburton noted, for "his wilds in Maine as sulky as a Bear."[8]

After such a long and divisive struggle over the northeastern boundary, the two diplomats settled the residual boundary issue west of Lake Superior with surprising ease. On this topic, Webster benefited from having no festering state issues involved and little interest from London in retaining the territory. British fur trading and fishing proponents found the boundary delineation crucial but were not joined in that sentiment by their government. As a result, Webster scored a major prize with very little effort; about 6,500 square miles of land, including St. George's (Sugar) Island in the northernmost reach of Lake Huron, came under the American flag. From the terminus of the settled line at the "most northwestern point of the Lake of the Woods," the boundary then dropped due south to connect with the existing border that followed the 49th parallel to the Rocky Mountains. Webster, of course, would never fully appreciate the value of his territorial prize. Decades later, rich mineral deposits, especially iron ore, were tapped in the Vermilion and Mesabi ranges, both within the border established in 1842.[9]

Webster and Ashburton had every right to be pleased in having resolved the troublesome northeastern boundary dispute, but that was only one of several problems threatening amicable relations between the nations. Although they had addressed these complications generally in their talks, there remained another US-Canadian boundary dispute in the Oregon Territory; the matter of the *Creole* and associated maritime issues such as the slave trade, right of search, and impressment; and the final dispensation of the *Caroline* and McLeod affairs. To secure the rapprochement Webster and Ashburton sought, all these issues would have to be addressed either as part of the treaty or, at least, as an addendum to the negotiations. Ashburton's first communication with Webster after his appointment had expressed confidence that "many if not all" of the differences between the nations would "vanish on candid explanation and discussion." The time had arrived to either validate this optimism or expose it as disingenuous or naïve.[10]

Of the remaining issues, the slave trade held the most potential to upset the cart, not only because it involved the sensitive subject of slavery but also because the practice itself touched sensitive issues in Anglo-American relations that had persisted for decades. Since the early days of the republic, the United States had struggled to have Britain at least acknowledge, if not fully honor, American maritime rights. Passions over British impressment of American seamen into the Royal Navy factored large in provoking the United States to war in 1812. Add to this the abusive British practice of visit and search at the heart of both impressment and the slave trade, and the two friendly negotiators faced a combination that might turn the positive

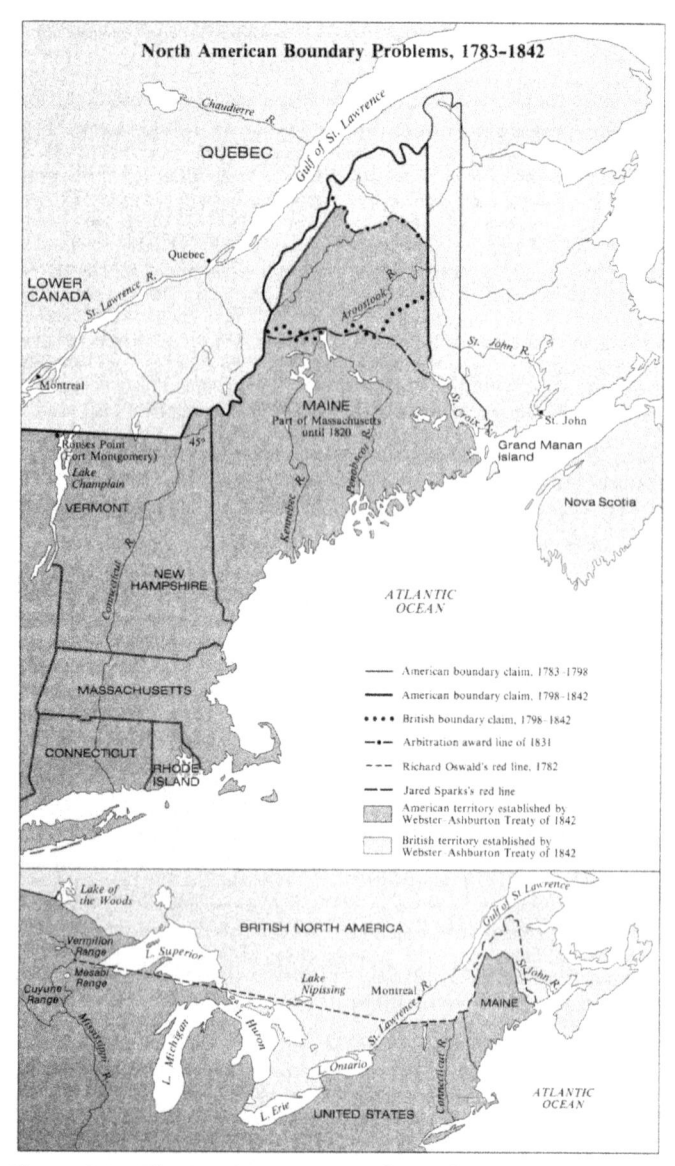

Figure 4.1. The Northeastern Boundary Dispute. From Howard Jones, *Crucible of Power: A History of American Foreign Relations to 1913* (2009).

conclusion of the boundary talks into a fractious termination of the proceedings altogether. Southerners felt confirmed in their belief by the liberation of the slaves in the *Creole* incident that Britain ultimately intended to conflate abolition of the slave trade with abolition of slavery itself.

To further complicate the matter, US minister to France, Lewis Cass, muddied the waters with a public (and unauthorized) pronouncement on how best to police the slave trade. He suggested that an American be posted on each of the British ships policing West African waters. The American would judge the legitimacy of ships flying American colors and control any action by the British cruiser to which he was attached. Although Ashburton entertained the odd proposal, with the caveat that the assigned American be a civilian, the Peel government rejected the suggestion out of hand. Practical implementation of such a procedure would have given an American de facto authority to countermand that of a British captain.[11]

The deep-rooted irritant of impressment further complicated the talks surrounding the slave trade; after all, it remained the core grievance associated with the right of search. Americans connected the British practice of visit and search with the forced removal of American sailors from American ships and induction into the Royal Navy, an intolerable assault on sovereignty and national self-respect. Webster approached the subject with his typically sound understanding of the law as well as an appreciation for the deep scars that the practice left on national honor. The Crown, he stated, could not require sovereign nations to submit to British municipal laws and statutes wherever on the planet Britain chose to enforce them. Foremost among these was the notion of "perpetual" allegiance to the Crown that attached the obligation of military service to nothing more than being British. This, the government maintained, vindicated the practice of impressment.[12]

The impasse that developed in Washington between Webster and Ashburton over impressment resulted more from the theory than the practice. There had been no incident of impressment since the Napoleonic Wars. Aberdeen confessed to Everett that he would be pleased to assure Americans that the practice would never recur but could not do so formally. Ashburton, likewise, "would gladly renounce it." But American honor was not the only intangible at play. British honor dictated that the Peel government hold to the tradition of military service to the Crown implicit in impressment; therefore, private assurance was as far as the foreign secretary could go. The dispute found no formal remedy in the treaty. Webster and Ashburton, at Everett's suggestion, agreed simply to exchange notes to record the positions of their governments on impressment. As they completed their respective communiqués at the end of Ashburton's mission, the British envoy expressed hope that a resolution would be forthcoming that might "set at rest all apprehension and anxiety" of the American people on the subject. This hope was realized in 1858, when the British government finally ended the practice.[13]

Having disposed of the impressment issue, the diplomats turned their attention to policing the illegal slave trade, an Ashburton priority that he hoped would bear "the very best fruit of this mission." Early in the deliberations, Webster had resurrected an 1820s scheme whereby both nations would "jointly" police West African waters. Unlike the Quintuple Treaty arrangement, the United States would consummate no pact, but rather act unilaterally, exercising its *own* discretion in enforcing its *own* laws. This, Webster noted, would be the "more manly and elevated" approach; the United States, thus, would go no farther than cooperating with Britain in policing the nefarious slave trade. Webster had not arrived at this position without due diligence. In April, he solicited details of operations off the African coast from two US naval commanders. As part of his information gathering, he asked their opinion on joint naval operations. The report provided significant detail, including estimates on the number and types of vessels required and confirmed for Webster that the magnitude of the slave trade was so great that no "material good can result without an earnest and cordial co-operation" between the United States and Great Britain.[14]

Ashburton agreed to Webster's joint-squadron compromise and its inclusion in the body of the treaty and successfully promoted it to Aberdeen in late April. Articles VIII and IX of the final treaty both addressed the slave trade: VIII provided for each nation to maintain a squadron of no less than eighty guns to patrol the African coast, and IX committed both signatories to "urge" all nations to close down markets for slaves, the demand for which perpetuated the trade in African labor. Although Webster committed the United States to this arrangement, in practice America's contribution went little beyond the promise on the page; the United States rarely fulfilled the obligation to maintain a force of eighty guns, and southern legislators routinely attempted to either defund or overturn this part of the treaty. The United States did not participate fully in suppression of the slave trade until the Civil War made moot the issue by eliminating the market for African labor in the United States.[15]

Despite Webster's complaint about the *Creole* incident lodged with the Foreign Office before Ashburton booked transport for America, the British envoy received no instructions on the matter. Perhaps the British were unaware that passions in the American South over the recurring incidents of British liberation of American slaves ran parallel with those of Maine over the boundary dispute. In February 1842, Mississippi officials forwarded resolutions to the state's delegation in Washington that demanded return of the property and held that the unlawful "search" by which the British authorities emancipated the blacks was "just cause for war." Webster knew southerners were angry and understood that this incident contributed to the charged environment clouding relations between the nations. British Bahamian authorities, as they had with the *Hermosa* in the fall of 1840, failed to respect American property rights over slaves in their jurisdiction—property that southerners felt should have been secured and returned. Webster knew the British had been under no legal requirement to return the slaves and, while the president repeatedly called for reparations, the authorities in Nassau likewise felt justified in their actions. Since slavery was outlawed in the Empire, the mere arrival of the *Creole* in British waters had converted the status of the blacks on board from slave to free. That some were charged with a criminal offense committed on the high seas was not a factor. Under international law, such crimes could only be tried in the country under whose flag the ship sailed. Since the United States did not have an extradition treaty in place with Britain, only accommodation, not law, would have prompted the return of the accused blacks to the United States.[16]

Everett had met with Ashburton in January in London and informed him that, although no extradition agreement was in place, Jay's Treaty (1794) had provided for such an arrangement. If the arrangement were revived, it might be applicable to the *Creole* affair. The notion of reinstituting an extradition arrangement appealed to the Crown as much as to the Americans. A few years before, the United States had refused to surrender two British murder suspects, and the US Supreme Court had ruled shortly before the *Creole* affair that an escaped murderer should not be returned to Canada. With both sides appreciating the need for an extradition protocol, Webster and Ashburton included it in the final treaty. Soon, both France and Prussia sought similar accommodations from Washington with the former succeeding in Webster's first term at State and the latter during his second incumbency in the 1850s. The disposition of the *Creole* matter itself remained beyond the reach of formal agreement and relied on an exchange of letters.[17]

As the two diplomats approached the *Creole* letters, Ashburton exposed a lack of optimism as he began his initial attempt on July 31: "Using the words of Walter Scott when he sent one of his novels to his publisher—I send you my Creole Damn her." Webster laid out his argument in a letter to Ashburton the following day, noting that the proximity of British territories to the American coastline would likely invite future incidents as American vessels, engaged in lawful commerce, might be "driven by stress of weather or carried by unlawful force into English ports." Since the British envoy had no authority to settle the matter, perhaps, Webster suggested, his lordship could provide instructions to the authorities in the islands to "regulate their conduct in conformity with the rights of citizens of the United States and the just expectations of their Government." Hopefully, this would prove adequate to discourage such problems in the future. If the issue were left unaddressed, Webster warned, a "future collision" similar to that of the *Creole* might disrupt the harmony reflected in their recent efforts.[18]

Ashburton struggled to find language that would satisfy both Webster's request and Tyler's rigid parameters. The president monitored Ashburton's communication with Webster and offered line-by-line edits on one occasion before laying it aside as likely inadequate to provide a resolution of the *Creole* dispute. The Virginian had routinely called for reparations since hearing of the actions of the British authorities in Nassau, and Ashburton feared that, out of deference to his fellow southerners, Tyler might block the slave trade convention. Although Ashburton had earlier felt London the better venue for resolving the *Creole* matter, he now doggedly pressed on "through at least a dozen attempts" before satisfactory language would be "at last but sulkily received by" the president. On August 9, the day of the treaty signing, he wrote to Aberdeen that "my great plague," the *Creole*, had been disposed of. Webster, in consultation with Justice Story, had earlier affirmed his belief that Britain's action stood on sound legal ground; hence, a letter including the instructions to British authorities with jurisdictions near the United States that promised "no officious interference with American vessels driven by accident or by force into those ports" was all that could be expected.[19]

The *Caroline* and McLeod matters, still grating on national honor in both countries, also required an exchange of deferential notes, each intimating an apology. Webster initiated the exchange on July 27, not with a fresh argument, but with his missive to British minister Henry Fox from the previous April and a relevant excerpt from President Tyler's recent message to Congress. In a brief introduction preceding the enclosed documents, Webster argued that the activities of the *Caroline* precipitating the attack at Fort Schlosser had no bearing on whether that attack was or was not justified. The attack itself was "wrong and an offence to the sovereignty and dignity of the United States," an offense to the "honour of the country" for which "no atonement or even apology has been made by Her Majesty's Government." In the lengthy message to Fox, Webster made it clear that simply (and unjustly) designating those on board the *Caroline* as pirates did not excuse the action taken against it. No nation, Webster held, has established more rigid constraints against individuals engaging in the internal conflicts of other nations than the United States. More to the point, an 1838 Act of Congress had specifically curtailed the involvement of Americans in the Canadian turmoil.[20]

In the Fox letter, Webster eventually targeted the question of self-defense, the only *plausible* rationale for the action taken against the *Caroline*. Could Her Majesty's Government, he asked, show that the activities of the *Caroline* left her Canadian subjects no recourse other than the attack on the steamship—that there was "no choice of means, and no moment for deliberation?" Had it been impossible to wait for daylight, to sort out the innocent from the guilty? Did the British subjects find it necessary to attack "in the darkness of night, while moored to the shore, and while unarmed men were asleep on board" before sentencing the ship "to a fate which fills the imagination with horror?" This, Webster held, was the heart of the matter; for only self-defense defined by tightly prescribed conditions could justify the attack on the *Caroline*.[21]

Ashburton replied the following day and, after taking issue with Webster's colorful rendition of the attack, focused on the matter of self-defense and the breach of territorial integrity. "The only question between us," Ashburton reasoned, "is, whether this occurrence came within the limits fairly to be assigned to such exceptions." Those limits, he added, were established by Webster as "that necessity of self-defence, instant, overwhelming, leaving no choice of means" but to engage the *Caroline* while docked in American waters. Ashburton wished to know at what point patience could reasonably be exhausted. US citizens had helped the rebels inflict pain on British subjects in Canada, and there was no indication that American authorities intended to do anything about it. Thus, Ashburton contended, the Canadian officials acted in the moment and in self-defense. The only culpability Britain could be asked to assume derived from the location of the attack. Territorial integrity, he acknowledged, was central to national sovereignty. But circumstances and not premeditation had placed the attack on the American side of the river. Nevertheless, Ashburton conceded, this action was regrettable. It was unfortunate, he admitted, "that some explanation and apology for this occurrence was not immediately made" and that the incident had been allowed to disturb the desired harmony with the government and people of the United States.[22]

Ashburton's decision to include the words *regret* and *apology* allowed the Tyler administration to set the matter aside and maintain harmony with London. In his reply on August 6, Webster once again visited the notion of self-defense before accepting Ashburton's claim that Britain had not intentionally disrespected the sovereignty of the United States.[23]

Finally, the exchange of letters between Webster and Ashburton also put to rest the issues raised by the McLeod affair. These issues involved both matters of jurisdiction and public versus private acts. Ashburton wished to know if the United States accepted the principle that individuals acting under orders of their government (public) could not be held personally accountable. If, as acknowledged by the Crown, the assault on the *Caroline* had been a public act, McLeod's incarceration and prosecution was illegitimate. Webster not only affirmed American adherence to the principle but also expressed regret over McLeod's prolonged ordeal. This case, Webster noted, was complicated by the jurisdictional tension between the state and federal government, and Congress had passed a remedy to prevent a recurrence in future cases. At the end of August Webster sent Ashburton a copy of the "Bill to provide further Remedial Justice in the Courts of the United States" to establish federal control over detention and prosecution of "subjects or citizens of a foreign State." This act, commonly known afterward as the "McLeod law," was privately drafted by Webster at the request of Senate Judiciary Committee Chairman John McPherson Berrien, and it represents an often-overlooked but significant accomplishment of Webster's first term at State.[24]

As the two diplomats finalized treaty terms and exchanged letters, only the Oregon Question remained on their agenda. Surely after healing the festered northeastern boundary, the two could sort out a remote territory that seemingly held few national interests and few subjects and citizens of either country. But like the northeastern boundary, that in the Northwest had a conflicted history. Both nations had laid claims to Oregon in the late eighteenth century, and a number of failed negotiations signaled the difficulty of reaching an easy compromise.

When Ashburton left for America, his instructions closely tracked previously rejected offers by London to set a boundary between US and British claims at the Columbia River. These terms, Ashburton reported to Webster in April, formed the limits of his instructions from the Foreign Office. This stricture did not bode well for an Oregon settlement. Besides forcing the United States to forfeit all territory north of the river, this line would leave the United States with no good harbor on the Pacific. To this problem, Webster had a possible, albeit unusual, solution. The American minster to Mexico, Waddy Thompson, believed that Mexico might be persuaded to sell the port city of San Francisco to the United States. If this could be arranged, the United States would have the required Pacific harbor and Britain could have its "great desideratum" at the northern bank of the Columbia River. Webster grasped this idea as a way to salvage the Oregon negotiation on the basis of Ashburton's Columbia line. When presented, Ashburton saw no reason his government would object to this so-called tripartite concept, but such an arrangement, he observed, would depend more on the attitude of Mexico City than London.[25]

In a dispatch to Aberdeen shortly after the meeting with Webster, Ashburton seemed confident that the Oregon issue could be resolved. He dismissed American interest in the territory, indicating that few Americans had settled there, that Indians would block any serious settlement in the area, and that Americans would not "for many years to come make any considerable lodgement on the Pacific." He also saw potential in the tripartite idea. This message to Aberdeen revealed Ashburton's woeful lack of understanding of the Oregon Question. First, the beginnings of Oregon Fever had already sent hundreds of Americans into the territory. Second, plenty of evidence existed that the northwestern tribes were not a deterrent to American migration to the territory. A consensus, in fact, was forming that the tribes on the coast chose "peacefully making a nuisance of themselves" over blocking the settlers. Third, the current state of US-Mexican relations suggested little hope of cooperation with the tripartite proposal. Finally, Ashburton seemed oblivious to the fact that his offer of the Columbia River boundary was less than a rejected British offer from the 1820s. At that time, British negotiators had offered the United States territory north of the Columbia River in the form of an enclave on the Olympic Peninsula, giving the United States the safe harbor on the Pacific that Webster sought.[26]

Uncharacteristically, Webster had not adequately prepared for the Oregon part of the Washington talks or fully appreciated the growing interest among the American people in westward expansion. Congress had ordered all documents related to the northwestern boundary talks published in 1828. Webster knew the information was available. In it, he would have been reminded of the enclave offer and realized that Ashburton brought less to the table than had his predecessors. Webster also had plenty of evidence that the Oregon Territory was geographically positioned to enhance America's Pacific trade. While Webster engaged Ashburton, the American consul in Honolulu, Peter Brinsmade, had written him regarding the value of Puget Sound and the Juan de Fuca Strait for developing American commerce in the Pacific and had asserted that portion of the coast was "of vastly greater importance than that of Maine to the Atlantic Coast." This prospect certainly should have piqued Webster's interest as a commercial expansionist. Further, if Webster believed he could substitute San Francisco for the Oregon harbors, he underestimated the expansionist zeal overtaking the American people. They did not have their eyes on either this piece of real estate or that one; they wanted both.[27]

To allow time for Webster and Ashburton to address these deficiencies in their understanding of the Oregon problem, the treaty would have to be postponed and talks extended deeper into the Washington summer. Neither Webster nor Ashburton expressed enthusiasm for this scenario for, as Ashburton feared, it ran the risk of unraveling all that had been accomplished, including the northeastern boundary settlement. Besides, Ashburton had suffered yet another month of "sleepless fever" and felt he could not physically endure the brutal heat and humidity much longer. An exit from Washington, he acknowledged, would bring him personal relief, but the unsettled Oregon Question would not do the same for Anglo-American relations. He confessed to Aberdeen that "a new and troublesome Boundary question may grow up on that distant shore at no remote period." Nevertheless, he lamented, Oregon must, "I fear, sleep for the present." The masterful accomplishment of Webster and Ashburton that set on track an Anglo-American rapprochement had left a hazard unaddressed with the potential of turning amity back to enmity. But that remained to be seen; at present, a historic document lay before them that reflected considerable effort and an enviable level of success.[28]

On August 9, 1842, Webster and Ashburton affixed their names to a treaty that heralded a new and harmonious relationship between the two English-speaking nations. Although there would be attacks from both political opponents and opportunists, most observers appreciated the significance of their achievement. The two negotiators had significantly advanced Anglo-American relations toward a friendship that continued to evolve for the remainder of the nineteenth century and throughout the twentieth. Rarely had there been so much of historic import accomplished in such a short period. The two diplomats had completely resolved the decades-old northeastern boundary; removed the prickly thorns of the *Creole*, the *Caroline*/McLeod affairs, and impressment; established cooperation on suppression of the slave trade; and formalized an extradition arrangement. Only Oregon remained unresolved. In addition to planting the seeds for lasting stability in Anglo-American relations, Webster's legal argument over the *Caroline* codified what constitutes national self-defense. Later established as the *Caroline* Doctrine, it would be used to assess justification for military preemption from Webster's nineteenth-century State Department to the United Nations of the twentieth and twenty-first centuries.[29]

Webster heightened his satisfaction over the accomplishment on the day of the signing by finally revealing to Ashburton the "evidence" that had held the envoy's curiosity since mid-June—*the red-line map*. One can only imagine the coy look on the secretary's face as he showed the map to his friend *after* the British envoy had signed over seven thousand of the twelve thousand square miles in dispute. Ashburton's gracious reaction must have been surprising, as he ironically betrayed a sense of relief that he had not known of the map before the signing. Had he seen the map during the negotiations, he would have been duty-bound to hold out for territory over which Maine might have taken the two countries to war. Perhaps his attitude is easier to understand if one remembers that his main goal, as expressed by Lady Ashburton, was to bring home a "treaty of peace in his pocket."[30]

If Ashburton remained magnanimous after learning of Webster's connivance, political opponents in both countries were not likely to take it so well. As news of the red-line maps surfaced, competing maps began to fall out of every tree shaken. For example, Democrat Thomas Hart Benton of Missouri shook the Library of Congress tree and out fell a map from the Jefferson collection, a most credible source since Jefferson had been a member (though not a participant) of the Paris peace commission. After chiding Webster for shameful tactics and accusing the secretary of surrendering too much of America to the British bully, Benton laid out his evidence: the Jefferson map, a Mitchell, showed a line ostensibly supporting the American claim. Why, he demanded to know, had Webster not used it to push the boundary northward?

Benton's colleagues in the Senate must have felt that his vision was failing. Although there was, in fact, a faint dotted line approximating the American claim, how had he not seen the bolder line that replicated the one in support of the British position that appeared on the Sparks map? Benton, as any good politician would, simply refocused his aim. If this were true and there was any validity at all to the red-line maps, he declared, "the concealment of them [by Webster] was a fraud on the British, and the Senate was insulted by being made a party to the fraud." Webster's assessment of Benton's speech on the treaty required few words: It was, he wrote Everett, "a huge mass of trash." On the charge of having perpetrated a "fraud on the British," Webster later reported tongue-in-cheek to the New-York Historical Society that "I did not think it a very urgent duty on my part to go to Lord Ashburton and tell him that I had found a bit of doubtful evidence in Paris, out of which he might perhaps make something to the prejudice of our claims, and from which he could set up higher claims for himself, or obscure the whole matter still further! (Laughter.)"[31]

All of the political preening by his political opponents as the ratification process moved forward had little impact on the fate of the treaty. Before the end of the year, pleadings from powerful Democrats like John C. Calhoun, who stressed the overwhelming importance of peace with Britain, ended the debate with a ratification margin of 39–9 in favor, a stronger affirmation than even Webster had expected. The Senate proceedings had not been open, so news of the maps did not reach the public until the debates appeared in the *Globe* at the end of the year. The public airing invited still more attacks from Webster critics.[32]

Perhaps the most serious vulnerability for Webster appeared the following March when another map surfaced, this one in the papers of Paris peace commissioner John Jay. It seemed apparent that the commissioners had consulted this Mitchell map in Paris in discussions with British representative Richard Oswald; it too had a strong red line, this one supporting the American boundary claim. Shortly after this revelation, Webster found an opportunity to defend his boundary. The New-York Historical Society hosted an event that was double billed. Webster shared the platform with seasoned diplomat and prominent figure of the early republic Albert Gallatin, who had, himself, engaged in early negotiations over the northeastern boundary. Webster seized the opportunity to address the Jay map and his handling of the boundary issue and drew welcomed support from the senior statesman.

Gallatin spoke first and defended Webster's compromise as well as his use of the Sparks map in the process. He opened his remarks with regrets that the Jay map had been used to attack the treaty: "It is much to be lamented that, after a conciliatory compromise, convenient and honorable to both countries, and apparently almost universally approved," that "an incident of so little real importance as the discovery of a certain Map . . . should have served as a pretence [sic] for renewing the discussion on the merits of the case." To the charge that Webster should have revealed the Sparks map to the British, Gallatin also found no merit in sharing evidence that would bolster the position of the other party. When Webster took the floor, he acknowledged the authenticity of the Jay map and confessed that "the conflict of these maps is undoubtedly a pretty remarkable circumstance." Then, after sketching the history of the boundary dispute, he defended his treaty, echoing Gallatin's sentiments that a fair compromise had been reached and that all parties concerned had gained. "I believe, or at least I trust with great humility," he concluded, "that the judgment of the country will ultimately be, that the arrangement in this case was not an objectionable one. (Applause.)"[33]

In London, advocates of the treaty also lauded its preservation of the peace and admonished their reticent colleagues to take it as they would "Castor oil, very much disliking it, but with Confidence that it will do good." Opposition leader Lord Palmerston, to no one's surprise, railed against the treaty and denounced Webster for hiding the map. Having returned to the agitated atmosphere of London, even Ashburton confessed that Webster's actions had produced a general feeling that "we have been duped" by the Americans.[34]

To further complicate the story, Henry Bulwer had been dispatched from London to Paris to find the original Sparks map and reported back to London that he had found two d'Anville maps, neither of which conformed to the one Sparks claimed to have seen. Bulwer then offered a shocking conclusion, one supported by the French archivist: "No such map as Sparks describes exists." On March 3, Aberdeen replied to Bulwer, "We have also made our discoveries here of Maps . . . which are interesting, but which tend to throw the whole argument from Maps into utter confusion."[35]

In March 1839, a request had been put before Parliament concerning "a Mitchell map" from the British Museum believed to show "the true line." Palmerston, foreign secretary at the time, thought he should have a look and so met with the British Museum's Keeper of Printed Books and found an interesting Mitchell map in the collection of King George III. This map contained notes in the king's own hand pointing out the "boundary as described by Mr. Oswald," a boundary that validated the American version of the border. This placed Palmerston in a similar position to that faced later by Sparks in Paris: What to do with evidence clearly supporting the claims of the other side? Unlike Sparks, the foreign secretary did not wrestle with the question but rather had a warrant issued to have the map moved to the Foreign Office where it remained hidden away throughout Ashburton's negotiations with Webster. Ashburton, now back home and completely caught up in the "battle of the maps," used his credentials as a British Museum trustee to access the catalogue where he tracked down the King George map by following Palmerston's warrant.[36]

In March 1843, Palmerston foolishly launched an attack on Ashburton and the Peel government, contending that the British envoy should have employed another map recently discovered in the State Paper Office "shewing the Boundary to be such as we claimed it." His bluster went too far when he cynically concluded, "Who knows, that on the sight of our red-lined map, Webster might not have exclaimed, 'Well, to tell the truth, we have got a red-lined map also . . . and I must fairly confess that it tallies exactly with yours.'"[37]

Peel defended Webster, asking why the American should have been expected to disclose the weak points of his case in the form of the Sparks map. In other words, why should he have been expected to show his cards? Then Peel played his own card. There was no Sparks map in the French archives that aligned with Franklin's letter, but the George III map had been unearthed and, even though it had been in Palmerston's possession throughout the negotiations, "he did not communicate its contents to Mr. Webster." Palmerston, thus, had gained little more from his attack than ridicule from the London press.[38]

The prime minister put an end to the battle of the maps by applying something rare among politicians—logic. Not one of the maps could be authenticated; they all could do no more than claim, at best, to have been consulted in preliminary discussions before the Treaty of Paris 1783 and, as a result, held little or no evidentiary weight. Webster was in complete agreement with Peel's assessment. He wrote to Everett that not one of these maps "settle the question; because they bear no marked lines, which may not have been merely proposals. In other words, none of them shows a line, clearly purporting to represent on the map, a boundary which had been agreed to."[39]

Over the next few years Democrats persisted in their efforts to discredit Webster, accusing him of everything from being Ashburton's unnamed informant to misappropriating the president's secret service fund. Beyond crass politics, there appeared to be some incriminating inferences, but no hard evidence, in a communiqué from Ashburton to Aberdeen written on the day of the treaty signing. In the note, a cryptic passage appeared that referenced the "money I wrote about," money that had subsidized Sparks's mission to the governors of Maine and Massachusetts. "My informant," he continued, "thinks that without this stimulant Maine would never have yielded." Who was this informant? Webster detractors claimed that the secretary had colluded with Ashburton to force a compromise that forfeited American territory. Making the accusation all the more salacious, money had passed hands, presumably some going to Webster. While the temptation of the combination of secrecy and money proved too tantalizing for Webster critics, neither the available record nor logic supports the charge. First, why would Webster, champion of nationalism, risk charges of disloyalty, if not treason, in order to transfer remote and disputed land to British Canada? Second, why would Webster invite Ashburton to see his ace card by showing him the Sparks map? It is apparent from Ashburton's June 14 letter to Aberdeen that he was not privy to "evidence [map], known at present to nobody." Besides, all of the British envoy's comments after the treaty signing substantiated the fact that he was just then made aware of Webster's "grand stroke." Lack of evidence rarely dissuades politicians from pressing the attack. The accusations of Webster's collusion with the British to sacrifice American territory followed him back to the Senate.[40]

In the interim, Webster continued, at personal political cost within Whig ranks, to manage Tyler's state department while enjoying widespread approval for the Washington (Webster-Ashburton) Treaty from the American people. Webster, perhaps more than most, relished praise, but one element of that praise ran counter to his intention. At this moment, the people jealously looked westward, and the rapprochement he had fashioned with Britain seemed to clear the way for a new expansionist vision. Webster did not share this vision but reduced it to an unfortunate consequence of his diplomatic triumph. While an increasing number of Americans, including Tyler, embraced expanding the republic, Webster feared that adding territory would place debilitating stress on America's republican institutions and heighten sectional tension over slavery. These tensions were closely tied to US relations with Mexico, which had remained volatile since Texas won independence and pressed for annexation to the United States in the mid-1830s. Any gesture toward expansion that involved Texas and the Southwest would place additional strain on relations with Mexico City. This attitude conformed to Webster's consistent opposition to annexation that he carried from Congress to the State Department. Now, however, his position was increasingly at odds with that of his president.[41]

On more than one occasion the secretary of state was called on to intervene on behalf of American citizens snared in the Texas-Mexico drama. In early June 1841, Texas president Mirabeau Lamar sent an expedition to Santa Fe to "encourage" the residents of New Mexico to break with Mexico and join Texas. The force of around three hundred, two-thirds of whom were US citizens, ran into difficulties soon after crossing into New Mexico. Lost, hungry, and struggling with the rugged terrain, they surrendered to the governor of New Mexico. Many of the poorly treated prisoners did not survive the subsequent march to Mexico City. By the time the motley crew arrived at the capital, word of the expedition had ignited American protests. Since one of the captives, George Wilkins Kendall, was editor of the New Orleans *Picayune*, it is small wonder that a sympathetic American press followed closely the agitation generated by the citizens of Louisiana.[42]

In response to numerous requests for relief from family, friends, and concerned politicians, Webster's office directed American minister Waddy Thompson to press for their freedom along with that of the Texans. This he accomplished, announcing the promised release of the Americans at the end of April and the emancipation of the Texans a few weeks later.

Webster and Thompson reprised this successful diplomacy later in the year for Americans who had joined Texas forces in an attack on the Mexican town of Mier, resulting in their surrender and incarceration in Mexico City. Efforts to free the American prisoners, some of whom were awaiting execution, required patient diplomacy that did not bear fruit until shortly before Webster left the State Department in May. Thompson wrote him in March 1843 that he had arranged the release of Kentucky senator John Crittenden's son, George, for whom Webster had exerted special effort. The last of the surviving Mier prisoners (some escaped and others died) were not freed until 1844.[43]

In the midst of the sundry repatriation efforts, an American naval officer, Commodore Thomas ap Catesby Jones, complicated Webster's diplomacy by raising American colors over the capital of California and declaring it US territory. In October 1842, the impulsive Jones seized Monterey on the basis of flawed reports that war had broken out between Mexico and the United States. With the two nations at war, the capture of Monterey, he determined, would dissuade opportunistic British warships prowling the area from taking California for the Crown. Within twenty-four hours Jones discovered his error, lowered the flag, and apologized as he withdrew his forces.[44]

With US-Mexican relations tenuous at best, Jones's action presented Webster with an added and unnecessary irritant. Webster and Thompson emphasized to the Mexican authorities that Jones had not acted on instructions of the US government but had simply made a mistake based on the erroneous report of war between the two nations: The action, the Americans contended, was no more than "the inconsiderate conduct of an individual officer." In late December, Thompson expressed "surprise [sic] and regret" equal to that of Mexican officials on hearing of Jones's unauthorized action in Monterey and assured the Mexican foreign secretary that the "fullest reparations"—to include "a full band of musical instruments"—would be forthcoming.[45]

Webster's additional expression of "deep regret" and feeling that the incident should not impede "amicable relations" did not satisfy the Mexican minister to Washington, who insisted that Jones receive severe punishment for his actions. "Does Commodore Jones esteem the peace of Nations so lightly," he inquired of Webster, "that on the strength of a mere rumor . . . he should consider himself authorized to act in arms against a friendly nation?" Jones, he added, deserved no clemency. Fortunately for the commodore, his punishment went no further than loss of command of the Pacific Squadron. Tyler felt that the Mexican minister's demand for retribution stepped "rather beyond the mark."[46]

Webster also faced problems associated with Cuba and a growing US strategic interest in the island, driven by both circumstance and geopolitical calculus. In July 1839, African slaves in transit out of Havana on the Spanish slaver *Amistad* staged a successful mutiny off the Cuban coast and demanded that the crew of the ship return them to Africa. The crew navigated the ship in a meandering pattern to give the Africans a sense that they were headed home while the ship instead cruised northward. After several weeks, it was spotted off the northeastern coast of the United States, seized, brought into port at New London, Connecticut, and held over for an admiralty court ruling. Against the backdrop of intense abolitionist sentiment, the "kidnapped Africans" were portrayed as a living illustration of the inhumanity of slavery and the determination of their status, whether cargo to be adjudicated or persons with rights, ultimately came before the Supreme Court. Unlike Joseph Story's disappointing action with the *La Jeune Eugenie* case in which he deferred judgment to the French, this time the judge, now associate justice of the Supreme Court, voiced the majority opinion that the slaver was in clear violation of treaty terms that prohibited the slave trade. Besides, Story added, the Africans were guilty of nothing more than exercising their inherent right of self-defense. Once freed, the funding for their return to Africa became an issue. When Webster could find no legal cover for expending government resources for transport to Africa, private donors underwrote their return in early 1842.

This proved awkward for Webster on a number of fronts. He clearly agreed with Justice Story that the Africans held natural rights and had fallen victim to the illegal slave trade. But his support was mitigated by the growing momentum of abolitionism and its implications for sectional discord. Beyond the direct connection of *Amistad* slaves with sectional tension, Webster also knew that Cuba presented an indirect link as well. Any talk of slavery mustered opposing sectional attitudes about the future affiliation of the Jewel of the Antilles. On the one hand, northern leaders opposed arguments for bringing Cuba under the American flag and thereby adding to the strength of the Southern slavocracy. On the other hand, southerners validated this northern concern by making acquisition of Cuba central to any and all expansionist schemes.[47]

When Webster declined an invitation to represent the *Amistad* blacks before the Supreme Court (a providential decision that landed John Quincy Adams in that role), he did so to maintain his broader political base; after all, he still harbored aspirations for the presidency. As would become abundantly clear, both his concern for the threat posed by abolitionists on sectional relations and the stability of the Union and his own political calculus required that issues such as those represented by the *Amistad* case be approached carefully.[48]

When *Amistad* demanded his attention at State, he addressed it strictly as a legal question. Spain had lodged a complaint with Webster's predecessor, John Forsyth, on the basis of Pinckney's Treaty (1795), and demanded compensation for losses suffered as a result of the *Amistad* mutiny. The claim included ship and *all* cargo—including the Africans. Webster rejected the application of Pinckney to the *Amistad* as well as an attempt by Madrid to have earlier claims excused to balance the *Amistad* losses. Of broader concern than the tiresome calculation of indemnity was that of the disposition of the island itself.[49]

America's geopolitical interest in Cuba ranged from mere geographic proximity to an appetite for the island's abundant resources. By the 1840s, the zeal for expansion had awakened interest in either acquiring or, at least, preserving Cuba for the United States. If the United States meant to keep European influence at bay in Latin America with the pronouncement of the Monroe Doctrine in the early 1820s, surely frustrating further European intrigue ninety miles from Florida was a worthwhile pursuit. Granted, Cuba belonged to a European nation, but Spain hardly presented a European power capable of threatening American interests. Britain was another matter.

When word came to Webster that the British had designs on exploiting Spain's weakness to encourage the Cubans to throw off Spanish rule, establish "a black Military Republic," and immediately come under the Empire's protection, he reacted quickly and forcefully. American chargé d'affaires Aaron Vail wrote from Madrid at the end of November 1841 that the Spanish minister of foreign affairs had affirmed reports of British intrigue on the island with the intent of emancipating the slaves. These reports, the chargé noted, "found an echo in the southern portion of the United States." This joined a Waddy Thompson letter with similar information to prompt a directive from Tyler to Webster to get Robert Blain Campbell, the new American consul to Havana, in place and have him "report . . . the condition of things." Webster wrote to Campbell in mid-January (copied to American minister Washington Irving in Madrid) detailing what he knew of the reports. While expressing hopeful skepticism that the reports were exaggerated, he informed the consul that the United States would stand by its commitments to Spain and would use force, if necessary, to frustrate British plans. This militant statement reflected Webster's apprehension that if "this scheme should succeed, the influence of Britain in this quarter . . . will be unlimited," a prospect clearly unacceptable to the United States. On March 14, 1843, Webster informed Irving that his skepticism had been warranted. Campbell assured him that the reports were "greatly exaggerated." Still highly gratified by the recently repaired Anglo-American relations, Webster must have been relieved to avoid an altercation with London over Cuba.[50]

Before leaving the State Department, Webster also addressed America's role in the Pacific, beginning with America's relationship with the Sandwich (Hawaiian) Islands. By the early 1840s, Americans had become the dominant foreign presence in Hawaii, integral to the economy and vocal proponents of the strategic importance of the islands for developing the China trade. In addition to American commercial investment, Christian missionaries had established an imposing number of missions and schools to proselytize and educate the Hawaiian people.

A clumsy move by the French in 1839 to forcibly extract concessions from the kingdom alerted Americans both at home and on the islands that Europeans might at any time seek to bring the Hawaiians under an imperial heel. Despite the alarms activated by French adventure, it still required three attempts by representatives of Hawaiian king Kamehameha III before Webster discussed formal relations with the kingdom. In early December 1841, two officials arrived from Hawaii and began a series of seven meetings with Webster. The Hawaiian delegation sought American recognition of their national independence but were unable to draw a commitment from Webster.

His focus did not narrow until they intimated that failure to secure recognition of Hawaiian sovereignty from the United States might force them into the British sphere as a Crown protectorate. The recent annexation of New Zealand and the Marquesas by Britain and France, respectively, certainly lent credibility to this prospect. Consequently, as the December meetings progressed, Webster relaxed his position; the United States, he stated, would acknowledge the legitimacy of the Hawaiian government. He further expressed the American "sense" that the islands should remain free of any "undue control" by outside forces. Webster stopped short of diplomatic recognition, stating that official contact would remain with the offices of the US consulate already in place. In a broader statement of US policy, Tyler echoed both Webster's advice and his words in a presidential message to Congress on December 30. Expressing a special interest in the islands as the nearest continental power and the most prolific commercial partner, Tyler articulated a noncolonization principle for the "Sandwich islands."[51]

In what became known as the Tyler Doctrine, the administration adopted a position for the islands that mirrored the one established by President James Monroe for Latin America. Other nations, Tyler declared, should resist intervention or intrusion in the affairs of the islands. He made clear that this included the United States; Washington had no designs on controlling the kingdom. Although unwilling to formally recognize Hawaiian independence, the United States did intend to support the preservation of that independence. Recognition followed two years later when Secretary of State John C. Calhoun formally acknowledged the independence of the kingdom of Hawaii. Webster's hand in fashioning the Tyler Doctrine cannot be overstated. He placed the islands clearly in America's orbit and set the course for an evolving and lasting relationship.[52]

The president's December message also set in motion the first steps toward opening formal US relations with China, steps designed and animated by Webster. American interest in China was, of course, not new, but it found a new earnestness in the early 1840s that required the articulation of a proper Sino-American foreign policy. The increased attention to China resulted from the confluence of three factors: American commercial interests, American missionary zeal, and, once again, the British.

By the time Harrison and Webster settled on the senator's appointment to State, all three factors had elevated American interest in China—none more so than Britain's waging of the Opium War between 1839 and 1842 that positioned the Crown as the dominant foreign influence in the Celestial Kingdom. During the war, American commercial interests lobbied the government to bring some order to US interaction with Peking. The missionary impulse found a dynamic voice in Peter Parker, who not only inspired the people but, more importantly, moved Webster. Before replacing John Forsyth as secretary of state, Webster met with Parker, who made an urgent appeal for the placement in Peking of an American diplomatic mission "without delay." In the fall of 1841, both Tyler and Webster talked with Parker and assured him of their determination to open diplomatic relations with China. They did not display Parker's level of urgency until a victorious Britain forced Chinese concessions in the Treaty of Nanking in late summer of 1842. The treaty opened four new ports and established a regular commercial arrangement, all under the heavy paw of the British lion.[53]

The president, now facing a stiff political wind, did not receive his requested support for a commissioner to China until March 1843. The administration first approached Everett, by now a seasoned and highly capable diplomat, but political opponents charged Webster with orchestrating Everett's redeployment from London to Peking to free up the post at the Court of St. James's for himself. At any rate, Everett declined the offer, and the appointment went to Massachusetts congressman Caleb Cushing.

Though nearing the end of his tenure at State, Webster still devoted considerable time and attention to the Cushing mission. He gathered materials from the Treasury on commercial activity with China and made a broad appeal for information from anyone willing to contribute to his and Cushing's understanding of how best to engage the Chinese. In April, Webster and Tyler went over an extensive list of gifts for the Chinese government, scribbling frequent notations on where they should be acquired or adding some descriptive comment. For example, a "Model of War Steamer" appeared fourth on the list with a note by Webster that read "full model of engine." Item number six, a "Model of Locomotive Steam Engine," carried the notation "not done." All this indicates an unusual level of attention. The list also included a small library of books and document sets with the notable inclusion of a volume on the northeastern boundary.[54]

When Webster drafted Cushing's instructions in early May, he demonstrated not only an intent to dilute Britain's influence and interpose American priorities but also an understanding of the diplomatic approach required to achieve success with Peking. Cushing's assignment was clear: negotiate a treaty for American access to Chinese ports and markets on an equal footing with the British. How to prosecute that assignment within the forms and customs of an Asian culture was not as clear. Webster coached Cushing on how to navigate the culture by balancing an American posture of strength with the respect and courtesy expected by the emperor. Meet with the emperor, Webster directed, as "a messenger of peace, sent from the greatest power in America to the greatest Empire in Asia." Cushing should make it clear that the United States was not a "tribute bearer" but a sovereign nation seeking only "the tender of mutual regard, and the establishment of useful relations." The commissioner should, Webster insisted, distinguish between the behavior of the United States and that of Britain. Clearly, the British pursued dominance at the tip of the bayonet. "You will take care to show strongly how free the Chinese Government may well be from all jealousy arising from such causes towards the United States."[55]

Webster's instructions to Cushing and his letter of resignation from the Tyler administration were both dated May 8, 1843. He saw the fruit of his China efforts the following year with Cushing's historic Treaty of Wanghia that granted most-favored-nation status to the United States. Although no longer at State, all associated with the milestone agreement knew that no one had more fingerprints on the project than Webster. His closing days at the State Department had produced opening days for America's Pacific and East Asia foreign policy.[56]

Having remained with Tyler at great political peril, Webster belatedly excused himself from an administration that was Whig when he joined but had gradually reverted to the president's Democratic roots. In fact, Tyler planned to seek the nomination of that party for the 1844 campaign. There was also the matter of Texas. Tyler's hope for a nomination that might return him to the White House hinged on the annexation of Texas. This Webster could not support. His opposition to adding a slaveholding Texas to the Union was firm. Likewise, Tyler was pleased to replace Webster with a more politically compatible cabinet member. At one point it appeared that a mission to London to settle the Oregon dispute would provide Webster an exit from the cabinet more palatable than resignation, but the House refused to appropriate funds. Thus Webster resigned, but with a tremendous sense of accomplishment.

In just over two years at State he managed an astounding level of success. He cleared away an impressive number of problems in Anglo-American relations that set the two nations on course to a unique rapprochement that evolved into the twentieth-century's "Special Relationship." Webster added to the epic accomplishment of the Washington Treaty a foundational structure for American influence in the Pacific and East Asia with the Tyler Doctrine and the Cushing mission. And finally, although it would require reassertion on his return to State in 1850, Webster laid the foundation for full government protection of American missionaries posted abroad. With much of this success visible at the time, only the most partisan would find fault in his decision to remain with "His Accidency" for as long as he did. But as he returned to politics, he was well aware that those "most partisan" could make or break his future.[57]

CHAPTER FIVE

From State to the Senate and Back Again, 1843–1850

> Generally, when a divorce takes place, the parents divide the children. I should be glad to know where I am to go.
>
> —Daniel Webster, September 1843

When Webster packed up his desk at the State Department and leased his Washington home, the Swann House, to incoming British minister Richard Pakenham, he faced an uncertain political future with his estranged Whig Party. Retreating to his beloved seaside estate in Marshfield, Massachusetts, he settled into a sabbatical while plotting his political redemption. He soon found a platform for renewing his party standing when he was invited to deliver another Bunker Hill address, this one on the occasion of the dedication of the completed monument in June 1843. No one, not even Webster, could reach the heights of his masterful 1825 performance. But that oration took the measure of a rising Webster; perhaps in 1843 it was enough for the son of Ebenezer to simply take the stage. "The whole occasion," Ralph Waldo Emerson reported, "was answered by his presence. . . . There was the monument, and there was Webster." Something about the simplicity of Emerson's observation acknowledged Webster's stature as the mature American statesman, no longer requiring affirmation. He spent the remainder of the summer at Marshfield regrouping and toying with the idea of a mission to London to promote trade reciprocity between the two nations, an idea that came to naught.[1]

The following fall, he found his moment of equilibrium with the Whig Party. In early November, Professor Moses Stuart invited him to speak at

Andover where, according to daughter Julia's diary, he set out to deliver "a Whig speech," and "all the world will be there." While not quite "all the world," still an enormous crowd that included reporters from Boston and New York gathered for the event. Seizing the opportunity, Webster proclaimed to the crowd: "I am a Whig, a Massachusetts Whig, a Faneuil Hall Whig, and none shall have the power, now or hereafter, to deprive me of the position in which that character places me." He then advanced in commanding fashion his Whig bona fides, and he completely closed the circle the following May with a speech at the national convention endorsing Whig Henry Clay for president. Afterward, Webster worked for the party platform by addressing rallies throughout the Northeast, which articulated party orthodoxy on banking and the protective tariff while inserting an occasional reflection on foreign policy.[2]

As the 1844 election approached, Webster grew increasingly concerned with the Democrats' reckless commitment to expansionism. Martin Van Buren had expected to secure the nomination but failed to appreciate the rising fever for expansion and found himself deadlocked with Michigan senator Lewis Cass. The standoff resulted in the nomination of a dark horse who more than appreciated the fever—he was infected with it. James Knox Polk, native of North Carolina, adopted son of Tennessee, and protégé of Andrew Jackson, embraced and aggressively pursued an expansionist platform that promised the "reannexation of Texas" and the "reoccupation of Oregon." The world soon found that expansion to Polk meant absorption of both the American Southwest and the Pacific Northwest—in other words, all territory from Texas west to San Diego and north to Alaska. Expansionism that held the potential, Webster feared, to undo the republic now had its champion in Young Hickory. For Webster, a return to an active role in the affairs of the nation after Polk defeated Clay in November must have seemed both inevitable and urgent.[3]

When Webster accepted Harrison's cabinet appointment in 1841, his Senate seat had gone to the capable Rufus Choate, who had not intended to make a career of the Senate and now wished to retire. The scenario that brought Webster to the Senate the first time in 1827 was poised to repeat. Party leaders invited him to return to the Senate upon Choate's resignation. Once again, however, Webster hesitated; he could not bear the financial loss he would suffer from time away from his law practice. His friends and supporters understood his less-than-subtle hint for patronage and moved to underwrite his return to Washington. This pattern of subsidization had become so common to Webster that Thomas Wrens Ward described him "as a sort of public property." So it was set: patrons "freely and cheerfully" established an annuity from which Webster would draw $1,000 monthly, with any residual serving as a life pension for the family. With funding arranged, Webster agreed to replace Choate as advocate for the Whig agenda in the Senate.[4]

As Webster awaited his election, Democrats pressed their expansionist agenda: Senator George McDuffie of South Carolina and Congressman Charles J. Ingersoll of Pennsylvania proposed in December a joint resolution for the annexation of the Lone Star Republic. This move, apart from the unconventional method, should not have surprised anyone familiar with Tyler's interest in Texas. In 1843, the president had hoped to make the annexation of Texas his ticket for an extended stay at the executive mansion. After accepting the intransigent Webster's resignation from State, he had Webster's successor, Abel Upshur, and, after Upshur's untimely death, John C. Calhoun, advance a treaty of annexation to add Texas to the Union.[5]

It is uncertain how Upshur might have finessed Senate approval of an annexation treaty, but clearly there was no hint of finesse in Calhoun's approach. The treaty, Calhoun believed, was about more than Texas—it was about the preservation of slavery. In a ham-handed exchange with British minister Richard Pakenham, Calhoun left no doubt that the annexation of Texas meant both the expansion and survival of slavery. The secretary, suspicious of British intent, cautioned the Crown through Pakenham to avoid any attempt to press Texas to abandon slavery. Calhoun knew that Britain preferred an independent Texas and had replied to Pakenham's suggestion of a joint Anglo-French-American effort to safeguard the independence of the republic with a wry smile. All attempts to allay Calhoun's concern failed. The secretary, Pakenham reported, perceived a British conspiracy to purge slavery and would not let the notion go. This became so obsessive that Pakenham finally gave up trying to persuade him, resigned that "there is nothing so hopeless as arguing with a person who is determined not be convinced."[6]

Calhoun's insistence on linking Texas with slavery was exposed when the Pakenham correspondence was included in treaty materials sent to the Senate that were then leaked by Senator Benjamin Tappan (brother of Arthur and Lewis Tappan of the American Anti-Slavery Society) to the New York *Evening Post*. When Webster read Calhoun's communication with Pakenham, he was appalled to see such "reprehensible sentiment, and unsurpassed nonsense, united. . . . What," he asked, "must he suppose this age will think of him & of us, too, if we adopt his sentiments?" Calhoun had, in effect, made Texas synonymous with slavery, assuring the treaty's defeat in June along with that of Tyler's hoped-for political reward. Before leaving office, the Virginian joined fellow Democrats in hatching an alternative plan to annex Texas via the McDuffie-Ingersoll joint resolution.[7]

As he had throughout the Texas debates of the 1830s, Webster continued to warn that the addition of the Lone Star Republic to the Union would fracture the nation by sections, start the fire bell of slavery ringing again, and lead to war with Mexico. No longer holding a political position, his ability to recast the narrative was limited. During the treaty discussion in the spring of 1844, he relied on ink for his attack. The reprinting of a Webster letter produced for Worcester County circulated widely and revisited his contention that the Constitution did not allow the incorporation of foreign territory into the Union. This strained interpretation ignored both Florida and Louisiana as well as arguments he himself had made before the Supreme Court. Perhaps more reasonable was his reminder of longstanding concerns that a republic, by its nature, would be weakened when extended over too great an expanse. Add to this the likelihood that Texas could not be added without both war with Mexico and, as he proclaimed at the convention in October, the indefinite prolongation of the evil of slavery, and his brief against Texas was complete. Webster met with like-minded opponents of annexation at Faneuil Hall at the end of January 1845 to spur a campaign to block the Texas resolution, but the Lone Star was coming in, and the impact it would have on both nation and party could not be avoided.[8]

Leading the Whigs in a chorus of opposition to Texas, Webster found, could not be done successfully when party members insisted on singing from different scores, if not entirely different hymnals. A division had emerged in the party between Conscience Whigs who opposed slavery on immovable moral principles and Cotton Whigs who identified New England looms with southern cotton and were prone to be more pragmatic than passionate about slavery. Webster struggled to maintain his influence with both. On the one hand, his consistent defense of slavery where the Constitution had sanctioned it satisfied the Cotton contingent while, on the other hand, his steadfast opposition to the expansion of slavery via the annexation of Texas resonated with the Conscience Whigs. His overarching concern was that the zeal of the latter would push them toward the attempted eradication of slavery itself and with it the destruction of the Union. Although the 1844 Whig platform had no Texas plank, Webster felt compelled to address it on the campaign trail. At Valley Forge he made his position clear: "Now, slavery, in this country stands where the Constitution left it . . . and I mean to abide by it. . . . I shall do nothing to interfere with the domestic institutions of the South. But," he continued, "that is a different thing, very, from not interfering to prevent the extension of slavery by adding a large slave country to this." Thus, Webster's position: halt the march of slavery westward while defending it where it stood.[9]

When Polk eked out the win over Clay in the 1844 presidential election, Webster's concern elevated to crisis level, spurred in part by Tyler's scheme to annex Texas by resolution. In late January, as the McDuffie-Ingersoll resolution moved forward, Webster participated in a state convention of several hundred delegates from across Massachusetts. Meeting on familiar ground in Faneuil Hall, Webster joined with Charles Allen to compose a statement opposing McDuffie-Ingersoll, ostensibly to send a consensus document to Congress in hopes of eroding support for annexation. Webster, again, offered his disingenuous constitutional argument before issuing the legitimate challenge that no constitutional authority existed for engaging a foreign nation by resolution. Congress had before it a proposal to negotiate with a sovereign nation for purposes of annexation, not by treaty but by the odd mechanism of a joint resolution. This, Webster argued, was indefensible. Process aside, Texas, he argued, should not be brought into the Union. Cotton and Conscience Whigs divided over the statement, with the latter calling for complete abolition and the threat of secession should the Texas resolution pass. The convention adopted the statement over abolitionist protest, and Webster added another bold, though fruitless, document to his growing anti-Texas portfolio. Less than a week before his return to the Senate in March 1845, the joint resolution passed. He continued to wage the battle even though the war was lost. In December, for example, when the new state's constitution appeared in Washington for congressional approval, he sustained his assault while admitting that antiannexation efforts were "a little late for Texas, but they may do for Cuba."[10]

By the time of Webster's return to the Senate, Oregon had replaced Texas as the burning issue. Migration of Americans along the Oregon Trail had escalated, with upward of three thousand joining the Willamette Valley settlers south of the Columbia over the previous year alone. The pressure persuaded Britain's Oregon contingent, the Hudson's Bay Company, to relocate its offices to Victoria on the southern end of Vancouver Island, far north of the Columbia River and, significantly, near the 49th parallel. In April 1844, Everett had written to Calhoun expressing his sense that a settlement might be reached between the two nations that set the boundary at 49° but left the southern tip of Vancouver Island to the Crown. The Peel government, he felt, wanted to compromise but could not appear to bow in the face of American blustering. Once again, national honor was at play. If the United States argued for the extreme 54°40' then settled for 49°, the appearance of concession by the United States might preserve British honor. In the fall of 1844, Calhoun and Pakenham engaged in a series of meetings that, in effect, narrowed the disputed territory to that lying between the Columbia River and the 49th parallel.[11]

After the election, both houses of Congress opened discussions for organizing a government for the entire territory of Oregon. Pakenham deemed this action a step toward bringing the territory "completely and exclusively to the jurisdiction of the United States." On February 3, 1845, the House passed an Oregon bill that included an amendment giving the required twelve-month notice for ending the joint occupation arrangement established in 1818 and renewed in 1827. The Senate, Pakenham predicted, was too caught up with Texas to follow on the House bill, but the broader message signaled by the House action should not be missed. The election of Polk had guaranteed an aggressive posture on Oregon.[12]

The following month, Polk's inaugural address confirmed Pakenham's fears: in it, the president claimed all Oregon. The British press, Everett reported, was fuming over Polk's address, with the *Times* declaring that "the territory of Oregon will never be wrested from the British Crown to which it belongs, but by War." Aberdeen instructed Pakenham to signal the Americans that Britain would "concede nothing to force or menace" and would be "fully prepared to maintain our rights." This comment followed a reminder to Pakenham of British naval strength in the Pacific and the deployment of a force under Sir George Seymour to the Oregon coast. In Parliament, Aberdeen, while hoping for peace, indignantly declared that "our honour is a substantial property that we can never neglect."[13]

Following Polk's address, Senator Lewis Cass called for an assessment of America's military preparedness, an unnecessary exercise that Webster felt only served to heighten war passions. At the time of the negotiations with Ashburton, Webster had been less concerned than his British counterpart with their failure to resolve the Oregon dispute, but now he feared the territory had placed his grand accomplishment in jeopardy. Once again, the cloud of war hung over Anglo-American relations.[14]

Amid the bluster from both sides, there remained openings for compromise. Aberdeen had more interest in the economic stability of the empire than in real estate in the Pacific Northwest. In the summer of 1845, the Peel government received word of the potato blight in Ireland that would lead to catastrophic famine with potentially debilitating consequences for all of Britain. The best hope to temper the impact was to open British markets to foreign grain. This meant repealing the cherished Corn Laws, a staple in British policy for generations. Peel believed that if honor could be assuaged, repeal of the Corn Laws might advance an amicable settlement of the Oregon dispute. "The admission of maize" from America, he predicted, would "go far to promote a settlement of Oregon." Furthermore, with the American Congress discussing tariff reduction, a reciprocal move toward free trade might quiet any wayward voices. Both nations seemed poised for a shift toward free trade. If either seriously contemplated war over Oregon, that consideration would yield to the prospective benefits of commercial interdependence.[15]

Although Webster could not be expected to recalibrate to the free trade calculus of his early years, he agreed that the rabble-rousing threatened economic prosperity, if not stability. At Faneuil Hall in November 1845 he issued assurances that war would find little enthusiasm beyond the passing rhetoric of hotheads. This reckless talk, he asserted, "confounds and confuses men in regard to their own business plans. What we want is settled peace, and the conviction that peace will remain until there is some just and sensible cause for war." Talk of war, Webster cautioned, was almost as hard on the economy as war itself. Later he complained to Boston friend and patron David Sears of the zealots in the western states eager to provoke London. They have "no cotton crops, & no ships," and are convinced that "war would create much employment among them, raise the price (as they think) of their provisions, & scatter money." Webster, nevertheless, remained confident that Calhoun's peace contingent (with Whigs in support) would relegate these western rowdies to a minority.[16]

Neither Washington nor London missed Webster's conciliatory tone. Pakenham conveyed Webster's remarks to Aberdeen along with newspaper reports that he felt were "all strongly deprecating any violent course" on the Oregon Question. Secretary of State James Buchanan, Pakenham reported, also expressed a sense that the dispute was "now more likely to be settled than six months ago." But, the minister interjected cynically, Buchanan "is a man whose civility I think sometimes gets the better of His sincerity." From London, American minister Louis McLane complained to Polk that these pacific signals, especially those exhibited by Webster and his fellow Whigs, were undercutting Washington's negotiating position.[17]

McLane need not worry; the following day, Polk shored up that position in his first message to Congress. The president directed the legislative body to issue notice to London that the United States intended to withdraw from the joint-occupation arrangement in Oregon. Many feared that notice would be the first step toward "Fifty-Four Forty or Fight," the belligerent slogan adopted by supporters of the all-Oregon position. Although Webster complained of Polk's mixed messages, this one was clear. He meant either to push the British out of Oregon completely or to leverage them into offering a compromise boundary at the 49th parallel. America's rights in Oregon, Polk asserted, could not be abandoned "without a sacrifice of both national honor and interest."[18]

Polk remained piqued at the curt rejection of a compromise he had Buchanan propose in the summer. Honor now dictated a stern face, looking "John Bull straight in the eye" and forcing Britain to come forward with its own compromise offer. In July, Buchanan had offered Pakenham a settlement at the 49th parallel with Britain retaining all Vancouver Island. Despite conflicting messages from Aberdeen that *might* have found merit in the proposal, Pakenham adhered to his rigid instructions and rejected it "without," an irate Buchanan noted, so much as "referring" it to London for "consideration." The president directed Buchanan to withdraw the offer. Pakenham's error in judgement reset the impasse, and the temperamental Polk returned to bluster and bluff as he waited for Peel to initiate a compromise.[19]

Here the matter stood as Webster and moderates worked to dilute the persisting war rhetoric reflected in the president's address of December 1845, and, Webster hoped, to "prevent all alarm." But alarm was not easily prevented when congressional firebrands sought to raise the president's defiant tone to a complete break with London, peace be damned. On February 10, 1846, the Senate opened debate on the notice resolution. William Allen, leader of the extremists and chairman of the Senate Foreign Relations Committee, supported a "naked" (simple notice to abrogate the joint-occupation agreement) resolution followed by American occupation of the entire territory. He ranted against the British for two days at the opening of debates and demanded to know which of his colleagues would yield on Oregon "from the mere dread of invasion by a rabble of armed paupers, threatened to be sent by a bankrupt government, whose whole power of the sword and the dungeon is required to stifle cries of famine at home, or to protect its own life, against the uplifted hands of starving millions." Americans, he continued, "will give you an answer which will make the British empire tremble throughout its whole frame and foundation." Calhoun joined Webster in attempting to suppress this dangerous rhetoric and Allen's persistent challenge to not be intimidated "by the cry, 'If you do this, war will follow.'" The president, Webster scolded, claimed "to be for negotiation, and yet is against taking anything but the whole of Oregon."[20]

It is no surprise that Webster promoted the 49th parallel compromise that would, in essence, complete the boundary he had set with Ashburton four years earlier. At the end of March, Webster again pressed from the Senate floor for an Oregon settlement. This could not be accomplished by continuing to twist the lion's tail with a notice resolution that read like an ultimatum. If some moderating language could be added, perhaps the British would read it as an invitation to compromise. This level-headed proposal joined the notice resolution as an amendment, but only managed, at best, to smooth the harsh edge. In April, Congress directed the president to issue notice, but in an atmosphere in which a dispute over territory had escalated to one of national honor, could either side afford to concede?[21]

Honor, that "substantial property," prevented Peel from yielding while London papers featured the rash words of American leaders. Honor alone, Lord Ashburton asserted, would bring the two nations to war. "I need not tell you," he wrote Webster in January, "that we are pacific if you will let us be so, for though we care as little, or probably less, than your men of sense do about Oregon we cannot afford to be kicked." The London *Times* warned that the president foolishly toyed with war with both Britain and Mexico. Surely the American people, the *Quarterly Review* cynically mused, "would not be guided by the madness of their present rulers."[22]

In late February 1846, McLane had warned of the heightened tension, reporting a British military buildup that he connected directly to the assault on British honor. Congress had recently become aware of the "warlike preparations said to have been lately in progress in England." In fact, on February 3, 1846, McLane reported the "immediate equipment of thirty sail of the line, besides steamers and other vessels of war" scheduled for North American waters. This news elicited a cabinet consensus to offer the 49th parallel to Britain with navigation rights on the Columbia, but Polk refused. He did, however, direct McLane to advise the Peel government that an offer from the Crown of the 49th parallel would find a favorable response.[23]

Webster simultaneously reinforced the compromise sentiment, recruiting Member of Parliament James McGregor as a conduit to assure Aberdeen that, despite the indelicate language of "rash, headstrong, and uninformed men," Polk would entertain a compromise offer of the 49th parallel. "In my opinion," Webster reported to Everett, "our government now waits only for the other to make that offer." In the face of such a proposal, he was confident "the people of the United States cannot be mad enough to go to war."[24]

This moderating climate combined with the conciliatory amendment to the notice resolution and assurances from John Russell that his party would not challenge an Oregon offer to provide Peel a face-saving path to compromise. When the notice resolution arrived, Peel greeted it as a good-faith gesture by the United States to resolve the dispute. Taking McLane's suggested proposal with only slight modification, Peel delivered the compromise offer. When McLane sent the proposed settlement to Washington, he raised a question about navigation rights for Britain on the Columbia and wondered if a counter offer was in order. Fortunately, when the proposal arrived, Polk ignored the counter-offer suggestion and put a treaty based on the British offer before Congress. The timing was critical. The United States was now at war with Mexico; there could be no more dawdling with the Oregon

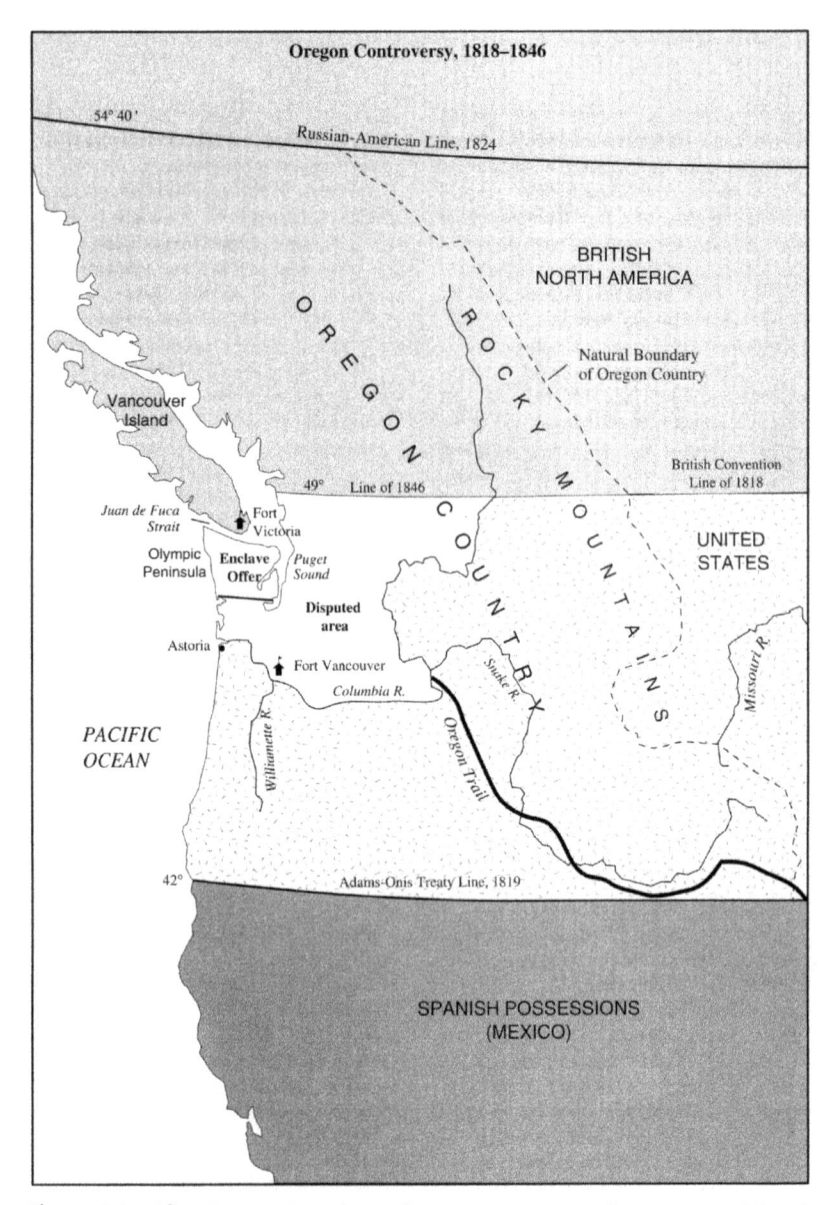

Figure 5.1. The Oregon Boundary Dispute. From Howard Jones, *Crucible of Power: A History of American Foreign Relations to 1913* (2009).

Question. In fact, Webster grew increasingly concerned that "this Mexican War cannot but cast a cloud over the prospect of an immediate adjustment with England."[25]

The Senate approved the subsequent Oregon Treaty on June 18, and McLane took it to the Foreign Office on July 17 for the formal exchange. Circumstances in London had changed, and Aberdeen no longer headed the Foreign Office. Lord Palmerston, the most animated British critic of America—and of Lord Ashburton's so-called capitulation to Webster on the northeastern boundary—was now foreign secretary and must have swallowed hard at having to host an event he surely saw as a parallel capitulation on the northwestern boundary. In Washington, Pakenham had invited Webster on the evening of the signing to a small celebratory dinner where elbows were bent in numerous toasts to the restoration of Anglo-American rapprochement.[26]

As the Oregon negotiations ended, so too did hopes of a diplomatic effort to prevent war with Mexico. The government of Mexico had recalled its diplomats in protest of the Texas annexation resolution in March 1845. Polk sent John Slidell to Mexico City in an attempt to find a peaceful solution, but the government refused to receive him—a move that Webster described as "highly unjustifiable." Polk deployed General Zachary Taylor to the Rio Grande to guard Texas against any Mexican intrusion—an order that, according to Mexico, located Taylor's army not in Texas but in Mexico. The Mexican government had never accepted the Rio Grande as the Texas border but instead argued that the Nueces River set the southern limits of the Lone Star Republic. By Mexican reckoning, Polk had marched a hostile force into their country. On April 24, Mexican cavalry attacked a small party of American dragoons north of the Rio Grande.

When word arrived in Washington, Polk informed his cabinet that hostilities had commenced, and on May 13, Congress responded to the president's request with a formal declaration of war. Of the two no votes in the Senate, one was lodged by Massachusetts—not by Webster, but by John Davis. Webster had made a trip to Boston in mid-April and had not yet returned to the capital. By the time he arrived in Washington, the war had begun and he, though opposing it in principle, accepted his practical obligation to support troops in combat. A week after the declaration, he wrote Fletcher that only a war for "national defence, [sic] or public rights & interests," warranted backing, not one of "ambition, or desire of aggrandizement, or acquisition of territory." But once the fighting had started, he would not withhold needed supplies.[27]

While war with Mexico drew Webster's attention, he was, at the same time, distracted by the late stages of an assault on his reputation and public standing instigated by Democrat Charles Ingersoll of Pennsylvania. Stimulated by a history of ill will toward his Whig colleague, Ingersoll seized on what he deemed questionable behavior by Webster while at the Department of State. Alleged obstruction of justice by Webster in the McLeod case found little traction. Ingersoll charged that Webster had perverted the New York trial by placing US Attorney Joshua Spencer in charge of McLeod's defense and had even arranged for payment of Spencer's fees.

In early April 1846, Webster mounted a rebuttal that contained both a veritable tutorial on the proper conduct of foreign affairs and a response to the charges. The matter of Spencer's pay was especially easy to dismiss. Evidence confirmed that Spencer's compensation was arranged by the British government. These accusations, Webster howled, came from an individual who had more than "a screw loose somewhere. In this case the screws are loose all over." While Ingersoll clearly received the sharp edge of Webster's ire, the senator identified Edward Stubbs, disbursement agent at State, as the "original mover of the mischief." Apparently, Stubbs alerted Ingersoll to some possible discrepancies arising from the McLeod case but had not intended to open a fishing expedition. When the McLeod charges waned, the Pennsylvanian turned his focus on misconduct that he claimed to have found in the Ashburton negotiations. Webster, Ingersoll alleged, had misappropriated funds from the president's secret service account, illegally diverted funds to manipulate the press in Maine and Massachusetts during the boundary dispute, and had embezzled $2,000 from State Department accounts. Now Ingersoll began to fish in earnest, having been "let loose among all the vouchers & papers touching secret service money."[28]

Ingersoll's aim was to neuter Webster politically through the novel action of a retroactive impeachment of his tenure as secretary of state. If successful, this would presumably (although there was no precedent to affirm it) cripple the senator's current and future ability to serve in public office. It did not help that all knew of Webster's dysfunctional relationship with money and his willingness to take favors to subsidize his lifestyle. William Yancey of Alabama attacked him over it, holding up the example of John Quincy Adams, who would not so much as take the gift of a Bible without paying for it. Unlike the pious Adams, Webster was guided by pernicious forces and, to emphasize the point, Yancey reprised Webster's nickname from youth, Black Dan, recasting it from his physical attributes of dark complexion, dark hair, and dark eyes to that of a dark and ignoble character.[29]

Ingersoll's collection of materials supporting his charges resulted in the empaneling of two House committees, the more critical of which would examine the evidence and grounds for impeachment. The other, surprisingly, was tasked with determining how exactly Ingersoll had collected the materials. Webster submitted his rebuttal to the investigating committee in May, admitting to, at most, careless accounting while probing his memory for odd bits and pieces of receipts and vouchers: "I have," he wrote Fletcher, "a sort of recollection" about paying Sparks an additional amount, but "whether I ever handed the additional sum over to Mr. Sparks or forgot or omitted it—I cannot say."[30]

Testimony to the impeachment committee opened with Stubbs, who Webster suspected "would not behave as he ought." But behave he did. Stubbs verified Ingersoll's numbers but found that, by the time Tyler left office, Webster had made a satisfactory accounting of all expenditures. In the end, everyone called supported Webster's innocence, concluding with Tyler who verified that he had signed off on all expenses and that Webster's conduct deserved no reproach. In June, by a vote of four to one, the committee found for Webster on all counts. "I look upon the whole thing as now thro, & perfectly well through," he reported to Fletcher, and confidently concluded, "the evidence will fully satisfy the public, both of the propriety of everything done by me, &. of Mr Ingersol's [sic] rascality, both in his charge, & in his mode of rummaging for evidence."[31]

In the meantime, the Democrats seized the opportunity to revisit the tariff and, as Aberdeen had hoped, eliminate the protectionist elements of the Tariff of 1842 in response to the repeal of the Corn Laws. The "great struggle about the Tariff," Webster wrote Fletcher, loomed in the background as a Polk priority. It was a matter of time before Webster's defense of the 1842 tariff ran him headlong into Treasury Secretary Robert Walker's free trade agenda. The basis of the tariff conflict was simple: Webster believed (as did his well-heeled patrons) that protectionism was essential to economic growth, while Walker argued that protectionism amounted to injurious government intrusion in the relationship of capital to labor, placing government on the side of manufacturing, "augmenting its wealth and power," and favoring it in "the struggle between man and man." Webster disagreed, contending that government intervention in the economy benefited all, capital and workman alike. Protective tariffs encouraged the moneyed class to invest "in such a manner as to occupy and employ American labor." The tariff, in other words, "favors every interest in the country" and reflected the constructive impact of proper government action. Argue though he would, Webster was an astute politician and knew that a coalition of the South and West that had buoyed the Democrats in recent elections would succeed in undoing the so-called black tariff of 1842. It was also clear that Britain's concession on Oregon, repeal of the Corn Laws, and the Walker Tariff were now linked.[32]

It was no coincidence that debate on the Walker bill began on the same day news of the repeal of the Corn Laws reached Washington and seventy-two hours after the ratification of the Oregon Treaty. Webster joined the debate on the day of the vote, July 28, 1846, attacking the bill that promised to "revel in the delights of taking away men's employment." The bill was not for the people, he argued, but "for the relief of the highest and most luxurious classes of the country, and a bill imposing onerous duties on the great industrious masses." In the debate, Webster was reminded of his commitment to free trade in his early years in Congress, to which he replied that "an honest man may change his opinion, and he may change it in two or three, as well as in twenty years." Webster knew the votes and that he was fighting a lost, though close, cause. The Walker Tariff passed the Senate 28–27. Once it cleared the House, the president signed it on the 31st and, perhaps to Webster's surprise, trade began to flow across the Atlantic rewarding farmers and consumers on both sides of the ocean.[33]

The month after the tariff bill was introduced to Congress and soon after the Ingersoll impeachment episode concluded, Webster recalibrated his focus and turned to the recently declared war on Mexico. After initially thinking that the conflict would be short-lived, he soon faced the reality that Polk's goals, while winnable against a weaker opponent, would in fact take time. He wrote his friend, Boston banker Franklin Haven, that the war "might be spun out, for some time" and might invite Europeans into the quarrel. A few weeks later, Webster delivered his first speech on the war in response to a funding request from the president. Since the nation was at war, Webster emphasized that he would not withhold necessary support. Regardless of cause or justification, all should reasonably "agree that the refusal of supplies would make no amends for what some lament, and would not hasten what I hope all desire."

As was the case in his attack on Mr. Madison's war as a young congressman, he insisted on knowing the president's end game. Echoing his 1813 challenge to Madison, Webster insisted on differentiating between a war for defense and a war of aggression. "There is not now," he pointed out, "a hostile foot within the limits of the United States." It seemed that American troops had gone from "an army of observation" at the outset to an "army of occupation," and now formed an "army of invasion." Given these circumstances, he proposed a suspension of military action to encourage a negotiated settlement. If Mexico agreed to negotiate, good; if not, "then, of course, she must have war, vigorous war, until she be compelled to adopt a different line of conduct." After all, it could not be the desire of the American people to "crush the republic of Mexico," a weak and unfortunate neighbor whose very institutions were modeled on America. To break Mexico and make it prey for some of the "thrones of Europe," he added, "is not a thought which can find harbor in the generous breasts of the American people."[34]

As the war dragged on and the fire in his belly for the presidency once again stirred, Webster's attack sharpened. At the Massachusetts Whig state convention in fall of 1847, he accused the president of fabricating the war by elevating bloodshed on either Mexican, or at best disputed, soil, to an attack on the United States that had to be repelled. Polk had, he complained, manipulated Congress into a war that violated the spirit of the Constitution's war declaration clause. Congress should thus demand that the president verify that the conflict aimed to repel a threat to the security of the nation. If Polk failed to do so, Congress should "pass resolutions against the prosecution of the war, and grant no further supplies."[35]

Meanwhile, on August 10, 1846, a House bill responsive to a $2 million funding request from Polk passed with an amendment attached by David Wilmot of Pennsylvania to block the extension of slavery into any territory acquired from Mexico. Coming on the last day of the congressional session, the Senate had very little time to comment before both houses adjourned. Thus, the bill lapsed with no action taken. The Wilmot Proviso, however, would not lapse. The congressman from Pennsylvania had opened a question that demanded attention. The war would expand the nation, but would it also expand the institution of slavery? Webster's initial answer was simple: Don't expand the nation and thereby eliminate the Wilmot problem altogether.

The following month at Faneuil Hall, the Massachusetts Whigs met to develop their platform and slate of candidates for the 1848 election. Immediately the fracture between Conscience and Cotton Whigs exposed the fissure in party unity. The Union, Webster warned his colleagues, was on the edge of a dangerous precipice and only "the intelligent, patriotic, united Whig party" could pull it back. Polk had violated his constitutional authority, and the Whigs must take care not to let an extreme position draw them away from the founding document as well. Webster consistently worried that the abolitionists in the party would squeeze southerners into a reactionary box that would force them to consider secession. As a result, the Wilmot Proviso was conspicuously absent from his speeches and public pronouncements.[36]

Legislators returned to Washington in December to find a new funding bill on their desks, the so-called Three-Million Bill. When the Senate took it up, the Wilmot Proviso once again appeared as an amendment from the House. Webster continued to argue against territorial acquisition but gained little support. Territory had already been won. The burning question now was Wilmot's. On March 1, 1847, Webster made one last attempt to rein in the expansionists: Massachusetts, he stated, "would strenuously resist the annexation of any new territory to this Union, in which the institution of slavery is to be tolerated or established." When he finally accepted the reality that there were only two possible outcomes in the Senate—territory with Wilmot's restrictions or territory with no restrictions—he supported the Proviso. In the end, the Senate voted down the Wilmot amendment and voted up the Three-Million Bill with no restrictions. Webster, unhappy with the vote of his northern friends, turned to his habitual pastime of seeking the presidency.[37]

In the spring of 1847, Webster staged a grand tour of the South to gauge support for a presidential run in 1848 while General Zachary Taylor staged a grand tour of Mexico garnering support for his own presidential bid. Greeted graciously by large crowds from Virginia to Georgia, Webster carefully tailored his messages to broader ecumenical themes. "Our duty," he told a Savannah, Georgia, crowd, "is to be content with the Constitution as it is, to resist all changes from whatever quarter, to preserve its original spirit and original purpose, and to commend it, as it is, to the care of those who come after us." Southerners heard, as was intended, the "as it is" comment as affirmation of their slave labor system. Clearly, Webster had no intention of meddling with the institution's constitutional protections. Despite the warm reception received across the South, there was no competing with the appeal of a war hero who, the Whig partisans believed, could win back the presidency. As an apolitical soldier, Taylor had the advantage of no controversial baggage; in fact, the baggage he did bring was that of a victorious warrior in a highly romanticized war for Manifest Destiny. Not even the godlike Webster could compete with that résumé. Massachusetts sent Webster as their pick to the Whig convention in Philadelphia in June 1848, but General Taylor drew the votes—no longer a winner of battles, but now a winner of wars.[38]

In February 1848, Nicholas Trist had negotiated the Treaty of Guadalupe Hidalgo, which transferred to the victorious United States the title to the entire Southwest from the Nueces River (Mexico's version of the Texas border) to San Diego. For this massive territory, the United States committed a paltry $15,000,000. Webster fought the treaty in the Senate, charging among other things that New Mexico and California (where unbeknownst to Webster gold had already been found at Sutter's Mill) "were not worth a dollar," but he fared no better than he had with the Whig nomination. The senator was trying to close a door that was off its hinges over a threshold crowded with expansionist Americans fired with patriotic passion for a republic extending from sea to sea.[39]

In the summer of 1848, Congress considered a wide range of options for pacifying diverse attitudes toward slavery and the Mexican Cession. New York Democrat Daniel Dickinson offered a resolution proposing the application of popular sovereignty to the territories. Under this concept, the people in the territory would decide whether to ban or to accommodate slavery. Polk believed the extension of the Missouri Compromise (36°30' latitude) line to the Pacific the most practicable solution. Some agreed with Delaware Whig John Clayton that the question was a matter for the courts, wherein federal judges might rule on actions brought by individual slaves. Although the Polk plan and the Clayton proposal found support in the Senate, neither of these approaches could rally adequate backing in both houses of Congress. Webster stood firm against the extension of slavery and so rejected all compromise plans. In debates over the bill to organize the Oregon Territory, Illinois senator Stephen Douglas offered an amendment to extend the Missouri line to the sea. Webster opposed the amendment: slavery would be a nonissue in Oregon, but the amendment would sanction slavery through much of the Mexican Cession. Under no conditions would he back the further "extension of the area of slavery upon this continent" or to any "increase of slave representation in the other house of Congress." Nevertheless, while expressing impatience with southern intransigence, he accused anyone from outside the South who dared "disturb the relation between master and slave" as "unconstitutional in their spirit," and "productive of nothing but evil and mischief."[40]

During the winter session, Webster engaged in a fruitless debate over a provisional arrangement for governing the Mexican Cession. In a tangle with Calhoun, who argued that the Constitution followed the flag into the territories, Webster reinforced his position that the territories were the purview of Congress and that the legislature alone would determine the degree to which the Constitution applied to the territories. Again, Webster distinguished between the states that existed at the time the Constitution was drafted and those states and territories that came after the Founders' government gaveled in.

Webster's frustration with an incongruous Congress and a Whig Party that had chosen a political neophyte for president paled in comparison with his personal suffering during the 1848 campaign season. His youngest son Edward had insisted on quitting his work with the Maine boundary commission and accepted an appointment as an officer with the Massachusetts

Volunteers. His father feared the "effects of the climate" on Edward more than the dangers of battle and, sadly, his fear was affirmed in early 1848. On February 23, he received news that Major Edward Webster had died in late January, not of combat wounds but of fever. He immediately sent the tragic news to Fletcher, cryptically opening the note, "Dear and Only Son." Their sister Julia, who was very close to Edward, was devastated: "He went forth to a wicked and cruel war," she cried, "& there he has died . . . a useless sacrifice." In her grief Julia called on "God, in his mercy" to "sanctify this great affliction to us all." She died of consumption in late April, and on the day that Webster gathered with the family for Julia's funeral, Edward's body arrived from Mexico. An inconsolable Webster that day set out two weeping elms—"Brother and Sister"—in memorial.[41]

Webster dutifully met his political obligations to both the party and Congress, but he demonstrated little enthusiasm for the Zachary Taylor–Millard Fillmore ticket. Fletcher had advised him to remain neutral, but Webster feared for both his party standing and the reckless Democratic candidate Lewis Cass, so he fell indifferently in line behind Taylor. The general, Webster believed, had little to suggest political competence but was a safer option than either Cass or the extreme abolitionists who would make the purging of slavery a litmus for the next president.

When Taylor won the election, Webster, tired of Congress, had a fading hope that he might influence the administration from a seat in the cabinet as secretary of state; but a few weeks before the March 5 inauguration, he conceded that a cabinet position would not be offered. Taylor proffered the post to John Clayton, a Whig who had shown more enthusiasm for the Taylor-Fillmore ticket. Webster understood this and wrote his friend Richard Milford Blatchford in mid-February that, even if offered a position, fealty dictated that he should remain with his friends on the outside, maintaining a "position of respect, friendship, and support of the incoming administration; but not a position in which I should be called upon to take part in the distribution of its offices and patronage." There was ample work ahead, and none more pressing for the Taylor administration and Congress than the disposition of California.[42]

Soon after the war ended, California, easily meeting the minimum requirements for statehood, advanced quickly toward that goal. Before Trist had signed his treaty to end the Mexican War in January 1848, reports circulated of gold at Sutter's Mill. The next year a rush to California added over eighty thousand to the territory's population. Webster friend and Whig colleague Philip Hone assessed the situation succinctly, describing "California gold and the cholera" as "two diseases equally infectious."[43]

Not one for nuanced solutions, Taylor determined that the best way to cool the fever over the new territories was to preempt the slavery agendas of sectional firebrands by quickly queuing both California and New Mexico for statehood. By the time of Taylor's first message to Congress in December, California had already begun the process and, without authorization, formed a free-state government. In his annual message, Taylor proposed moving forward with statehood. The general, like all military officers, was accustomed to issuing orders and having them followed with straightforward efficiency, two words not commonly associated with congressional behavior.[44]

   The question of California statehood occasioned one of the most dramatic moments in congressional history and provoked so-called statesmen to overwrought pronouncements, volatile language, and frequent challenges to duel. Southerners had already planned a meeting in Nashville for the following June, ostensibly to decide whether or not to remain in the Union. In this increasingly toxic atmosphere, the Senate once again looked to the time-tested skills of Henry Clay, "The Great Compromiser." In fact, the debates over California found all three of the Great Triumvirate on the floor of Congress for the last time. Calhoun was near death and struggled to make it to his seat; gaunt and feeble, wrapped in a cloak, and unable to find the breath to speak, the old nullifier relied on a reader to have his position heard. Clay was old and frail but, at seventy-three, tenaciously determined to breach the gulf with one last compromise.

   Before delivering his proposal to the Senate in January 1850, Clay, fighting a nasty cough, trudged through a frosty Washington evening to Webster's house to seek his counsel. It was urgent that the differences between the North and the South be reconciled. Further delay, he feared, would threaten the survival of the Union. Would Webster, he asked, stand with him on a compromise? Webster agreed, reflecting after Clay left that his old colleague believed that "Providence had designed his return to the Senate" so he could supply "the means and the way of averting a great evil from our country." At the end of the month, Clay presented his compromise to the Senate, offering something for both sides. For his northern colleagues, he proposed the acceptance of California's admission as a free state. For southerners, the remainder of the Mexican Cession would be organized with no constraints on slavery. For northerners, the compromise would end the slave trade in Washington, D.C., but southerners would be secured in their rights to have slaves at the capital. For southerners, Congress would not interfere in the interstate slave trade, and a new and effective fugitive slave law would be put into effect. Finally, Congress would address the agitation between Texas and the New

Mexico Territory by compensating Texas for accepting a boundary favorable to New Mexico.[45]

Ironically, Webster at first did not see the crisis potential over California statehood and dismissed it as "mischievous." Preoccupied with pleadings before the Supreme Court, it took several weeks for him to realize that talk of disunion coming from both sections had put the nation in peril. In the third week of February 1850, his view of conditions shifted from mischief to emergency as he vainly sought "weapons to beat down the Northern and Southern follies, now raging in equal extremes." Perhaps, he determined, it was time for an unrestrained pro-Union speech that gave no quarter to the extreme positions of either section. In other words, he should reprise his skills as a diplomatist, not between two nations but between two sections flirting dangerously with separation.[46]

He scheduled his performance for the seventh of March, and as happened so often in his career, the advanced notice assured a packed chamber: even Calhoun managed to totter to his seat, although tardy and unnoticed. For three hours Webster held forth, declaring that he stood before the body "not as a Massachusetts man, nor as a Northern man, but as an American," earnestly calling "for the preservation of the Union." During the speech Webster referenced Calhoun and, not seeing him, lamented that his health did "not allow him to be here." After a second reference, the South Carolina senator mustered enough energy to rise slightly from his chair and announce to Webster's surprise that "the Senator from South Carolina is in his seat." Later in the speech, when Webster quoted a letter from then Secretary of State Calhoun to the American chargé d'affaires in Texas suggesting that the goal of Texas annexation was "to strengthen the slave interest of the South," the old senator rose to defend himself. After the exchange, Webster complimented him as one who would "never disguise his conduct or his motives," to which Calhoun replied, "Never, never." Furthermore, Webster noted, "What he means he is very apt to say." Calhoun responded, "Always, always." This would be Calhoun's last exchange on the floor of Congress. Webster joined Clay as pallbearer for Calhoun's funeral a few weeks later.[47]

Webster's objective was not to engage the fading Calhoun but to promote a compromise to relieve the sectional threat facing the Union. It is a characteristic of some, Webster acknowledged, to believe that right and wrong are "absolute; absolutely wrong, or absolutely right" and that the distinction between the two can be determined "with the precision of an algebraic equation." On the issue of slavery, however, the rigidity of a mathematical formula had never been possible: variables did not remain constant but

Figure 5.2. "Daniel Webster Addressing the United States Senate," March 7, 1850. Courtesy of the Library of Congress Prints and Photographs Division, LC-USZ62-1414.

changed to accommodate circumstances. Positions in both the North and South, he pointed out, had shifted since the founding of the republic. The North, for example, acquiesced at times (most recently by accepting the annexation of slave-holding Texas) to what northerners now deemed reprehensible. The South, before the "the age of cotton, became the golden age," had signed onto the Ordinance of 1787 barring the expansion of the "inhuman and cruel" institution into all territories under congressional authority. Now southerners planned to meet in Nashville and, "over the bones" of Andrew Jackson, discuss seceding from the Union over the possible restriction of slavery from lands under congressional authority. Contemplation of secession seemed especially foolish, Webster noted, since "an ordinance of nature" would inherently bar slavery from the Southwest and, consequently, make Wilmot's proviso moot. Albeit assuming that nature would save him, Webster had, for the sake of reconciliation, been willing to withdraw his longstanding opposition to the extension of slavery.[48]

In the manner of the experienced diplomatist he had become, Webster reduced the problem to pragmatic compromise. Neither section could hold firm to its line without risking the fracturing of the Union itself. Both, he argued, must yield. If his experience as chief negotiator at the State Department had taught him anything, it was to set the priority and compromise as necessary on all ancillary points. On the present matter, those determined to champion abolition would, historian Irving Bartlett has stated succinctly, "destroy slavery at any cost and leave the Union to Providence. Webster would preserve the Union at any cost and leave abolition to Providence." For the sake of this sacrosanct cause, the senator admonished his colleagues to rise to their moment with destiny and "not be pigmies in a case that calls for men." Separation of the sections could not be pursued short of a violent war. The only peaceful path, therefore, lay in a compromise that would permit all involved to "enjoy the fresh air of Liberty and Union."[49]

Webster knew his speech would meet headwinds of criticism from both sides, and once again, he had to restore his Whig standing. Conscience Whigs would, among other criticisms, reject his argument that slavery in the South and the enforcement of fugitive slave laws were both validated by constitutional authority. Even his lifelong admirer Edward Everett could not sanction his morally tepid position on slavery. The once fawning Emerson now pronounced the senator devoid "of moral faculty" and his "eulogies of liberty" mere "sentimentalism & youthful rhetoric."[50]

Cotton Whigs were displeased with his chastisement of southern colleagues for threatening secession. Reacting to these attacks, Webster asked friends to circulate a letter favorable to the speech. Everett refused, but about a thousand others signed the letter that Webster described as "too good, too good. . . . I don't deserve the one hundredth part of what it says," but, he added, post it immediately. He did not help his cause among Bostonians when, on his return to the city in late spring, he admonished abolitionists to "conquer their own prejudices" and adhere to the fugitive slave law.[51]

While proponents of the Compromise of 1850 struggled against an obstinate Louisiana slaveholder in the executive mansion, circumstances took a tragic turn that sent Webster from the Senate back to the State Department. In the sweltering humidity of Independence Day, the president attended an event at the unfinished Washington Monument. Seeking relief from the heat, Taylor returned to the residence where he overindulged in an odd mix of food and drink that resulted in a deadly attack of gastroenteritis. On July 9, at the president's passing, New Yorker Millard Fillmore moved from vice president to president and immediately sought experienced advisors. For secretary of state he approached Webster, who accepted with little hesitation before offering what became a final goodbye to Congress on the seventeenth. As for the Compromise, it now had an advocate in the place of an adversary in the White House and, after Webster's confirmation on July 22, a force in the executive branch capable of driving it forward.[52]

Figure 5.3. Millard Fillmore. Courtesy of the Library of Congress Prints and Photographs Division, LC-DIG-pga-10236.

The urgency presented by a potentially violent altercation between Texas and New Mexico over the boundary dispute gave Webster an immediate opportunity to press the Compromise. A squabble over the border had run hot and cold since the end of the Mexican War. Texas attempted to exert control over Santa Fe, and New Mexico called on Washington to quickly organize the territory to secure it against Texans. After his predecessor had requested that the state legislature grant him unlimited force to protect the Texas claim, Governor Peter H. Bell moved to deploy adequate militia to safeguard Texas interests and establish Lone Star authority in the disputed area. When Fillmore sent word that federal troops would repel Texan encroachment into New Mexico, southern politcos offered to send military assistance to Texas if needed. Webster knew that this powder keg, like the one on the Maine-Canadian border over ten years before, should be quickly defused. He restrained Bell while sending former colleagues a clear signal that the president intended to use force in Texas, if necessary, and that Congress should move quickly to pass the compromise bills.[53]

A few days later, Stephen Douglas of Illinois piloted the compromise to success by breaking it into pieces, thereby allowing each, in turn, to win adequate support for passage. The Texas boundary bill secured approval first. If Webster had influenced Congress on the Texas-New Mexico matter, there is ample evidence that the various remaining bills that now made up the Compromise of 1850 reached the president's desk without his aid. His ability to steer legislation diminished with the Seventh of March Speech and ended when he left the Senate. Nevertheless, the compromise legislation moved forward, and Fillmore, in his first message to Congress in December, proclaimed the elements that now formed the Compromise of 1850 "a final settlement."[54]

Unfortunately, both Webster and the Compromise would be short-lived, but before the former's lights dimmed, he had another chance to add to an already impressive legacy in US foreign relations. During the third week of July, Webster returned to the second-floor offices of the Southwest Executive Building to resume the duties of secretary of state—duties that would require him to address the continued American expansionist impulse, a Europe that had undergone a seismic shift toward liberalism, and technological advances in communication and transportation, all affecting the mechanics of diplomacy and setting the stage for a Webster performance remarkably different from that of his first stay at 15th and Pennsylvania.

CHAPTER SIX

Last Turn at the "Old High Table," 1850–1852

> Who better than he has grasped and displayed the advancing tendencies and enlarging duties of America? Who has caught—whose eloquence, whose genius, and whose counsels, have caught more adequately the genuine inspiration of our destiny?
>
> —Rufus Choates, July 1853

Before returning to the "old high table in my little room" at State, Webster resumed his career-long pattern of soliciting financial support. Knowing from experience the trappings inherent in the top cabinet position, he would require adequate funding to subsidize the style and posture of secretary of state and to offset the losses he would incur from lack of attention to his legal practice. This expectation was met once again by friends and patrons. In addition to several thousand dollars arranged by Webster supporters, a letter from New York merchant and Webster friend George Griswold the following January confirmed that forty New Yorkers had signed onto a plan committing $500 each to ease Webster's move to the State Department. Accusations soon circulated that he was a "stipendiary of the bankers and brokers" who stood to profit from forthcoming transactions to satisfy pecuniary commitments to Mexico from the Treaty of Guadalupe Hidalgo. As in the past, the charges died in Congress and served only to remind those inclined to notice the fiscal cloud under which Webster had lived for most of his career.[1]

At the time of Webster's second incumbency at State, the nation had no international threats or impending foreign policy crises as had been the case the last time he served in a presidential cabinet. In fact, he later noted to his friend and legal associate Richard Blatchford that the foreign policy climate for the United States had never been "more quiet," producing "no disturbing breath on the surface." The "diplomatic gentlemen here," he noted, were "all amicably disposed." If this were the case, why did so many feel compelled to invest in a cabinet position for Webster? The answer does not lie in possible international crises, but rather in an immediate domestic one—preservation of the Union. As one of the president's principal advisers, Webster was in a pivotal place to apply the balm of compromise to the wound of sectional division. A few days before assuming his State Department duties, he wrote Nathan Sargent that his mission was simple: restoration of "peace and harmony to the Country." And who better than Webster to heal the Union, a mission that, more than anything else, defined his adult life.[2]

Fate (and bad cherries) had replaced the intransigent Taylor with Fillmore, who so favored compromise that he had informed Taylor that he would follow his conscience and not administration orthodoxy should the Senate require a vice-presidential tie breaker. Now, as president, his support for compromise reached considerably farther than a tie-breaking vote. Webster was pleased with Fillmore's Whig pedigree and his abilities and devotion to the goals of stability that Webster shared. The two men enjoyed a simpatico defined by understanding and clear communication; the president, Webster noted, is "a good-tempered, cautious, intelligent man, with whom it is pleasant to transact business." It seemed to impress Webster that the president followed the scriptural admonition to "be not puffed up." While the two were required to address issues in foreign policy, Webster did so with the Compromise of 1850 always in the foreground, often coloring the administration's response even to matters beyond the nation's shores.[3]

One of the first foreign policy concerns facing the Fillmore administration was left to Webster by his predecessor John Clayton and affirms Webster's appropriation of international matters for his domestic agenda. The year 1848 marked a watershed moment in European liberalism, with uprisings against the old hierarchy and demands for radical change in governance across the continent. In Hungary, Louis Kossuth led his people in an independence movement against their Austrian masters that demonstrated legitimate potential for Hungarian sovereignty. The inclination of the American people, as with the Greek movement twenty years before, was to applaud such movements and to urge their elected leaders to offer encouragement if not outright support.

President Taylor and Secretary Clayton sent A. Dudley Mann in the summer of 1849 on a covert mission to Hungary to ascertain Kossuth's potential for success. If Mann's assessment were for a positive outcome, he was instructed to extend America's support by formally recognizing Hungary's independence and follow with commercial treaties between the United States and the new nation. While Mann was en route, Russia intervened to shore up Austrian control of Hungary, and the movement collapsed with Kossuth and followers fleeing to exile in Turkey.[4]

US intrusion into what Austria considered an internal matter did not end with the suppression of the revolution. The Austrians had managed, through surreptitious means, to obtain a copy of Mann's instructions and were furious at Washington's attempted interference in the Hungarian uprising. In his December message to Congress, Taylor continued to salt the wound with an expression of America's desire to "welcome Hungary into the family of nations" and an acknowledgment that he had "invested an agent . . . with power to declare our willingness promptly to recognize her independence in the event of her ability to sustain it." The following March he made the correspondence from the Mann mission available to the Senate. The Austrians, already irritated by what they had seen from the intercepts, filed a formal complaint. The Chevalier J. G. Hülsemann, Austria's chargé d'affaires in Washington, had lodged an informal complaint, but now he was directed by his government to file an official protest with Secretary of State Clayton. His directive from Vienna arrived at the time of the president's death and, in "compliance with the requisitions of propriety," he delayed the complaint until the Fillmore administration had been constituted.[5]

Within the first weeks of his return to State, Webster learned of the coming complaint and attempted to dissuade Hülsemann from filing it. The new secretary cautioned that a strongly worded message from Vienna would necessitate a strongly worded response from the Fillmore administration. Nevertheless, Hülsemann was intent on following his directive. The official complaint, afterward known as the Hülsemann Letter, arrived at Webster's office the first week of October. It was, as Webster feared, abrasive and required a frank reply.

Despite the president's signature now inscribed on all the various bills forming the Compromise of 1850, Webster knew that the threat to the Union was only momentarily calmed and not removed. Whigs in both New York and Massachusetts, the respective home states of Fillmore and Webster, rejected the compromise and targeted the extension of slavery and the fugitive slave law for special repudiation. Concerning the latter, Webster's support provoked Emerson to assert that Webster's "fame ends in this filthy law," and Boston Whigs refused to allow Faneuil Hall to host an event honoring the secretary. Webster had demonstrated a resilient ego over the course of his professional life. It was, however, the Union's resilience that concerned him now; South Carolina continued to intimate secession. In this climate, Webster determined to craft a response to Hülsemann, not to pacify the Austrian but to pacify the angst of Americans by rallying patriotic passions against disrespectful words from a foreign pen. Hülsemann supplied those words.[6]

The Hülsemann Letter offered Webster the first opportunity to turn his position at State into an advocacy platform for domestic harmony. After derisively pointing out that the Mann mission was at variance not only with international law but also with America's policy of nonintervention, the chevalier accused the Taylor administration of deploying Mann as a spy. Clayton's subsequent contention that the mission was a mere quest for reliable facts could not be reconciled with the secretary's directive. Mann's instructions, Hülsemann noted, condemned Austria's "iron rule" while portraying the rebel leader Kossuth "as an illustrious man."[7]

Nevertheless, the Austrian government had been willing to excuse the transgression as a simple matter of American "ignorance" of the Hungarian situation until Taylor made public the Mann instructions. The public airing of the documents in the Senate required a formal protest. Hülsemann concluded the chastising letter with a less than subtle threat that this type of intervention might blow back on the United States, exposing the nation "to acts of retaliation and to certain inconveniences, which could not fail to affect the commerce and the industry of the two hemispheres." Hülsemann's reference to Mann's description of Austria's "iron rule" over Hungary exposed his government's illicit acquisition of Mann's original instructions. Webster informed Fillmore in January that the term *iron rule* had been redacted from the documents presented to the Senate.[8]

Webster, enjoying a respite at The Elms, took the better part of three months to craft a response, soliciting input from the small State Department staff, guests at The Elms, and, as was his custom, the reliable Edward Everett. Of the contributions to the secretary's response to Hülsemann, those of William Hunter, the State Department's chief clerk, and Everett were most prominent. In fact, after Webster's death, Everett laid his draft and Webster's final version side by side to show the remarkable similarity. Nevertheless, Webster presented it as his own, and there is evidence that critical points and the tone of the reply were indeed his.[9]

A few days before Christmas, Webster sent the reply to the Austrian legation offices. It was, as he later conceded to George Ticknor, "boastful and rough," but he made no apologies. Webster intended "to tell the people of Europe who and what we are, and awaken them to a just sense of the unparalleled growth of this country." In taking this approach, he sought to "touch the national pride, and make a man feel *sheepish* and look *silly* who should speak of disunion." Webster opened his reply to Hülsemann by indignantly scolding the Austrian for his comments about the president's interaction with the Senate. The internal message between two branches of the American government, he noted, contained no "public manifesto, to which any foreign state was called on to reply." In other words, what business was it of Austria to interpose a protest into the internal procedures of the American government? This, Webster chided, seemed to be no less than Austrian interference "with the domestic concerns of a foreign nation; the very thing, which is the ground of its complaint against the United States."[10]

Defending former secretary Clayton, Webster argued that Mann's mission was completely within the parameters of proper behavior; the agent had been sent to investigate conditions in Hungary—conditions that naturally concerned the United States as they did the entire Atlantic world. It had not been his purpose to assist in the detachment of Hungary from Austria, but only to open relations should that detachment occur, and "the new government should appear . . . to be firm and stable."[11]

Webster could have drafted a quick and concise reply to Hülsemann if he had only wished to defend the Taylor administration, but his objective was to exploit the moment for domestic purposes. Boasting of the greatness of the American Union and its popular government, he disparaged, by comparison, an archaic European monarchical system bent on perpetuating the notion that human rights were no more than "grants and indulgences from crowned heads." The United States, Webster noted, had offered no defensive response when "his late Austrian Majesty, Francis II" clearly targeted the American system in 1821 with his remark that "the whole World has become foolish, and leaving their ancient laws, was in search of imaginary Constitutions." And it was certainly unnecessary to offer a defense now of a United States of America with "a rapidly increasing population, a flourishing commerce, sound public credit, and amply protected personal property rights." The "power of this republic, at the present moment, is spread over a region, one of the richest and most fertile on the Globe, and of an extent in comparison with which the possessions of the House of Hapsburg, are but as a patch on the earth's surface." America's maritime presence reached ports throughout the world, he continued, and her citizens enjoyed "life, liberty, property and all personal rights," secured "by just and stable laws."[12]

Webster clearly intended to showcase the model republic that had emerged in North America, demonstrating to the world the rectitude of popular governance. He had apprised Everett that he aimed to seize the occasion "to show the world, the difference between the fundamental principles of our Government, and those of the arbitrary monarchies of Eastern Europe." It was no wonder, he wrote Hülsemann, that the American people exhibited an interest in movements such as that in Hungary; after all, the movements drew inspiration from principles formed and implemented in the United States. While avoiding active "interference with the political changes in Europe," Americans could not "fail to cherish, always, a lively interest in the fortunes of Nations, struggling for institutions like their own." Americans did so not out of any hostile intent, but "because they regard such constitutions and such National Independence, not as imaginary, but as real blessings."[13]

Webster had waxed romantic about the Hungarian uprising in late 1849 when he announced at a rally in Boston that "we have all had our sympathies much enlisted in the Hungarian effort for liberty. We have all wept at its failure." Having demonstrated to his satisfaction, and hopefully to that of contentious Americans, the superiority of American republican institutions, he invoked American honor in direct response to the chevalier's explicit threats.[14]

Webster rejected accusations that Mann had been a spy subject to Vienna's reprisal and the threat that such interference in Austrian affairs might provoke commercial retaliation. If the Austrian government had "subjected Mr. Mann to the treatment of a spy," Webster asserted, and carried "any such lawless purpose into effect . . . the Spirit of the People of this Country, would have demanded immediate hostilities, to be waged by the utmost exertion of the Power of the Republic, military and naval." Furthermore, a sovereign nation could not subject "the language, in which it may instruct its own officers" to the scrutiny of a foreign power and still claim to be independent. Finally, Webster dismissed Austria's "hypothetical" commercial retaliation with the firm and concise assertion that "the Government and people of the United States are quite willing to take their chances, and abide their destiny." During the second week of March, Hülsemann sent a reply to Webster reiterating his government's position on the Mann mission, but Webster's first statement had served his purpose, and he deferred to Fillmore's directive to offer a brief and courteous reply and let relations between the two nations calm.[15]

Meanwhile, Webster's rejoinder to Hülsemann had made more of a ripple than a splash with American nationalism and domestic harmony. Apart from an occasional letter of agreement and mention by the press, perhaps the most attention it received was in London where the American minister to the Court of St. James's, Abbott Lawrence, paid for its printing and circulation in pamphlet form. A similar suggestion met Clay's decisive opposition in Congress. Still, some observers applauded Webster's tone as a masterfully crafted reminder of America's exceptional nature. Artist and inventor Samuel F. B.

Morse (no stranger to communication), for example, expressed pleasure at Webster's verbal drubbing of "the insolent but impotent Austrian."[16]

Although tension between Vienna and Washington relaxed somewhat after the exchange of notes in early spring, an incident involving exiled rebel leader Louis Kossuth retightened that tension. Kossuth had been given refuge in Turkey following the collapse of the rebellion and became the subject of conversation between the Sultan's representative, Amin Bey, and Webster during the Turk's state visit to the United States in the fall of 1850. Webster extended every courtesy to the Turkish naval officer, arranging for accommodations in Washington and entertaining him in Webster fashion, both in the capital and at his home at Marshfield. He hoped to exploit the high-profile opportunity to propagate union. Amin Bey, like other foreign visitors, Webster proclaimed, was not welcomed by a factionalized republic or "a dissevered and broken country"; he was, rather, the "guest of the United States of America."

All the pomp and circumstance surrounding the visit of a Turkish leader, of course, had no impact on Vienna apart from the occasional mention of Turkish benevolence at having given sanctuary to Kossuth and Hungarian rebels. This all changed when Fillmore directed Webster to open negotiations with Constantinople to permit Kossuth and companions to come to America. The Turkish government agreed, and a year after Amin Bey's visit, on September 10, 1851, Kossuth and an entourage of four dozen began their journey to the United States. They arrived to great fanfare in December, heralded by their greeters in New York as torchbearers of freedom and liberty. Perhaps, thought Kossuth, enthusiastic citizens of the American republic could breathe life back into his deflated movement.[17]

Webster had to be careful to balance his promotion of American nationalism with the preservation of America's longstanding policy of nonintervention in European affairs. The more excitable Kossuth became, the more convinced he might become that the United States would somehow assist in the liberation of Hungary. It was not the aim of the United States, Webster explained, to deliver republican institutions to other peoples; it was rather the aim of this nation "to make proselytes by our example, to convert man to republicanism by showing what republicanism can do in promoting the true ends of government." In keeping with his mission to glorify the Union, he portrayed America as a sun "in the political firmament." America, he boasted, produced light, "the warming influence of which all shall feel and know."[18]

Webster's plan to offer American moral and philosophical backing while withholding anything that might be construed as physical support was soon tested by Kossuth's presence in Washington. The Hungarian icon arrived after Christmas, greeted like no foreign guest since Lafayette. After dining with the president, he was joined by Webster the first week of January at a banquet in the Hungarian's honor at the National Hotel. A bipartisan group of congressional leaders hosted the event. With all this attention, it is small wonder that Kossuth's expectations rose for American intervention. In fact, he envisioned a joint intervention by the United States and Britain to counter Russia's intrusion on the side of continued Austrian dominance of his people. Despite his determination to give Kossuth "no encouragement" and his promise to react to any talk of intervention with "ears more deaf than adders," Webster's address to the banquet gathering seemed an unwavering endorsement of Hungarian independence.[19]

After raising a glass to toast Hungarian independence, Webster lauded Kossuth's role in leading the fight and derided the Austrians for their commitment to the oppressive European model of "autocratic power, maintained by arms and force." Fortunately, he enthused, that system was in decline, supplanted by the increasing appeal of popular government. Reminding the gathering of his support for Greek independence as a young congressman, he revisited the jingoistic remarks from his reply to Hülsemann that espoused principles he would hold for as long as "the sun and moon endure, and while I can see the light of the sun and the moon." If unwilling to intervene by deed, Webster certainly felt comfortable intervening by word, advising Austria to confine "the limits of her power to her hereditary and German domains," as an independent Hungary established "our American model upon the Lower Danube." *The National Intelligencer* reported that Webster endorsed "Hungarian self-government," and further, "Hungarian control of Hungarian destinies, Hungarian independence and Hungary as a distinct nationality among the nations of Europe." Lewis Cass reinforced the sentiment that the bounty bestowed on the United States required that Americans not remain "blindfolded, with our arms closed, and see tyranny prevailing."[20]

Webster's comments not only lacked diplomacy, they were the very model of indiscretion. A banquet guest might have attributed the sensational delivery to the exuberant atmosphere or, perhaps, to Webster's zeal to demonstrate both his and his country's "exceptionalism" in a moment unfettered by tact or prudence. But this was the deliberate Daniel Webster, the celebrated voice that had rarely in his professional life uttered unvetted remarks, and he did not do so on this occasion. His words were planned, calculated, and intentional.

His indelicate rhetoric was not so much aimed at the audience at the National Hotel but at voters in the approaching presidential election. As expected, Webster had spent a considerable amount of 1851 shoring up his political support and had, in November, launched his campaign at Faneuil Hall, running as the embodiment of "the Compromise, the Union and the Constitution."[21]

Had Webster been a private citizen or even a member of Congress, his remarks would have simply dissolved into the mix of countless such expressions emanating from across the country, but he was America's top diplomat. Despite Kossuth's failure to garner more than moral support from Americans or to soften Fillmore's rigid devotion to nonintervention, the entire scene was such an affront to Vienna that Hülsemann felt compelled to express his ire directly to the president. Webster had delivered "a revolutionary address," Hülsemann contended, that "openly held out encouragement to Hungary, spurring her on to a new rebellion" as he audaciously toasted "the speedy emancipation of that Kingdom."[22]

When Hülsemann met with the president and targeted Webster's remarks as just cause to terminate his relationship with the secretary of state, Fillmore found himself in the awkward position of having to distance himself from his cabinet member's address. Webster's words, Fillmore explained, were not delivered in his official capacity as secretary of state and did not express the views of the government. Hülsemann was so agitated by Webster's public display that he left the country after informing Fillmore that he would not return to Washington until Webster had been dismissed from State or the next election brought in a new administration.[23]

Webster's address might have elicited positive feedback from his American fans and satisfied his aim to promote himself and the cause of Union, but it did so at the expense of US-Austrian relations. He let it be known as he prepared his address that his goal was not to walk delicately around Austrian sentiment but rather to shield himself from any potential political attacks for being lukewarm on liberty. He had confided to Fillmore that he would attend the banquet because he "should not like unnecessarily to provoke popular attack." After the speech, he wrote Blatchford that his purpose had been to maintain consistency with his prior characterization of the decaying European monarchical system, and "to take care that our political opponents shall have no well-founded charge against us for coolness in the cause of liberty."[24]

In this aim, he was successful. Various newspapers, including the *New York Herald*, applauded his bold position in support of Hungarian independence and his salute to Kossuth. But all this came at a cost to US-Austrian relations. Hülsemann's departure from Washington had created a de facto interruption in diplomatic relations; and, as threatened, he did not return until after Webster's death when the alleged source of the rupture was "buried in the grave of that great statesman."[25]

While Webster's commitment to a domestic agenda assured that the Hülsemann-Kossuth affair would be far from his finest hour as a diplomatist, his effort to restructure the State Department in the Fillmore administration to conform to the posture and increased responsibility of a rising power provided one of his most enduring successes. The spoils system he unapologetically exploited in his first term was not a sustainable model for a department tasked with managing expanding American interests and associated foreign policy. The US diplomatic corps, for example, was populated by "politicians in timely exile," deep-pocketed campaign donors, and "superannuated generals, and journalists." When Webster returned to State in 1850, the entire staff, including the secretary, numbered less than twenty. Pay was low and workload high. No salary schedule existed, and diplomatic posts often remained vacant because poor compensation could not attract qualified applicants. Webster worked to set competencies for the State Department staff that included language proficiencies and, not surprising, ample knowledge of geography and history. Many of Webster's reforms would not take effect until after his death, long after he had addressed a new complication resulting from Spain's tenuous control of the Jewell of the Antilles.[26]

Before leaving the Senate, Webster's attention had been drawn once again to Cuba, another reminder of the disparate agendas of the North and South. Cuba, since the early surge of Manifest Destiny, was embraced as a natural slave-holding complement to the southern states, and efforts had been made by southerners to extend American territory in that direction in the face of northern resistance. Polk attempted to buy the island from Spain for $100,000,000, but Madrid declined the offer. This may have dissuaded official efforts to acquire the island, but it did not prevent filibusters supported by southerners from launching their extralegal adventures. In clear violation of America's commitment to nonintervention, Americans led by Venezuelan mischief-maker Narciso López made numerous attempts to detach the island from Spain and bring it into the US orbit. Cuba was vulnerable. Spain maintained control by a heavy hand, taxing the Cubans into poverty and withholding even rudimentary civil rights. These woeful conditions invited adventurers such as López to incite revolution. He attempted unsuccessfully to do so on at least three occasions; but when Spain took his ships and declared his contingent of mostly American citizens to be pirates, Secretary Clayton indignantly called for their release. While still in the Senate, Webster reminded Florida senator David Levy Yulee of America's commitment to Spain's sovereignty over Cuba as well as the US obligation to defend that commitment against filibusters violating American neutrality.[27]

After replacing Clayton at State in July 1850, Webster negotiated the release of the López prisoners and promised Calderon de la Barca, Spanish minister to the United States, that the Fillmore administration would put an end to filibustering. As a demonstration of his sincerity, he provided Calderon with orders that went out to government officials to actively curtail filibustering. Despite Webster's assurance to Blatchford in April 1851 that the Cuban adventure would "all blow out," the López expeditions based out of New Orleans received local support, and when attempts were made to prosecute, friendly southern juries refused to convict.[28]

López launched his final expedition out of New Orleans in early August 1851 with around five hundred men, again consisting mostly of American citizens. The flotilla managed to circumvent Webster's deterrence efforts but, on arrival in Cuba, the filibusters met, not cheering revolutionaries, but defeat at the hands of Spanish forces. Authorities decided to make this the last López expedition by either imprisoning or executing him and his followers. As for the leader, he was garotted as a public display of the grizzly consequences of challenging Spanish rule. Attorney General John J. Crittenden's nephew was among those executed.

In New Orleans an explosive scene played out over the brutal ending of the López expedition. Angry residents trashed the Spanish-language newspaper offices and the headquarters of the Spanish consul, ripped the Spanish flag into pieces, and desecrated the queen's portrait. Calderon insisted that Webster have the US government provide reparations for the destruction. Webster agreed and apologized for this reckless display of "disgraceful acts, and a flagrant breach of duty and propriety." He informed Calderon that not only would the consul be welcomed back to New Orleans but also that he would be greeted with a salute to the Spanish flag. Furthermore, he intended to recommend that Congress appropriate funds to compensate those who had suffered the loss of property. Congress complied with Webster's request and arrangements followed, indemnifying victims of the New Orleans mayhem.[29]

Webster might have calmed Spanish concerns over the incidents in Cuba, but Britain and France viewed the filibusters as evidence of continued instability on the island, and both responded by moving naval assets to the area. When Webster received word that their deployment contemplated searching ships under the American flag as part of a bilateral plan to police filibustering, he could not believe they would seriously consider such an offense. Any such action, Webster stated emphatically, would "be regarded by the United

States with grave disapproval, as involving on the part of European sovereigns combined action of protectorship over American waters."[30]

This revived Webster's concerns over designs on Cuba by more capable European powers, especially Britain, and led him to reassert America's no-transfer policy. Cuba in the hands of a weak Spain was far preferable to the prospects of Britain drawing a strategic island in the Florida Straits into its sphere. When invited at Spain's request to join Britain and France in a tripartite guarantee of Spanish retention of Cuba, he reiterated both America's unilateral commitment to Spanish control of the island and its longstanding principle of avoiding "agreements with other States . . . except such as affect directly the interests of the United States themselves."[31]

A number of the other foreign policy issues demanding Webster's attention had been left unresolved by Clayton, many of which Webster would likewise leave for his successor, Edward Everett. First, there was the issue of the recently concluded Clayton-Bulwer Treaty between Washington and London addressing Anglo-American conflict in Central America. Before the ink was dry on the treaty negotiated by Secretary of State Clayton with British minister to America Henry Bulwer, both sides had begun to read between the lines, issue disclaimers, and to reinterpret the intent of the words on the document. For example, Bulwer convinced Clayton to agree that neither Belize nor British Honduras were subject to the treaty terms; but what exactly was Belize? Did it include the Bay Islands? And what of Britain's control over the Mosquito Coast and commitment to serve as protector for the so-called king of the Mosquitoes? Bulwer clearly thought he had preserved Britain's dominant position in this piece of Nicaragua and the important harbor at the mouth of the San Juan de Nicaragua River. Clayton had a completely different interpretation that considerably diluted Britain's influence on the Mosquito Coast. Also, border disputes abounded among the Central American states, the resolution of which remained strategically important to both Britain and the United States. Webster acknowledged to Fillmore in early 1851 the potential the "entanglements . . . with these little republics" held for creating problems in Anglo-American relations. The misunderstanding with Britain over Nicaragua, he cautioned, made Central America "the most delicate and important point in our foreign relations."[32]

Webster attempted to clarify matters with Bulwer by concluding an agreement whereby Britain would release Greytown to Nicaragua, whose government would then acknowledge Britain's position on the remainder of the Mosquito Coast and open commercial relations with the United States. While this negotiation was underway, an incident at the port of San Juan del Norte undermined the effort. In early 1852, an American steamship refused to pay harbor fees and, while attempting to leave the port, was stopped by a British warship with a shot across the bow. The British forced the American ship to pay the paltry sum of $123 before leaving the harbor. Webster, feeling that this affront demanded a response, instructed Abbott Lawrence, American minister to London, to make clear to Foreign Secretary Lord Palmerston that the United States would not "consent to the collection of port charges at San Juan by British ships of war, or that their collection should be enforced by them." The minor incident escalated in part because it happened at the same time Britain and France had deployed ships to guard Cuba. Fillmore sent a warship to Greytown to add bite to Webster's bark. Before year's end, Webster wrote Lawrence expressing disbelief that London would hazard a breach with Washington over "this miserable little town." His disbelief was ultimately shared by new British foreign secretary Lord Granville, who authorized Bulwer's replacement in Washington, John Fiennes Crampton, to settle these differences. In April 1852, Webster and Crampton produced a multilateral treaty among the United States, Britain, Costa Rica, and Nicaragua to solve the outstanding problems in the region. Unfortunately, Nicaragua declined, and the matter stood unresolved.[33]

Another issue left to Webster by Bulwer and Clayton involved the warring inhabitants of Hispaniola and a European intervention scheme. The conflict began in 1844 shortly after Webster's first term at State when the Spanish-speaking half of Hispaniola broke away from Haiti and founded the Dominican Republic. Under duress from the Haitian ruler, Dominicans ultimately requested intervention from Britain, France, and the United States. When Webster returned to State, Bulwer pressed him to join in a tripartite project to force Haiti to concede to the division of the island, and to compel an end to the violence by threatening Haiti with a naval blockade. While Webster did not agree to participate in the coercion of the Haitians, he did acquiesce to mediation efforts and, those failing, tacit approval of a blockade of major Haitian ports. The Fillmore administration further ordered the US Navy to cooperate with the Europeans "in all measures short of actual coercion." The pressure convinced the Haitians to accept an extended truce, but the matter remained unresolved, and within three years the conflict had resumed. In terms of American foreign policy, Webster's decision not only to accept European intervention in the Caribbean but also to join as a minor partner ran counter to the strictures of the Monroe Doctrine. Always the pragmatist, once he assumed European intervention a *fait accompli*, he determined that US participation offered the best safeguard for American interests.[34]

Meanwhile, Webster began the next chapter of the Tyler Doctrine, expanding American interests in the Pacific from Hawaii to Japan. Between his departure from State and his return, the United States had acquired Oregon and California and with them major Pacific harbors from San Diego to Puget Sound. If Webster had projected the need for an American presence in the Pacific while serving in Tyler's cabinet with no entrepôt on the Pacific coast, dramatically altered geopolitical realities now demanded a critical role for US commercial power in the exploitation of Pacific and East Asian markets. Seemingly content with the continued success of his earlier China policy, he turned his focus to unlocking the "double-bolted" Japanese Empire.

Webster needed little persuasion in early 1851 when approached, first by Aaron Haight Palmer, director of the American and Foreign Agency of New York, who for some time had been promoting aggressive tactics to intimidate Japan into granting American commercial access. Captain James Glynn reinforced this call to open Japan to US trade, encouraging Fillmore to send a naval officer with the diplomatic acumen to appreciate the balance between intimidation and respect. The object was not to put the Japanese on the defensive but to seek "trade and its necessary accommodations." The prospect of opening Japan, Webster believed, fit into a commercial vision that would link steam trade "from China and the East Indies to Egypt, thence through the Mediterranean and the Atlantic Ocean to England, then again to our happy shores." While casual attempts had been made during the administrations of both Jackson and Polk, when Webster returned to State the only western access to Japan remained a Dutch port at Deshima—an exclusive position, Glynn noted, the Dutch would be keen to preserve. Given the US frontage on the Pacific and trade prospects with East Asia, the secretary believed the time was right to end that monopoly by the addition of the American flag to Japanese harbors.[35]

When distressed Japanese sailors were rescued by an American ship and deposited at San Francisco in 1851, it seemed a fortuitous opportunity for an entrée to the empire. This "rescued-seamen" device, although practical under normal circumstances, had not proved successful with the Japanese in the past. On more than one occasion, American captains had returned shipwrecked Japanese sailors as a pretense for opening Japanese ports only to be thanked and told not to come back. Nevertheless, in May 1851, Webster had the secretary of the navy direct Captain John H. Aulick to transport the sailors from San Francisco to Japan and to seize the opportunity to open negotiations for "commercial relations with the Empire of Japan, or at least of placing our intercourse with that island upon a more easy footing." Webster's instructions for the mission included a promise that the United States would treat "Natives of Japan" in the same humane manner as that reflected by the experience of the returned sailors and would expect "similar treatment of such of its own citizens, who may be driven on the Coasts of Japan." Furthermore, Aulick was to assure the emperor that the United States had no desire to "interfere with the religion of other countries," but only to enter an arrangement of "Amity and Commerce."[36]

Webster's directive was not about religion, or even friendship—it was about Pacific trade and the coal that increasingly fed it. Aulick was to press to have Japanese ports opened and American commerce, sailors, and property treated fairly. Most importantly, he was to secure Japanese coal that would enable American steamers to ply the California-to-Canton trade efficiently. "The interests of commerce, and even those of humanity," Webster declared, required that Americans engaged in the emerging steamship network be able to purchase "not the manufactures of his (the Emperor's) artizans [sic] or the results of the toil of his husbandmen," but rather coal, "a gift of Providence, deposited, by the Creator of all things in the depths of the Japanese Islands, for the benefit of the human family." If the Emperor persisted "in following out its system of exclusiveness," Aulick was to propose that they transport their coal "to a neighboring island . . . where the steamers could supply their wants, avoiding thus the necessity of an intercourse with any large number of the people of the country."[37]

Before the mission began, fate intervened and Aulick, accused of misconduct in an unrelated matter, was replaced by Commodore Matthew Calbraith Perry. In January 1852, the president endorsed Perry's appointment to command the East India Squadron and authorized Webster to direct him to carry out the treaty mission to Japan. Two months later Webster informed Perry that the Dutch were forwarding maps and charts to assist in his mission. When Webster learned later that the maps and charts had not been made available, he had the chargé in The Hague inform the Dutch that, while Perry's mission was not intended to interfere with their arrangements with Japan, a lack of cooperation by their people in Deshima would relieve Perry of "any obligation to protect or to regard the interests of Hollanders in Japan in any proceedings which he may adopt for the purpose of carrying out the views of this Government."[38]

Webster did not live to see Perry's successful negotiation of the Convention of Kanagawa in 1854, but his participation in developing the mission secured for him a pivotal place in the opening of Japan. Perry, it should be noted, exercised latitude with his methods that ran contrary to Webster's more restrained diplomacy. Later suggesting that Webster had authorized him to act as he saw fit, Perry adopted a harsher posture that included broad discretion over the exercise of military force. While Perry's perspective (validated by revised instructions from an interim secretary of state dated two weeks after Webster's death) ran counter to Webster's established approach to the Pacific, it in no way alters the fact that Webster's role in the Perry mission completed a "great chain" in US-Pacific policy that the New Englander had initiated during his first incumbency at State in the early 1840s. A decade in the making, the Perry mission produced, as historian Kenneth Shewmaker has contended, "the final link in an interlocking chain that had in large measure been forged by the statesman from Massachusetts."[39]

Webster also reinforced the Hawaiian link in his Pacific chain. In the late 1840s the French increased their pressure on Hawaii, and on one occasion they had briefly seized Honolulu. In June 1851, Webster received word from an American missionary on the islands that the French were poised to use force if necessary to control the Kamehameha III government. From the same source he learned that the American commissioner to Hawaii, Luther Severance, had promised to accept the transfer of Hawaii to the United States in the event of French military intervention. Stunned at the apparent chaos in Hawaii that could produce the loss of the islands to France, a naval conflict with France over the islands, or a potential annexation request, Webster took prompt action.

Soon after Webster became aware of the turmoil, he outlined US policy in a letter to Severance. To ensure that all primary parties were clear on Washington's position, copies of the Severance communiqué were posted to London, Paris, and Honolulu. In the missive, Webster noted that the islands had increased in importance since the conceptualization of the Tyler Doctrine in the early 1840s. Not only were they geographically vital to American interests, they were far more economically connected to the United States than to any other nation. The presence of the US Navy would safeguard the independence and security of the islands against foreign intrusion. While Webster clearly wanted the bluster of the July 14 letter exhibited to Britain and France, his private correspondence with Severance was meant to rein in the excitable commissioner. Reminding Severance of the constitutional constraints on the application of force against a sovereign nation, Webster cautioned him to refrain from encouraging or directing American naval assets to engage the French.

Webster learned from Severance that the Hawaiian king had issued a preemptive request for annexation to the United States in the event of a French attack. Severance expressed enthusiasm for such a prospect, asking Webster whether the United States might avoid the "'manifest destiny' principle" by acquiescing to the Hawaiian's "voluntary offer." This voluntary offer, Webster directed in his confidential letter, should be returned to the king and assurances communicated that the goal of the United States was not annexation but rather preservation of the kingdom's independence.[40]

Although the Hawaiian authorities were satisfied with the US response, France was not. The French felt that Webster had intervened in a legitimate attempt by their representatives to address grievances with the Hawaiians and had done so with the tacit threat of armed force. Legitimate or not, Webster's posture on this occasion mirrored that of a decade before. In this he was consistent. The Europeans had been repeatedly reminded that the islands were primarily an American concern; critical to the United States, they would be protected from European designs to either erode the king's authority or to bring the islands under an imperial flag. In both the Japanese initiative and the Hawaiian response, Webster had reinforced America's role in the Pacific, establishing a foreign policy priority that would deepen with time and from which the United States would never retreat.[41]

In the summer of 1852, Webster revisited another initiative from his first term at State by seizing an opportunity to reaffirm his belief that American citizens should receive the protection of the US government wherever they traveled regardless of purpose. While serving in the Tyler administration in early 1842, Webster had responded to concerns expressed for American missionaries operating in the Ottoman Empire by advancing the nationalist notion that the flag and its protection followed *all* Americans, including those engaged in religious missions. His successors did not sustain this principle; so, when Webster became aware in 1852 of the difficulties suffered in Greece by Protestant missionary Dr. Jonas King, he reinforced his position that American missionaries were no less citizens of the United States than those engaged in any other undertaking and deserved "all proper succor and attentions of which they may stand in need, in the same manner" as that of "other citizens of the United States."[42]

King was a missionary who had resided in Greece since the late 1820s and had twice faced Greek legal proceedings that appeared to treat him unjustly. On the most recent occasion, in 1852, a Greek court (upheld by the Areopagus) convicted him of disparaging the Greek Orthodox Church, levied an excessive fine, and expelled him from the country. Webster, despite Fillmore's reticence, dispatched George Perkins Marsh, US minister to the Ottoman Empire, to Athens to ascertain the true facts of the case and to see that Jonas King's rights were protected. As an indication of the gravity the United States attached to the matter, the navy was asked "to keep one or more vessels of the Mediterranean squadron in the neighborhood of that place, and subject to your [Marsh's] order."[43]

Marsh reported in August that he deemed it "past all doubt, that the government of Greece" had "treated Dr King with flagrant injustice and bad faith," and that "the legal tribunals of Greece" were "guilty of an abuse of the principles of justice, and a perversion of the rules of law, as flagitious as any that ever disgraced the records of the State chamber." Based on Marsh's report, the United States argued for a reversal by the Greek authorities followed by a substantial indemnity for King and the lifting of his exile. After Webster's death, Everett followed through on the matter for his old teacher and friend and solidified Webster's foreign policy principle of equal protection for all American citizens abroad.[44]

In contrast to his first incumbency at State, Webster's second term included two epic failures, both in the Americas, and both displaying uncharacteristic bellicosity from the seasoned diplomatist. Among the issues inherited by Webster from Clayton was unfinished business with Mexico concerning transit across the Isthmus of Tehuantepec, a project Webster had vigorously advocated in the Senate. The long-desired transcontinental connection had "awakened, with new life" after the "golden" state of California joined the Union. The transit idea had a convoluted history that began with an 1842 grant from Mexico to Mexican contractor José de Garray authorizing him to connect the two coasts via a twenty-league-wide swath across the isthmus. Over the next several years this grant became an impediment to American designs for a trans-isthmian railroad. Evidence of this first surfaced when Mexico rejected a Nicholas Trist attempt to secure an American project during his negotiations ending the Mexican-American War. The Garray grant, Mexican authorities explained, made the American project and requested concession redundant.[45]

The same year that Trist concluded his peace treaty at Guadalupe Hidalgo, Garray conveyed his grant to British speculators who then sold it the following year to Peter and Louis Hargous of New York. The Hargous brothers sold controlling interest to a group led by Judah P. Benjamin and organized as the New Orleans Tehuantepec Company. By the fall of 1849 this circuitous process had landed the project on the desk of Secretary of State Clayton, who shared the investors' concerns that Mexico might not honor the original grant.

In September, Clayton directed Robert Letcher, the US minister to Mexico, to pursue an agreement with Mexico that would protect "the capitalists who may undertake" the Tehuantepec project. In the third week of June 1850, Letcher concluded a convention with the Mexican government that provided for American protection of the isthmian project should conditions warrant and Mexico requested assistance. The ratification of the convention was contingent on the formal consent of the current holders of the Garray grant, which, in essence, gave the Hargous brothers a veto over the US-Mexican agreement.

Before Webster returned to the State Department in July, Letcher's treaty had arrived in Washington and awaited the new secretary's action to advance the project. Webster found Letcher's treaty acceptable, but Peter Hargous (official holder of the Garray grant) called for greater assurances of US protection as well as increased latitude for the company in managing the project. Webster acquiesced and directed Letcher to renegotiate according to Hargous's wishes. If applied, these changes would have made the isthmus an American protectorate. Perhaps forgetting that Mexico would not be inclined to negotiate away more territory to an America that had recently taken half of the country by force of arms, Webster had Letcher attempt to intimidate the Mexicans into accommodation. This clumsy approach guaranteed failure of both the revised treaty and the convention previously accepted.

When both Hargous and the US Senate consented to the original terms, the Mexican congress refused to act. Instead, Mexico moved to annul the original Garray grant and restrict the activities of the Americans in the area. Webster refused to detach the grant concessions from the treaty and in April employed incendiary language to impress upon the Mexican minister to Washington that failure to honor the grant would mean "war between the two nations." This clearly was not Webster's intent; neither he nor Fillmore deemed the matter worthy of war. Nevertheless, Mexico, referencing its Texas experience, annulled the Garray grant in May and expelled the company operatives from the area.[46]

In mid-July, Benjamin approached Fillmore to inform him that his company meant to defend its position by force if needed and planned to deploy five hundred men to the area. If an altercation occurred, the United States would be required to either defend its citizens or join in their suppression. Benjamin left his meeting with Fillmore and made his way to Marshfield to present his case to a vacationing Webster. The secretary opposed Fillmore's intimation that Benjamin replace Letcher in Mexico City, instead composing new instructions for Letcher that would up the ante for Mexican approval of the convention.[47]

In the new orders, Webster reasoned that the convention might be connected with Article 11 of the Treaty of Guadalupe Hidalgo, which committed the United States to restrain the native population under its jurisdiction from causing mischief across the border in Mexico. Although giving assurances that the United States intended to adhere to the commitment, it was clearly beyond the capability of the US military to police the tribes. Webster received authority from the president to offer up to $3 million to extricate the country from its Article 11 responsibility; and in mid-August 1851, the secretary further directed Letcher to link the offer to a revival of the original Tehuantepec treaty. This ploy failed, as did his legal argument that Mexico had reneged on its contract obligations by annulling the grant.

Webster's efforts with Mexico were not only complicated by Indian incursions across the border but also by American filibustering expeditions into Mexico. Staging from Brownsville, Texas, the Mexican national José Maria Jesus Carvajal persisted in his efforts to extract pieces of the republic from Mexican control, launching several adventures in the early 1850s. By the time Letcher returned to Mexico with his new directive in fall 1851, ineffective border control by the Fillmore administration, increased suspicions of American intentions, and the reckless Carvajal had guaranteed a coalition against the Tehuantepec treaty.

Even subtle threats of force by Fillmore did not move the Mexican government; in April 1852, only one vote out of seventy-two prevented the treaty's rejection from being unanimous. Webster continued to press through early summer, but Mexico had already called his bluff. Both he and Fillmore ultimately acknowledged that the Mexican government's decision had been completely within its rights and the Texas experience justified the skepticism. Although Webster's handling of Mexican policy demonstrated none of the diplomatic finesse he had routinely shown in other matters, it conformed to his approach to Mexico in his first term. His dismissive attitude toward Mexicans as steeped in corruption and lacking the diplomatic acumen necessary for reasonable compromise made it impossible for Webster to consider that their position might be legitimate. Webster had done nothing to improve relations with Mexico and bequeathed to his successors a strained relationship with the United States' southern neighbor.[48]

Webster's second major diplomatic failure was undertaken in the shadow of declining health, both mental and physical. The disappointment suffered from the inability to generate enthusiasm for a presidential nomination conspired with later stages of cirrhosis, routine application of prescribed arsenic, and a recent concussion suffered in a carriage accident to make his last months at State a struggle both physically and mentally. In the midst of this decline, a letter arrived at his desk in June from the captain of the *Philomela* and guano trader, James C. Jewett. He and interested parties inquired if the Lobos Islands' distance from the Peruvian coast placed them in international waters and open to Americans.

Rather than taking the matter under advisement, Webster replied within seventy-two hours that the islands were not only outside the three-mile limit of territorial jurisdiction but were as likely discovered by an American captain in 1823 as by either Spain or Peru. As such, US citizens had the right to the guano and could count on the protection of the US Navy to secure that right. This message, to Webster's later consternation, led Jewett and associates to send a flotilla of about forty armed ships and over one hundred workers—all under the protection of a US warship—to collect approximately $40 million worth of resources claimed by a friendly nation. Webster had unwittingly adopted a policy that flirted with a US-Peruvian armed confrontation.[49]

Had Webster applied his customary due diligence, he would have conceded that Peru not only claimed the islands but had a decade before established guano as an important Peruvian resource and developed an elaborate trading scheme involving both British and Peruvian firms. The issue of guano was far from obscure, and a modest effort would have established Lima's claim both to the islands and to the enormous reservoir of bird lime that made them immeasurably valuable. By the time of Webster's second term at State, an obsession with the fertilizer had developed in the agricultural sectors of the US economy, one shared by Webster at his Marshfield operation.[50]

Shortly after returning to the State Department, Webster began working to redeem a recently failed treaty negotiated by Clayton and Peruvian minister to the United States, José Manuel Tirado. The treaty failed to win Lima's approval because of a provision that obligated Peru to adjust the current system of guano supply and invite the United States into the revised system. In fall 1850, Webster directed the American chargé d'affaires in Lima to press for fairer trade conditions for guano and wrote to agricultural expert, author, and promoter of guano, Solon Robinson, attacking Peru's unfair distribution system. In December, Fillmore referenced the fertilizer's importance in his first annual message to Congress, suggesting that its access for the American farmer should be underpinned by government action.[51]

Webster continued to press the matter with Lima until the summer of 1851, and then let the matter drop. When Jewett approached him the following June, it is difficult to understand—even given Jewett's subterfuge in making his inquiry about uninhabited islands with no mention of Peru—how Webster failed to make the connection with Peru's lucrative guano trade. Instead, he had steered blindly into a diplomatic conflict.

During the second week of August, the secretary of state, now visibly weakened from the multiple assaults on his health, learned that Peru had claimed the islands and had for years required all parties engaged in the collection of guano there to present a valid Peruvian license validating their action. The Peruvian minister to America, Juan Ygnacio de Osma, had attempted to persuade Webster in early July of Lima's sovereignty over the islands, tracking that jurisdiction not from the 1820s but from the Incas; but Webster dismissed the plea. A few days later Fillmore, who would later feign ignorance of his secretary of state's authorization to Jewett, instructed him to slow the process and, writing from Elms Farm, Webster promised to "consider the subject further."[52]

In August, Webster, having directed his close friend Hiram Ketchum to search in vain for evidence of American possession of the islands, admitted that the encouragement he had issued to Jewett might have been premature. He then attempted to revisit the muddled policy and its implications. Of all the issues he faced in the State Department, he admitted to Ketchum, none had ever "given me so much disturbance, as this Lobos business." He did not admit to Peruvian sovereignty over the islands; but stunned at the news in mid-August of the magnitude and militancy of Jewett's Lobos expedition, he quickly sent new instructions to the guano merchant informing him that there would be no protection provided and that his vessels would be subject to Peruvian statutes and authority.[53]

On the same day, Webster wrote to Osma once again attempting to reinforce the validity of American claims to the islands. American captain Benjamin Morell, the secretary of state declared, had discovered not only the islands but also the guano in 1823; and even before Morell's voyage, American fishermen (in particular those engaged in the seal trade) had used the islands since the last decade of the eighteenth century. Then, in an attempt to turn guano into gold, Webster proposed a settlement. In his last communiqué as secretary of state, he directed the American chargé, John Randolph Clay, to accept Peruvian sovereignty over the islands in return for a favorable arrangement for Americans that provided a moderate rate for guano.[54]

By this time, Webster had been overwhelmed with evidence from both Peruvian and American sources that the islands belonged to Peru. Both Osma and his brother had effectively laid out the history of the islands, the latter tracing discovery to Francisco Pizarro in 1526 and exploitation of the islands to the Incas. William Miles, a businessman from New York with extensive ties to Peruvian commerce, so impressed Webster with the breadth of his knowledge substantiating Peru's ownership of the islands that the secretary of state, as his final official order, dispatched Miles to Lima to deliver revised instructions to Clay. The chargé must have assumed the Miles mission was in response to a June 24 dispatch he had sent to Webster. In fact, his dispatch had arrived in early August, but it never made it to Webster, who was on holiday at the time. Clay's letter alerted the State Department that Britain had deployed ships to challenge ownership of the Lobos de Afuera. Perhaps, Clay opined, Webster could exploit the British threat by offering to exchange US respect for Peruvian sovereignty for guano prices favorable to American consumers. Apparently, William Hunter, who was overseeing State at the time, did not forward the message. As it happened, the message carried by Miles was very similar to what Clay had recommended.[55]

As incongruous as it must have appeared to Miles as an advocate for Peru's position, he was to inform Clay that the United States was not ready to acquiesce on the issue of sovereignty. Peru should allow the Jewett expedition to proceed unharassed with the collection of guano and provide the United States with a more favorable trade arrangement; the United States would then consider acknowledging Peru's claims to Lobos Afueco. The barter of recognition for fair trade echoed Clay's recommendation. The relevant missing piece was the incentive of American intervention against the British threat. Without this incentive, the offer was no more attractive than previous appeals for fair prices on guano. Miles must have felt he had taken an uninspired and futile mission to Lima that would accomplish little more than disappoint Clay with the apparent ineptitude at State.[56]

Fillmore had long before determined that Webster had erred dramatically in this episode and attempted to console him in late September with the opinion that Hunter's omission of Clay's June 24 dispatch might justify or at least explain the secretary's relentless insistence on American claims. Webster later declined the president's invitation to rationalize his misstep and, choosing statesmanship over pretense, accepted full responsibility for the debacle. "If, in your fortunes hereafter," he wrote Fillmore, "it shall become necessary to say, that the Lobos proceeding was mine, say so, & use this letter as my acknowledgement of that truth."[57]

By the time of Fillmore's letter and his mea culpa, Webster had settled in at Marshfield, having left Washington for the last time, and although the president made a gesture of keeping him informed, Charles M. Conrad was now acting secretary of state. It became his task to ameliorate the crisis with Peru. He sent word to Clay on September 21 that the United States now acknowledged Peru's ownership of the Lobos. Webster's friend and former student, Edward Everett, succeeded him in the Fillmore cabinet and formally extricated the United States from the Lobos incident on November 16, writing to Osma that "all the objections taken by the late Secretary of State" had been withdrawn.[58]

Fortunately for Webster, the Jewett mission ended without incident. The affair left enough of a blemish on Webster's diplomacy as it stood; had hostilities erupted leading to bloodshed, the blemish might have dwarfed his otherwise stellar accomplishments as one of the nation's more ardent defenders of peace. Webster's triumphant final return to Marshfield was not diminished by the Lobos; his friends and neighbors greeted him as the imposing figure whose evolution they had witnessed over decades of service to the law and the nation.[59]

In a supreme irony, Webster's last months led him full circle back to an Anglo-American dispute in the Northeast, a dispute that once again involved local passions, newspaper machinations, interpretations of the Paris treaty of 1783, and of course, maps. The negotiators in Paris at the end of the War for Independence had addressed the issue of American fishing in Canadian waters. During the talks, the British had pressed for the word *liberty* to be substituted for the word *right* to describe American access; this edit, they argued, would not alter the meaning but simply be more palatable to British subjects. In practice, the Crown interpreted "liberty" not as "right" but privilege, a distinction that over time placed American fishing interests at the mercy of London's discretion. Unlike a right, a privilege could be withdrawn, as it was in the War of 1812.

The issue had seemingly found resolution in the Convention of 1818; but once again, varied interpretations of diplomatic language had frustrated practical implementation. Although the 1818 agreement repeated the word *liberty*, it added a commitment to grant Americans fishing privileges in perpetuity; but where? The agreement depended on maps to set specific parameters for American fishing. American fishermen would not be permitted, the agreement read, within "three marine Miles of any of the Coasts, Bays, Creek, or Harbours of His Britannic Majesty's Dominions in America." This, sadly, raised cartographic questions similar to those that so long dogged the Maine–New Brunswick boundary dispute: What qualified as a "bay," and what base measure determined "three marine Miles"? The Americans made these determinations by following the contours of the shoreline, while the British argued that the demarcation traced from headland to headland. This distinction would alter the definition of the US fishing range by miles. In fact, this difference of opinion had earlier resulted in the detention of an American vessel *ten miles* from the shoreline of the Bay of Fundy in 1843. At that time, however, the atmosphere of conciliation from the Webster-Ashburton negotiations led Lord Aberdeen to concede to the American interpretation of the line, and fishing continued without further incident.[60]

Here the matter stood until the British decided to use fishing access as leverage to maneuver the United States into a trade reciprocity agreement with Canada. British minister Henry Bulwer raised the matter with Webster in mid-September 1850, but the secretary of state saw no benefit to Americans in a reciprocal arrangement with such a limited Canadian market. British authorities then determined Washington might appreciate the benefit more when attached to the lucrative Northeastern fishing industry. In mid-April 1852, the Crown deployed a squadron of ships to Canada to enforce the headland delineation of the fishing range and, according to British prime minister Lord Derby, to awaken "Brother Jonathan" to the urgency London attached to Canadian reciprocity.[61]

This action may not have awakened Brother Jonathan, but it did rouse Webster and his fellow anglers. On holiday for his health in New Hampshire, Webster responded to a notice of the ship deployment from British minister John Fiennes Crampton by inviting him to meet either in Boston or Marshfield to address this serious situation that was "full of danger." Meanwhile, he advised, Crampton should watch for "an official publication by me" in the Boston papers. Engaging foreign policy by newspaper proved a serious mistake—a mistake compounded by the missive's "actual" place of origin; Webster did not return to Washington but composed his letter to the editor articulating the American position while convalescing at Elms Farm. To authenticate the letter as official, Webster backdated it as though posted from Washington. Exacerbating this inappropriate approach, he proposed that Crampton meet him to discuss the issue, not at the State Department, but in Boston or Marshfield.[62]

Webster informed Fillmore of his plan and, though unorthodox, the president did not express concern until seeing Webster's policy statement on public display in the *National Intelligencer*. An editorial opened with a warning to American fishermen that they were subject to seizure under Britain's newly implemented restrictions, but it followed with the comforting assurance that the country had "not yet been deprived of the invaluable services of Mr. Webster." This self-promoting preamble was not the problem; in the published letter marked "official," Webster appeared to concede the British position. The American commissioners in 1818, he confessed, had accepted the British headland definition: "It was," Webster acknowledged, "an oversight in the Convention of 1818, to make so large a concession to England." It seemed clear to most that Webster's inartful word choice of *oversight* and *concession* amounted to official acquiescence to the Crown's latitude to do whatever it wished about American fishing in Canadian waters.[63]

When congressional leaders read these remarks, many were stunned that Webster had issued such a reckless public pronouncement—and worse still, while away from Washington. The attempted subterfuge of backdating the letter only added to the agitation. In the Senate, Louisiana firebrand Pierre Soulé derisively repeated Webster's words, denouncing him as having surrendered the "whole" American position. Andrew Butler of South Carolina chastised the secretary for conducting business while away from Washington and through the newspapers rather than through the official channels of government. He was especially disturbed that Congress had not been consulted.

Amid the barrage of attacks, the strongest (and perhaps surprising) defense of Webster came from William Seward, author of the anti-slavery "higher law" doctrine and the secretary's old nemesis from the McLeod affair. It should be clear to anyone familiar with Webster's résumé, Seward reminded his colleagues, that his intent was not to yield to the British position but to alert American fishermen of the British threat. Webster's allusion to the failure of the 1818 commissioners to insist on more verbal precision was not meant to concede the British point, but to demonstrate the British propensity to exploit illusory loopholes. Besides, Seward concluded, the body of Webster's work over his career established his commitment to American interests and guaranteed "a future of fame unapproachable and inextinguishable."[64]

Meanwhile, Fillmore expressed his concern and that of the cabinet and directed Webster to return to his office for consultation. But Crampton had arrived at Boston and agreed to travel with Webster to Marshfield, so Webster committed to resolving the issue in the more comfortable climate and confines of coastal Massachusetts. The two traveled by train from Boston to Kingston where, to Webster's satisfaction, an enormous crowd welcomed him and lined his carriage route to Marshfield. Arriving at the house, the secretary addressed the crowd with assurances that he would protect the fisheries, "the very nurseries of our navy," and secure the rights of the fishermen "hook and line, bob and sinker."[65]

While Crampton no doubt enjoyed the gracious hospitality of Marshfield, his official mission was impaired by a lack of direction from London. If Webster had hoped for an Ashburton moment, he was disappointed. The fishing conundrum he had inflated with his letter and continued rhetoric would not be resolved in casual talks with Crampton. The British minister did provide some unexpected relief in a promise to direct Canadian officials to relax enforcement of restrictions on American fishing, after which Webster wrote

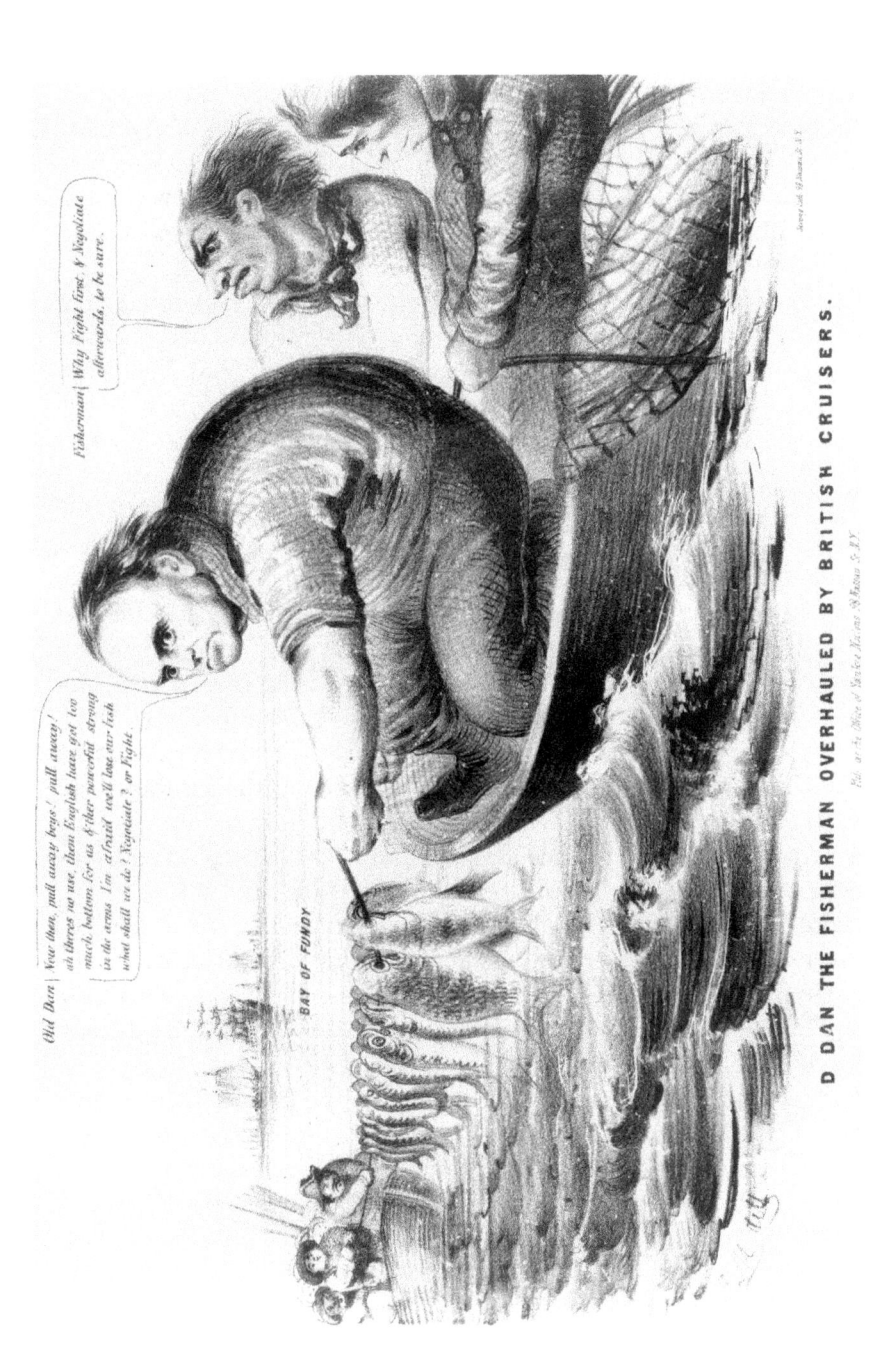

Figure 6.1. "Dan the Fisherman Overhauled by British Cruisers," Office of Yankee Notions (New York), 1852. Courtesy of the Library of Congress Prints and Photographs Division, LC-USZ62-8879.

Fillmore that there was nothing left to do "at present." By the time Crampton issued his promise, there was more than one naval presence capable of provoking an incident; Fillmore had ordered Commodore Matthew Perry to the area with an armed steamer to ensure the protection of American interests. Fortunately, the presence in Canadian waters of warships of both nations did not escalate tensions. In fact, it appeared that Crampton and Fillmore had rescued Webster from the diplomatically awkward moment by combining to secure American fishing interests.[66]

From London, Derby conceded that the scheme to use fish as bait for a US-Canadian trade agreement had resulted in a dangerous overreach. Before delivering a lengthy primer on the British position and Lord Aberdeen's 1845 proposal to American minister to Britain Edward Everett, British foreign minister Lord Malmesbury directed Crampton to inform Webster that the secretary had mischaracterized recent actions by Her Majesty's Government and that no "unfriendly feelings between the Subjects and Citizens of the two Countries" had been intended. After a tutorial on the previous agreements, he ended with yet another appeal to an adjustment "of the System of commercial intercourse between the United States and Her M's North American Colonial Possessions." Malmesbury's note to Abbott Lawrence three days later was more concise and basically reversed the recent decision that had provoked the current problems. At least for the moment, American fishermen could return to Canadian waters under the Aberdeen terms. Thus, American fishing "privileges" resumed as though the recent crisis had not occurred. Now Webster might, in a calmer climate, pursue a more orthodox path to resolution.[67]

After pondering resignation from his cabinet position and dismissing the notion of replacing Abbott Lawrence as American minister to London, Webster unhappily left the comfort of Marshfield for Washington during the second week of August. Welcomed back by surprisingly "cool . . . and quite agreeable" weather, and gracious cabinet colleagues, Webster exuded confidence that the Anglo-American fishing dispute would soon be resolved. He wrote Richard Blatchford later in the month that he had his "great halibut hook" lodged securely in the issue and would see it through. At the end of the month, the secretary began to prepare a note to address the matter, but his failing health left it an incomplete draft. Unlike the grand achievement in Anglo-American relations during the early 1840s, the final resolution of the fisheries dispute, as with other loose ends, was left for Edward Everett to manage as Webster's successor at State.[68]

After less than a month in Washington, Webster left the capital for the last time in early September. There followed a month of decline at Marshfield during which his doctor informed George Ticknor that Webster's illness was terminal, "a mortal disease in some one of the great organs of the abdomen." In mid-October, Webster acknowledged his approaching death by composing for his dear friend Edward Curtis the words for his gravestone. On October 18, Webster wrote his last letter. Addressed to Fillmore, it was almost apologetic that his health would not permit him to finish out the last days of the administration. "But let not this embarrass you," Webster lamented; instead assume "my Resignation as always before you, to be accepted, any moment you please."[69]

At half past two in the morning on October 24, Daniel Webster drew his last breath. He predicted his own fate, having announced the previous morning that his death would come that night. One of his last gestures offers a glimpse at Webster's often-concealed affectionate side. Two days before he died, a gold ring arrived from a Boston jeweler. It was inscribed "D.W. to S.S. Oct. 1852." Webster had ordered the ring for Sarah Smith, his African American nurse, who had also attended to daughter Julia. As he slipped the ring onto her finger he asked her to "wear it in memory of me and Julia."[70]

Everett's epitaph to Webster would not rest on the unresolved fisheries matter, Mexico, or even the Lobos affair, which he considered a terrible lapse in both management and judgment; nor would it likely take notice of the tenderness exhibited to Sarah Smith and other close friends and family present at his passing. Everett would, as most fair-minded examiners, relegate Webster's late missteps to a minor footnote in a most significant legacy as a master of statecraft.

Epilogue

> The sea, the rocks, the woods, gave no sign that America and the world had lost the completest man.
>
> —Ralph Waldo Emerson, October 1852

> Daniel Webster, the world without you will be lonesome.
>
> —Marshfield neighbor, October 1852

Born into modest circumstances on a New England farm, Daniel Webster rose to greatness in the emerging republic as one of the most influential statesmen of his age. His commanding voice spoke books of quotable phrases alive with passion and forged in the depths of an imposing intellect. His words captivated audiences from farm platforms to Faneuil Hall in his adopted Boston, on the floors of both houses of Congress, and before the Supreme Court. Known by every student of history for his eloquent orations that brought poets to tears, challenged presidents, took world leaders to task, and silenced Colonel Hayne with "liberty and union, one and inseparable, now and forever," Webster was, in the assessment of poet and philosopher Ralph Waldo Emerson, "the completest man." Despite falling out with Webster over the Seventh of March speech, Emerson confided to his journal after Webster's death that "nature had not in our days, or not since Napoleon, cut out such a masterpiece." But as with the French emperor, larger-than-life figures are inherently complicated. This was certainly the case with Black Dan.[1]

From the moment he stopped into Christopher Gore's law office in 1801, Webster began building a portfolio and developing a network of influence that would assure a future in both law and government. As a legal mind and student of the Constitution arguing before the Supreme Court, his performance and record of success are unassailable, weaving principles and precedents into the fabric of the republic with enduring influence. His arguments before John Marshall's Supreme Court prevailed in such landmark cases as *Dartmouth College v. Woodard* (1819), protecting the sanctity of contract and vested property rights, and in *McCulloch v. Maryland* (1819) and *Gibbons v. Ogden* (1824), establishing the supremacy of the federal government—with the latter extending federal authority over the nation's commerce.

A critical player in American politics, Webster proved instrumental in the development of the second party system by assuming a leadership role in first the National Republican Party and then the Whig Party. Like many of his contemporaries, he abhorred the nature of political parties but succumbed to their inevitability after the fractious election of 1824. When the Jacksonians coalesced in opposition to John Quincy Adams, former Federalists and opponents of Jackson's loutish populism produced the National Republican alternative. Joining with Clay, Webster quickly emerged as a leader of that party and the subsequent Whig iteration, instituting a party alignment that prevailed for the next quarter century. But while the anti-Jacksonians honored Clay with more than one presidential nomination, Webster was passed over time and again. He had charisma, intellect, and an enviable résumé, but his New England pedigree narrowed his base and discouraged national party leaders from backing his nomination. His attempt to broaden his support by assuaging Cotton Whigs with concessions on slavery failed to secure the nomination in his final disappointment in 1852.

Although law was his avocation, he developed an interest in and understanding of America's role in the world and routinely imported thoughts on that role into his speeches and writings. From his early college addresses to the Rockingham Memorial, he consistently affirmed his grasp of geopolitical intricacies and an ability to distill those intricacies into moving images. Ascending to the national stage during the War of 1812, he articulated an opposition to war—especially offensive war—which he viewed as constitutionally aberrant, a position to which he remained faithful throughout his lifetime.

On economics and nationalism—two subjects that would merge to define much of his career—he evolved. He began his career dedicated to a New England constituency that required open trade for its commercial interests, causing him to argue persuasively against protectionism and to "tacitly" align with the states' rights' canon of the Hartford Convention in 1814. As the economy of New England shifted to one benefiting from protectionism, so too did Webster's attitude. By the 1820s, he had committed to a protective tariff schedule and the broader political agenda of the so-called American System. As the champion of economic nationalism, Webster effectively articulated the vision before the Marshall Court and both houses of Congress that the federal system did not arise from the states but from the people, producing a seamless authority animating a perpetual Union. With this, his transition was complete.

His advocacy of economic nationalism, however, did not translate to an aggressive foreign policy advanced at the tip of a bayonet. He promoted instead a noninterventionist policy that avoided political intrusion in the affairs of other nations while fully engaging commercially. Webster believed America should seize every opening "to explore new channels for commerce, and to increase the intercourse of nations."[2] While he appreciated the interdependent nature of international relationships, he rarely missed an opportunity to remind foreign and domestic audiences of the superior framework that produced and maintained the American Union. Finally, though opposed to the unbridled expansionism of Manifest Destiny, he embraced the practical commercial benefits that accrued from territorial acquisitions and the broadening of American influence.

His creditors—to whom he left unsatisfied debts at his death—might feel that his greatest deficiencies were his fiscal foibles, but no Webster deficit was more disconcerting than his tepid position on slavery. While one can effectively argue that pragmatism drove his sacrifice of abolition on the altar of Union, his proactive efforts in and attitude toward the Thomas Sims case that forced a runaway slave back to chains and a public whipping in Georgia cannot be defended. Webster appeared satisfied to see Sims marched to the wharf for transport to Savannah, not appreciating the irony that his path crossed the very square where former slave Crispus Attucks had fallen in the Boston massacre.[3] When Charles Sumner had heralded Webster as "Defender of Peace" in 1846, he expressed hopes that Webster would apply his talents to the eradication of slavery and earn the grander title "Defender of Humanity." Webster's gracious response to Sumner a few weeks later dashed those hopes, and his support for rigid enforcement of the Fugitive Slave Law reflected in the Sims case served as a tragic reminder that his talents would work against, not for, Sumner's cause.[4]

Fortunately, demonstrations such as the Sims incident were the exception to the rule domestically and completely absent from his diplomacy. Nevertheless, neither a history of hostility to slavery, solid credentials against the slave trade extending back to the *La Jeune Eugenie* case early in his career, nor steadfast opposition to the expansion of the peculiar institution provided sufficient defense from the charges of unprincipled compromise by his peers following the Seventh of March speech. Ironically, this approach to the fragmenting Union, grounded in a calculated give and take, proved his most dependable attribute as a diplomatist. At a time that demanded fidelity in domestic affairs to one of two sides, weighing means against ends was not permitted. In international affairs, it was essential; as a pragmatist it was, in Webster's words, "the exercise of calm reason."[5]

His intimate understanding of and respect for the rule of law, his appreciation for the need to balance compromise against broader national interests, and a personal style that allowed him to move easily from the grand stage to the parlor all ensured an overall record for Webster as one of the more able and important diplomatists of the nineteenth century. In his official capacity at State—first under Harrison/Tyler from March 5, 1841, to May 8, 1843, then under Fillmore from July 23, 1850, to his death on October 24, 1852—Webster's pragmatism informed almost every effort, resulting in an impressive list of accomplishments, many of which had lasting impact on American foreign relations. Among these is his often-overlooked attempt to bring structure and professionalism to a State Department too small and inefficient for a republic with global reach. Shortly after his death, many of his initiatives to address those deficiencies became policy, including a graduated pay schedule and the creation of the position of assistant secretary of state. Few who held that office invested more in the organization and effectiveness of the department than did Webster.

His contributions as a diplomatist reached from the woodlands of northern Maine across the Pacific to East Asia, sowing the seeds of a developing American commercial empire and a critical rapprochement with an estranged Britain. When he accepted Harrison's invitation to join his cabinet, Webster was intimately familiar with the issues plaguing Anglo-American relations and had hoped to play a role in their resolution with a diplomatic appointment to the Court of St. James's. Accepting Harrison's invitation to head the State Department and continuing with Tyler after the president's death, Webster dedicated himself to applying practical compromise to issues ranging from the Maine–New Brunswick border issue and Aroostook War to the *Caroline* incident and companion McLeod affair that had dogged the two capitals since 1837. He also engaged the United States in the cooperative curtailment of the African slave trade and arranged for maritime protection against unlawful search and impressment in response to the *Creole* affair. He attained his proudest diplomatic legacy with Lord Ashburton through a combination of adept diplomacy, skullduggery, and charisma—an accomplishment that set Anglo-American relations on a firm path to lasting rapprochement and won for him the title Defender of Peace. When he and Ashburton signed the treaty that bears their names and exchanged letters to satisfy the ancillary disputes, they cleared the way for what would develop over the next century into one of the most important alliances in world history. When Winston Churchill designated the close association of the United States with Great Britain "The Special Relationship," students of history understood that "special" had come neither easily nor quickly. It had grown, in part, from seeds planted by Webster a century before. Also, as part of the 1842 negotiations, Webster had produced the *Caroline Doctrine*, codifying the notion of national self-defense as a tenet in international law—a tenet adopted and routinely applied to justify preemptive actions throughout the twentieth century. His final legacy associated with the boundary dispute drew on his legal, political, and diplomatic skills. He drafted and piloted through Congress the Remedial Justice Act, preventing a repeat of the jurisdictional conundrum of the McLeod case.

His articulation of the Tyler Doctrine in his first term as secretary of state and its reinforcement in his second term set the stage for American inroads into the China markets, the opening of Japan, and the establishment of US hegemony over the Hawaiian Islands. In December 1842, Webster orchestrated what amounted to an addendum to the Monroe Doctrine, extending its protection against foreign intervention to the Hawaiian Islands. When the president codified this policy in his annual message, he not only garnered a strategic locus for the expansion of American Pacific commerce but also fixed the United States as the chief guarantor of the territorial integrity of vulnerable states from European exploitation. Webster pressed American interests deeper into the Pacific by drafting instructions for the Caleb Cushing mission that resulted in the Treaty of Wanghia and prepared the way for America's developing commercial relations with the Chinese Empire. When he returned to State under Fillmore, he further expanded America's Pacific commerce by initiating the Perry Mission to Japan and reinforcing America's role in the Hawaiian Kingdom.

In the Western Hemisphere, Webster, except for the Hispaniola anomaly, adhered to the principles of the Monroe Doctrine. For instance, soon after Monroe pronounced Adams's noncolonization principle, Webster led the call for US participation in the Panama Congress of 1826. In both terms at State, his policies protected Cuba from transfer either in spirit or fact to a major European power and dissuaded filibustering efforts from destabilizing the island. While a member of the Fillmore cabinet, he pressed American leadership in foreign disputes involving Latin America, and, though failing to substantially raise prospects for a Central American canal, he kept Washington central to the discussion.

Finally, few public figures are afforded multiple tracks from which to craft their legacy. Webster, "the completest man," enjoyed several. His legacy from a political track did not, as is typically the case, survive politics. In other words, what he gained on one hand he lost on the other. And on this track all of his blemishes were exposed. His legal track, however, secured for him a legacy second to none, with his name attached to some of the most influential legal decisions in the nation's history. As an orator, he had few rivals—not just among peers but throughout the English-speaking world. As a diplomatist, his steady hand through most of his two terms at State established him as one of the more consequential secretaries ever to hold the office. His general profile has, perhaps, ebbed and flowed in many ways with the mood of American exceptionalism through the years. Nevertheless, if, as Howard Jones has noted, a statesman's stature derives from "the size of his shadow," Webster's place among the great American statesmen in both domestic and foreign affairs is beyond challenge.[6]

Chronology

1782
January 18 — Daniel Webster is born in Salisbury, New Hampshire.
1800
July 4 — Webster delivers the Independence Day address in Hanover, New Hampshire.
1801
August 26 — Webster graduates from Dartmouth College.
1803
May 18 — Napoleonic wars begin.
1804
July 20 — Webster begins work in the law office of Christopher Gore.
1807
December 22 — Jefferson signs Embargo Act.
1812
June 18 — Congress declares war on Great Britain.
August 5 — Webster delivers Rockingham Memorial.
November — New Hampshire elects Webster to US House of Representatives.
1813
June 10 — Webster introduces resolutions challenging the justification for war.

1814

March 12	Webster makes his first argument before the Marshall Court.
December 24	Commissioners sign peace treaty in Ghent, Netherlands.

1815

January 8	Andrew Jackson defeats British army in New Orleans.

1816

August 14	Webster moves his family to Boston.

1818

February 22	Webster argues on behalf of the Bank of the United States in *McCulloch v. Maryland*.
March 10	Webster argues on behalf of Dartmouth College before the Marshall Court.

1819

February 22	Adams-Onís Treaty is signed in Washington.

1822

January	Webster begins representation of clients before the Spanish Claims Commission.
November 4	Webster is elected to represent Boston in the US House of Representatives.

1823

December 2	James Monroe announces the noncolonization principle (Monroe Doctrine).

1824

January 19	Webster speaks in Congress recommending US support for Greek independence.
February 4	Webster argues *Gibbons v. Ogden* before the Marshall Court.
November	Webster is reelected by Massachusetts to the House of Representatives.

1825

April 14	Webster speaks in Congress in support of US participation in the Panama Congress.

1827

June 8	Webster is elected to represent Massachusetts in the US Senate.

1830

January 26–27	Webster issues second reply to Robert Y. Hayne in the US Senate.

1833

January 16	Webster is returned to the Senate by Massachusetts.
December 16	Webster is appointed chairman of the Senate Committee on Finance.

1839

January 27	Webster is reelected by Massachusetts to the Senate.
May 18–December 19	Webster tours Britain and visits the continent.
July 18	Webster addresses the Royal Agricultural Society at Oxford.
October 16	Webster meets with and offers legal counsel to Baring Brothers.

1840

September 10	Webster delivers Bunker Hill Declaration.
November 12	Alexander McLeod is arrested in New York.
December 11	Webster agrees to serve as secretary of state on Harrison's cabinet.

1841

March 6	Webster begins service as secretary of state.
March 12	British minister to Washington demands release of McLeod.
April 4	Harrison dies.
April 6	Tyler is sworn in as president.
April 24	Webster articulates the doctrine of national self-defense.
September 13	Tyler appoints Everett minister to Britain.
October 12	McLeod is acquitted.
November 24	Hawaiian Kingdom seeks recognition from the United States.

1842

February 2	Webster extends US protection for American missionaries abroad.
April 4	Lord Ashburton arrives in Washington to begin negotiations.
June 18	Webster-Ashburton talks begin.
August 9	Webster completes landmark negotiations with Ashburton and signs the Webster-Ashburton Treaty (Treaty of Washington).
August 29	Congress passes Webster law assigning jurisdiction to the federal government for crimes involving citizens of foreign countries committed under authority of their government.
August 29	Treaty of Nanking is signed.
December 19	Webster crafts the basis of the Tyler Doctrine in a letter to Hawaiian representatives Haalilio and Richards.

1843

March 2	Discussions are initiated with Prussia for extradition arrangement.

May 8	Webster initiates the Caleb Cushing mission to China.
May 8	Webster tenders resignation from Tyler cabinet.
June 17	Webster delivers Second Bunker Hill address.
August 8	Cushing mission departs for China with Fletcher Webster serving as mission secretary.

1844

January 23	Webster issues letter articulating opposition to Texas annexation.

1845

January 15	Webster is reelected to the Senate.
January 16	Senate ratifies Treaty of Wanghia with China.
March 1	Joint resolution of Congress annexes Texas.

1846

April 9	Congress initiates investigation of allegations of misconduct by Webster while secretary of state.
May 12	Congress issues declaration of war on Mexico.
June 18	Senate ratifies the Oregon Treaty.

1848

February 2	Mexico accepts terms of the Treaty of Guadalupe Hidalgo.

1849

March 5	Taylor is inaugurated.

1850

March 7	Webster delivers speech in the Senate in support of Henry Clay's compromise proposal.
April 19	Clayton-Bulwer treaty is signed.
July 9	Taylor dies.
July 10	Vice President Fillmore is sworn in as president.
July 23	Webster begins second incumbency as secretary of state.
September 12	Bulwer proposes reciprocity arrangement between the United States and Canada.
September 20	Compromise of 1850 is enacted.
December 21	Webster issues the Hülsemann letter.

1851

January 25	United States signs Tehuantepec convention with Mexico.
May 22	Mexican government nullifies the Garray grant.
June 10	Webster drafts instructions for the American mission to Japan.
July 10	Webster negotiates Costa Rica treaty of friendship and commerce.
July 14	Webster restates the Tyler Doctrine in his instructions to Luther Severance.

August 11	Narciso López lands filibuster expedition in Cuba.
December 2	French Second Republic is overthrown by Louis Napoleon.
1852	
January 7	Webster delivers Kossuth speech at a banquet honoring Louis Kossuth's visit.
January 22	Webster directs Commodore Matthew C. Perry to lead the mission to Japan.
April 7	Mexico rejects the Tehuantepec convention.
April 30	Webster negotiates the Webster-Crampton convention.
June 5	Webster writes James C. Jewett concerning access to guano on the Lobos Islands.
June 16	Webster completes extradition convention with Prussia.
July 19–20	Webster letter on fisheries appears in Boston *Courier* and New York *Daily Times*.
July 20	Webster-Crampton convention is rejected by Nicaragua.
July 25	Webster begins talks on fisheries disputes with John Crampton at Marshfield.
August 30	Webster sends William Miles on a special mission to Peru.
September 2	Webster leaves Washington for Marshfield for last time.
October 24	Webster dies at Marshfield.

Notes

Preface

1. In 1846, Charles Sumner acknowledged Webster's recent diplomatic success to a gathering of Whigs in Boston by designating him "Defender of Peace." *Works of Charles Sumner*, 15 vols. (Boston: Lee and Shepard, 1870–1883), 1:314–15.

Chapter One

1. It is no surprise that the breadth and depth of Daniel Webster has enticed so many biographers to record his life. A condensed list of the most essential include: Irving H. Bartlett, *Daniel Webster* (New York: Norton, 1978); Maurice Glen Baxter, *One and Inseparable: Daniel Webster and the Union* (Cambridge, MA: Harvard University Press, 1984); Richard N. Current, *Daniel Webster and the Rise of National Conservatism* (Boston: Little, Brown, 1955; Prospect Heights, IL: Waveland Press, 1992); George Ticknor Curtis, *Life of Daniel Webster*, 2 vols. (New York: D. Appleton and Company, 1870); Edward Everett, *The Life of Daniel Webster* (New York: J. A. Hill, 1904); Claude Moore Fuess, *Daniel Webster*, 2 vols. (Boston: Little, Brown, 1930); Robert Remini, *Daniel Webster: The Man and His Time* (New York: Norton, 1997); Kenneth E. Shewmaker, ed., *Daniel Webster: "The Completest Man"* (Hanover, NH: University Press of New England, 1990).

2. Bartlett, *Daniel Webster*, 12–13; Remini, *The Man and His Time*, 29–35.

3. Bartlett, *Daniel Webster*, 17.

4. Daniel Webster, "Autobiography," in *The Private Correspondence of Daniel Webster* (hereafter *PC*), Fletcher Webster, ed., 2 vols. (Boston: Little, Brown, 1857), 1:10.

5. Quoted in Bartlett, *Daniel Webster*, 22.

6. Daniel Webster, *An Oration, Pronounced at Hanover, New-Hampshire, the 4th day of July, 1800* (Hanover: Moses Davis, 1800).

7. James W. McIntyre, ed., *The Writings and Speeches of Daniel Webster* (hereafter *W&S*), 18 vols. (Boston: Little, Brown, 1903), 15:486.

8. Daniel Webster, "Autobiography of Daniel Webster," PC, 1:18–19; Remini, *The Man and His Time*, 71.

9. Remini, *The Man and His Time*, 75–76; Bartlett, *Daniel Webster*, 42; Webster recorded his exchange with Gore and his father's reaction in "Autobiography," PC, 1:22–23.

10. Webster to James Hervey Bingham, January 19, 1806, PC, 1:221.

11. See *American State Papers, Foreign Relations* (*ASPFR*) (Washington: Gales and Seaton, 1832), 3:269–70; "Voices of the Northern Neutrals," *Literary Digest*, October 30, 1915, 983. The general sentiment that Britain arbitrarily set maritime rules was commonly held long before the quoted phrase appeared during the Great War; *W&S*, 15:537–47; Remini, *The Man and His Time*, 80–81. Napoleon's decree issued an equally unenforceable blockade of the British Isles by directing the seizure and condemnation of all ships touching a British port. The emperor's so-called Continental system would, he hoped, shut off British trade with the continent and play havoc on the Crown's commerce.

12. Webster to Jacob McGraw, January 12, 1807, PC, 1:223–24; Remini, *The Man and His Time*, 86.

13. Jefferson's response to the *Chesapeake* incident on July 2, 1807, ordering all British ships from American waters, was transmitted to Congress in early November. See *ASPFR*, 3:24–25; For details on Jefferson's economic response to harassment of American commerce, see Louis M. Sears, *Jefferson and the Embargo* (Durham, NC: Duke University Press, 1927); Quoted ibid., 178.

14. Baxter, *One and Inseparable*, 30; Daniel Webster, "Considerations on the Embargo Laws, 1808," in *W&S*, 15:564–74.

15. These conditions included American acceptance of the previously rejected Rule of 1756, permission for British warships to ply American waters, and the continuance of Non-Intercourse on the French. For a detailed study of the Erskine Agreement within the context of the general decay in Anglo-American relations in the years leading to the war, see Bradford Perkins, *Prologue to War: England and the United States, 1805–1812* (Berkeley: University of California Press, 1961).

16. Roger H. Brown, *The Republic in Peril: 1812* (New York: W. W. Norton, 1964), 22–29.

17. *W&S*, 15:596.

18. *W&S*, 15:600–610.

19. Quoted in Bartlett, *Daniel Webster*, 56.

20. Merrill D. Peterson, *The Great Triumvirate: Webster, Clay, and Calhoun* (New York: Oxford University Press, 1987). See also, H. W. Brands, *Heirs of the Founders: Clay, Calhoun, Webster and the Struggle for Democracy* (New York: Doubleday, 2018).

21. See Webster's "The French Decrees" in W&S, 14:3–7; Baxter, One and Inseparable, 42; Remini, The Man and His Time, 108; The Debates and Proceedings in the Congress of the United States, 13th Cong., 1st sess., 149–51.

22. Baxter, One and Inseparable, 43; The Debates and Proceedings in the Congress of the United States, 13th Cong., 1st sess., 149–51. Grundy's speech appears ibid., 120–29; Quoted ibid., 126.

23. Perkins, Prologue to War, 335–37; Annals of Congress, 13th Cong., 1st sess., 149–52, 319–28, 330–31, 351–83, 387–98.

24. See Monroe's report of July 12, 1813, in ASPFR, 3:608–12; Remini, The Man and His Time, 110; Baxter, One and Inseparable, 45–46.

25. Daniel Fletcher Webster was born at the end of July and joined three-year-old Grace Fletcher in the Webster household. Sadly, Grace would only live to the age of seven. Webster and his wife would have three more children, but of the five, only Fletcher outlived his father.

26. Quoted in Remini, The Man and His Time, 114.

27. Annals of Congress, 13th Cong., 2nd sess., 940–50; Remini, The Man and His Time, 113–14.

28. Donald R. Hickey, "American Trade Restrictions during the War of 1812," Journal of American History 68, no. 1 (December 1981): 517–38; Baxter, One and Inseparable, 50–51.

29. Baxter, One and Inseparable, 53; Quoted ibid., 61.

30. Annals of Congress, 13th Cong., 3rd sess., 482, 720–50; Remini, The Man and His Time, 127–28; Daniel Webster, "On the President's Message Relative to the French Decrees," January 3, 1814, W&S, 14:8–10.

31. Daniel Webster, "The Conscription Bill, December 9, 1814," in The Papers of Daniel Webster: Speeches and Formal Writings, Charles Wiltse, ed., 2 vols. (Hanover, NH: Dartmouth, 1986), I:24–27; Remini, The Man and His Time, 128; Wiltse, Speeches and Formal Writings, 1:30.

32. Wiltse, Speeches and Formal Writings, 1:31; Remini, The Man and His Time, 129–32; Webster biographer Irving Bartlett noted that "the ironic thing about Webster's first years in Washington is that the man who became not only famous but venerated by whole generations of Americans as a spokesman for American nationalism began his career by opposing the war which more than any other single event in the first quarter of the nineteenth century made national sentiment possible." Bartlett, Daniel Webster, 69. There was little wise in the actions of the Federalist supporters of the Hartford Convention. The incident contributed to the precipitous decline of the party as a factor in national politics. Webster would be late to appreciate this.

33. Baxter, One and Inseparable, 65–66; Remini, The Man and His Time, 140–44.

34. W&S, 16:47; Bartlett, Daniel Webster, 79.

35. W&S, 11:8.

36. Wiltse, Speeches and Formal Writings, 1:45–59; Bartlett, Daniel Webster, 80–81, 90; Remini, The Man and His Time, 169–71.

37. Fuess, Daniel Webster, 1:272–73.

38. Daniel Webster, "Basis of the Senate," in W&S, 5:8–25; Fuess, Daniel Webster, 1:276–79.

39. John Adams to Daniel Webster, December 23, 1820, quoted in Fuess, Daniel Webster, 1:284 and Curtis, The Life of Daniel Webster, 1:193–94; Remini, The Man and His Time, 178; For Ticknor's assessment of the speech, see Curtis, The Life of Daniel Webster, 1:192–93; Everett is quoted in Fuess, Daniel Webster, 1:287. Everett was destined to play a major part in both Webster's personal and professional life, including his role as diplomatist.

40. General Jackson accused the two British subjects of complicity in the grievances assigned to the Seminoles and had them executed; for details on the Adams-Onís Treaty, see Phillip Coolidge Brooks, Diplomacy and the Borderlands (Berkeley: University of California Press, 1939); James E. Lewis, The American Union and the Problem of Neighborhood: The United States and the Collapse of the Spanish Empire (Chapel Hill: University of North Carolina Press, 1998).

41. Andrew J. King and Alfred S. Konefsky, eds., The Papers of Daniel Webster: Legal Papers, 3 vols. (Hanover, NH: University Press of New England, 1982–89), 2:176–77.

42. Webster to Peter Chardon Brooks, February 24, 1819, ibid., 201; for documents associated with the Spanish Claims, see "The Spanish Claims Commission," ibid., 175–275.

43. "The Spanish Claims Commission," 202–3.

44. "The Spanish Claims Commission," 265; Remini, The Man and His Time, 189.

45. King and Konefsky, Legal Papers, 2:228.

46. Webster to Jeremiah Mason, April 19, 1824, The Papers of Daniel Webster: Correspondence, ed. Charles Wiltse, 7 vols. (Hanover, NH: Dartmouth, 1974) 1:357.

47. William P. Mason, reporter, "Report of the Case of the Juene Eugenie Determined in the Circuit Court of the United States, for the First Circuit, at Boston December 1821" (Boston: Wells and Lilly, 1822), 3.

48. Mason, "Report of the Case of the Juene Eugenie," 7.

49. "Notes: International Norms and Politics in the Marshall Court's Slave Trade Cases," Harvard Law Review 128, no. 4 (February 2015): 1184.

Chapter Two

1. Colonel Perkins (and others) to Webster, October 18, 1822, PC, 1:321. This letter bears the signatures of five nominating committee members officially inviting Webster to "throw down" his law books "and enter the service of the public" by representing the Suffolk District in Congress; Claude Moore Fuess, Daniel Webster, 2 vols. (Boston: Little, Brown, 1930), 1:309–10; Maurice Glen Baxter, One and Inseparable: Daniel Webster and the Union (Cambridge, MA: Harvard University Press, 1984), 97.

2. Annals of Congress, 18th Cong., 1st sess., 1108; The Papers of Daniel Webster: Speeches and Formal Writings, Charles Wiltse, ed., 2 vols. (Hanover, NH: Dartmouth, 1986), 1:87; Baxter, One and Inseparable, 99; Fuess, Daniel Webster, 1:312.

3. Webster to Everett, November 16, 1823, December 5, 1823, January 2, 1824, in *PC*, 1:327–38.

4. Baxter, *One and Inseparable*, 100; Edward Everett, "Life of Ali Pacha," *North American Review* 18, no. 42 (January 1824): 106–39. In December 1823 Everett participated in a meeting for the Relief of the Greeks in Boston in which he disseminated his knowledge of the conflict; Fuess, *Daniel Webster*, 1:312; Robert Remini, *Daniel Webster: The Man and His Time* (New York: Norton, 1997), 214–19; *The Debates and Proceedings in the Congress of the United States*, 18th Cong., 1st sess., 805–6.

5. *Annals of Congress*, 18th Cong., 1st sess., 914, 917–18; Baxter, *One and Inseparable*, 100–101.

6. *Annals of Congress*, 18th Cong., 1st sess., 1084–99. Webster delivered his speech before the House Committee of the Whole; *The Great Speeches and Orations of Daniel Webster*, Edwin P. Whipple, ed. (Boston: Little, Brown, 1879), 57–76; Wiltse, *Speeches and Formal Writings*, 1:92–93, 97; Fuess, *Daniel Webster*, 1:313; Baxter, *One and Inseparable*, 102.

7. The debates appear off and on in *Annals of Congress*, 18th Cong., 1st sess., 1105 (Poinsett), 1112 (Randolph's Pandora's box reference), 1150 (Bartlett's dismissal). The Don Quixote comment attributed to Bartlett is drawn from Remini, *The Man and His Time*, 217.

8. *Annals of Congress*, 18th Cong., 1st sess., 1214. The committee adjourned on January 26 with the resolution left to die on the table; See also Baxter, *One and Inseparable*, 103–4; Joseph Hopkinson to Webster, January 23, 1824, *PC*, 1:341; H. A. Dearborn to Webster, May 4, 1824, in *The Letters of Daniel Webster*, ed. C. H. Van Tyne (New York: Haskell House, 1969), 104.

9. *Annals of Congress*, 18th Cong., 1st sess., 959–65. The tariff bill was introduced to Congress in the second week of January; Fuess, *Daniel Webster*, 1:317fn; Remini, *The Man and His Time*, 219–22; For Webster's opinion and comments, see Daniel Webster, "The Tariff, April 1–2, 1824," in Wiltse, *Speeches and Formal Writings*, 1:114–60.

10. Webster to Jeremiah Mason, April 19, 1824, *W&S*, 16:84. Webster wrote to Mason, "My great business of the session remains yet undone, that is, to get through the law for paying the Spanish claims." Quoted ibid.; Fuess, *Daniel Webster*, 1:318 fn; Remini, *The Man and His Time*, 228.

11. Henry Warfield to Webster, February 3, 1825, and Webster to Henry Warfield, February 5, 1825, *W&S*, 17:377–80.; Ibid., 379. A note attached to Webster's letter states that he read his reply to Warfield to Adams in order to get Adams's informal commitment to having Federalists actively participate in governing under his administration; See also, Bartlett, *Daniel Webster*, 104–5; Overshadowed by the presidential selection, Webster also had a few noteworthy achievements in this session. He led Story's crusade to codify the criminal statutes and spoke in support of key elements of Clay's American System. As an advocate now for internal improvements such as the National Road, he was advancing American nationalism, the central theme of his career. See Remini, *The Man and His Time*, 243–44.

12. Whipple, *Speeches and Orations*, 125–35; Bartlett, *Daniel Webster*, 111; *National Intelligencer*, July 17, 1830. It is interesting that the reporter's reflection chose Thomas Gray's words. Gray would be a favorite of Webster and one that he called for in his deathbed delirium: "Poet, poetry; Gray, Gray." Fletcher responded with Gray's "Elegy" that begins, "The curfew tolls the knell of parting day." Quoted in Remini, *The Man and His Time*, 760.

13. Webster to Joseph Story, December 31, 1825, W&S, 17:401. Webster wrote to Judge Joseph Story to update him on the Judiciary Committee's effort to reform the court. In the letter he made the observations on Panama; See also, Fuess, *Daniel Webster*, 1:329–30; Baxter, *One and Inseparable*, 120.

14. *Register of Debates*, 19th Cong., 1st sess., 1241.

15. *Register of Debates*, 19th Cong., 1st sess., 1301–2. Webster's resolution was accepted on February 3, 1826; For McLane's amendment, see ibid., 2009; Wiltse, *Speeches and Formal Writings*, 1:202.

16. *Register of Debates*, 19th Cong., 1st sess., 2011–21; Wiltse, *Speeches and Formal Writings*, 1:205.

17. Wiltse, *Speeches and Formal Writings*, 1:226; For Adams's "ripe fruit" comments, see Chauncey Ford Worthington, *Writings of John Quincy Adams*, 7 vols. (New York: MacMillan, 1917), 7:372–73; Wiltse, *Speeches and Formal Writings*, 1:234–35.

18. Baxter, *One and Inseparable*, 123.

19. Henry Clay to Daniel Webster, November 10, 1826, James Hopkins and Mary Hargreaves, eds., *The Papers of Henry Clay*, 10 vols. (Lexington: University Press of Kentucky, 1973), 5:889.

20. Baxter, *One and Inseparable*, 138.

21. Justice Story to Webster, January 27, 1827, W&S, 17:446; See also, Fuess, *Daniel Webster*, 1:348–49; Webster's May 9, 1828, speech, *Register of Debates*, 20th Cong., 1st sess., 750–65; Remini, *The Man and His Time*, 296–99.

22. Remini, *The Man and His Time*, 305–11.

23. Foot introduced his resolution on December 29, 1829. *Register of Debates*, 21st Cong., 1st sess., 3–4; For Hayne's speech, see *Register of Debates*, 21th Cong., 1st sess., 43–58, 82–92.

24. Quoted in Remini, *The Man and His Time*, 324.

25. Whipple, *Speeches and Orations*, 231, 257; "Liberty" lines can be found in Ibid., 269.

26. Remini, *The Man and His Time*, 334–36

27. *Register of Debates*, 22nd Cong., 1st sess., 981–88; Jackson's veto message was received by Congress on July 10. Ibid., 1220; this was, in fact, personal to Webster whose winning argument in *McCulloch v. Maryland* (1819) affirmed the constitutionality of the National Bank.

28. *Register of Debates*, 22nd Cong., 1st sess., 1229–32, 1240; Quoted in Bartlett, *Daniel Webster*, 131; See Remini, *The Man and His Time*, 343–55; Bartlett, *Daniel Webster*, 130–31; Baxter, *One and Inseparable*, 194–208.

29. Webster opposed Van Buren's appointment on his alleged deferential attitude to the British while secretary of state. Pointing out concessions to Britain that Van Buren had issued through American minister to Britain Louis McLane over trade with the West Indies, Webster accused him of kowtowing to the Crown as though London dispersed trade accommodations as an allowance rather than in deference to the rights of a sovereign nation. See speech in W&S, 6:89–96; Remini, *The Man and His Time*, 372. South Carolina rewarded Hayne with the governorship.

30. W&S, 13:40–43; Remini, *The Man and His Time*, 377; See James D. Richardson, ed., *A Compilation of the Messages and Papers of the Presidents*, 20 vols. (Washington, DC: Bureau of National Literature, 1917), 2:1183–84, 1192–95.

31. *Register of Debates*, 22nd Cong., 2nd sess., 519–53; Baxter, *One and Inseparable*, 214.

32. W&S, 6:183, 210; The entire reply to Calhoun appears Ibid., 181–238.

33. *Register of Debates*, 22nd Cong., 2nd sess., 808–9; Baxter, *One and Inseparable*, 220.

34. See details in Richard Current, *National Conservatism*, 81–87; Remini, *The Man and His Time*, 418–24.

35. W&S, 8:34; Current, *National Conservatism*, 95.

36. Quoted in Remini, *The Man and His Time*, 429.

37. Webster to James Hervey Bingham, August 24, 1835, *The Papers of Daniel Webster: Correspondence*, Charles Wiltse, ed., 7 vols. (Hanover, NH: Dartmouth, 1974) 4:49–50; Andrew J. King and Alfred S. Konefsky, eds., *The Papers of Daniel Webster: Legal Papers*, 3 vols. (Hanover, NH: University Press of New England, 1982–89) 2:325; Webster to H. W. Kinsman, May 28, 1830, Van Tyne, *Letters*, 158. Wheaton would, that same year, begin an eight-year appointment as chargé to Denmark.

38. Jackson's impatience escalated to the extreme, and Webster and Clay worked with others to block extravagant defense spending proposed by Democrats in the House. In the process, Webster set off an issue with Adams that was long lived. See Baxter, *One and Inseparable*, 240–42; King and Konefsky, *Legal Papers*, 2:324–43. There are a number of Webster letters running up to the January 12 speech to the Senate verifying Webster's designs on the various claims. He opens his speech in response to allegations of those designs with the disclaimer that "I have not the slightest interest in these claims," Edward Everett, *Works of Daniel Webster*, 6 vols. (Boston: Little, Brown, 1851), 4:152. For the entire January 12, 1835, speech, see ibid., 152–78; See also Remini, *The Man and His Time*, 433.

39. Webster to John Davis, April 7, 1836, Wiltse, *Papers: Correspondence*, 4:100.

40. Samuel Price Carson to Webster, March 30, 1836, ibid., 99; for US-Mexican diplomacy during the critical years of Texas' secession from Mexico, see Eugene C. Baker, "The United States and Mexico, 1835–1837," *The Mississippi Valley Historical Review* 1, no. 1 (June 1914), 3–30.

41. Comments on Texas from a March 15, 1837, speech in New York can be found in W&S, 2:205–7.

42. *Register of Debates*, 24th Cong., 1st sess., 1415–16; Webster to Everett, May 7, 1836, Wiltse, *Papers: Correspondence*, 4:110.

43. *Register of Debates*, 24th Cong., 1st sess., 1527–28.

44. Remini, *The Man and His Time*, 447; Samuel Houston to Webster, November 20, 1836, Van Tyne, *Letters*, 209. By fall, the climate in Texas had so calmed that Texas president Sam Houston wrote Webster a letter of introduction for Santa Anna with the request that, on the general's appearance in Washington, he be received and treated with the respect due his rank; Remini, *The Man and His Time*, 464. Later, in 1837, when the nation entertained an annexation request from Texas, Webster rejected the notion of expanding American territory as anathema to the "interest and happiness of the whole Union," especially considering it would be accompanied with the expansion of slavery, "a great moral, social, and political evil." Quoted ibid.

45. Webster to Hiram Ketchum, May 12, 1838; George Ticknor Curtis, *The Life of Daniel Webster*, 2 vols. (New York: D. Appleton and Company, 1870)

46. Webster to Hiram Ketchum, May 12, 1838, Curtis, *The Life of Daniel Webster*, 1:576. For example, Senator Samuel McKean presented memorials from citizens of Pennsylvania beseeching congressional leaders to invalidate the treaty and block its enforcement. *Journal of the Senate of the United States of America, 1789–1873*, April 13, 1838; Webster, Calhoun, and Clay were among the no votes. *Journal of Executive Proceedings of the Senate*, 4:546.

47. Remini notes that Webster's disappointments might be connected to his decision to write his will in the month of the election. The date on the will is simply November 1836, but whether it came before or after Van Buren's victory by now was moot. The handwriting revealing the election results had appeared on the wall months before Remini, *The Man and His Time*, 452; Bartlett, *Daniel Webster*, 148.

48. *W&S*, 2:238.

49. Remini, *The Man and His Time*, 485.

Chapter Three

1. Hunter Miller, ed., *Treaties and Other International Acts of the United States of America, 1776–1863*, 8 vols. (Washington, DC: United States Government Printing Office, 1931–1948), 2:152; Howard Jones and Donald A. Rakestraw, *Prologue to Manifest Destiny: Anglo-American Relations in the 1840s* (Wilmington, DE: SR Books, 1997), 4–6; John P. D. Dunbabin, "'Red Lines on Maps' Revisited: The Role of Maps in Negotiating and Defending the 1842 Webster-Ashburton Treaty," *Imago Mundi: The International Journal for the History of Cartography* 63, no. 1 (January 2011): 40–42; No study of Anglo-American relations during the 1830s and 1840s would be complete without consulting Howard Jones's *To the Webster-Ashburton Treaty: A Study in Anglo-American Relations, 1783–1843* (Chapel Hill: University of North Carolina Press, 1977).

2. William F. Ganong, "A Monograph of the Evolution of the Boundaries of the Province of New Brunswick," *Transactions of the Royal Society of Canada* 7, no. 2

(January 1901): 139–449; For details of the arrangements discussed at Ghent and the commission effort that followed, see ibid., 287–89; Jones and Rakestraw, *Prologue to Manifest Destiny*, 6–7.

3. J. Chris Arndt, "Maine in the Northeastern Boundary Controversy: States' Rights in Antebellum New England," *The New England Quarterly* 62, no. 2 (June 1989): 205–6; Lord Palmerston sketched out the competing Anglo-American issues associated with the border in a letter to British minister to the United States Henry Fox. See Lord Palmerston to Henry Fox, July 6, 1837, Lord Palmerston's Letter-Books, Additional Manuscripts, Series B, 48495, LXXIX, British Library, London.

4. Francis M. Carroll, "Kings and Crises: Arbitrating the Canadian-American Boundary Dispute in the Belgium Crisis of 1830–1831," *The New England Quarterly* 73, no. 2 (June 2000): 194–98; the Senate then narrowly supported reopening talks but reached an immediate impasse when it attempted to link the boundary negotiations with a British concession of American navigation rights on the St. John. See Jones and Rakestraw, *Prologue to Manifest Destiny*, 8.

5. James D. Richardson, ed., *A Compilation of the Messages and Papers of the Presidents*, 20 vols. (Washington, DC: Bureau of National Literature, 1917), 3:485–87; C. P. Stacey, ed., "A Private Report of General Winfield Scott on the Border Situation in 1839," *Canadian Historical Review* 21, no. 4 (December 1940): 407–14; Jones and Rakestraw, *Prologue to Manifest Destiny*, 23–26.

6. Jones and Rakestraw, *Prologue to Manifest Destiny*, 31.

7. *New York Herald*, January 4, 1838; *Halifax Pearl*, April 6, 1838. The *Halifax Pearl* carried the report from Quebec along with the recent exchange between Fox and Forsyth.

8. Timothy D. Johnson, *Winfield Scott: The Quest for Military Glory* (Lawrence: University Press of Kansas, 1998), 130–32; Jones and Rakestraw, *Prologue to Manifest Destiny*, 33–34.

9. John Forsyth to Henry Fox, January 5, 1838, Department of State, Notes to Foreign Legations, National Archives, Washington, DC.

10. Jones and Rakestraw, *Prologue to Manifest Destiny*, 37–38.

11. *Congressional Globe*, 26th Cong., 2nd sess., 173; Henry Fox to Daniel Webster, March 12, 1841, Kenneth E. Shewmaker, ed., *The Papers of Daniel Webster: Diplomatic Papers* (hereafter *DP*), 2 vols. (Hanover, NH: Dartmouth, 1983), 1:42–44.

12. Jones and Rakestraw, *Prologue to Manifest Destiny*, 8–13; For a detailed account of the conflict, see Howard Jones, "Anglophobia and the Aroostook War," *New England Quarterly* 48, no. 4 (December 1975): 519–39; William R. Manning, ed., *The Diplomatic Correspondence of the United States: Canadian Relations, 1784–1860*, 4 vols. (Washington, DC: Carnegie Endowment for International Peace, 1940), 3:29.

13. Claude Moore Fuess, *Daniel Webster*, 2 vols. (Boston: Little, Brown, 1930), 2:72; Jones and Rakestraw, *Prologue to Manifest Destiny*, 14–16.

14. Jones and Rakestraw, *Prologue to Manifest Destiny*, 17; Winfield Scott, *Memoirs of Lieut.-General Scott, LL.D.* (New York: Sheldon & Company, 1864); Johnson, *Winfield Scott*, 134–35.

15. *Cong. Globe*, 25th Cong., 3rd sess., 258–59; Ibid., 314.

16. For Webster's opposition to Van Buren's appointment to London, see *W&S*, 6:89–96.

17. See memorandum in Charles Wiltse, *The Papers of Daniel Webster: Correspondence* (Hanover NH: Dartmouth, 1974) 4:346. See Webster's speech in *W&S*, 5:178–217; Webster to Samuel Jaudon, March 29, 39, PC, II:45; See Memorandum, March 10, 1839, and "A Scheme for the Settlement of the Northeastern Boundary," April 1839, Van Tyne, *Letters*, 215–18. Webster also reflected his pessimism in a brief account of his meeting with Poinsett and the president "that the President might think my notions too much inclined to a war aspect." Quoted ibid., 215.

18. See Charles M. Wiltse, "Daniel Webster and the British Experience," *Proceedings of the Massachusetts Historical Society* 85 (1973): 68. Ward contributed $500 to the trip; Robert Remini, *Daniel Webster: The Man and His Time* (New York: Norton, 1997), 486–87. For the influence of Baring Brothers on both Webster and the nation see Jay Sexton, *Debtor Diplomacy: Finance and American Foreign Relations in the Civil War Era, 1837–1873* (New York: Clarendon Press, 2005).

19. London *Times*, June 4, 1839; Remini, *The Man and His Time*, 488; Maurice Glen Baxter, *One and Inseparable: Daniel Webster and the Union* (Cambridge, MA: Harvard University Press, 1984), 296; Webster to Edward Curtis, June 12, 1839, Wiltse, *Papers: Correspondence*, 4:369.

20. Webster to Hiram Ketchum, September 20, 1839, ibid., 94; Remini, 493; *W&S*, 2: 285–89.

21. Webster to Charles Henry Thomas, October, 14, 1839, Wiltse, *Papers: Correspondence*, 4: 402–3; Baxter, *One and Inseparable*, 297; Baring Brothers to Webster, October 12, 1839, Wiltse, *Papers: Correspondence*, 4: 401–2; Webster to Baring Brothers, October 16, 1839, ibid., 405–7; Remini, *The Man and His Time*, 497; Baxter, *One and Inseparable*, 298; Wiltse, "Webster and the British Experience," passim.

22. Fuess, *Daniel Webster*, 2:78–79.

23. Webster to John Henry Manners, Duke of Rutland, November 16, 1839, Wiltse, *Papers: Correspondence* 4:409–10; Webster to Everett, October 16, 1839, ibid., 408.

24. Webster to Joshua Bates, March 26, 1840, Wiltse, *Papers: Correspondence*, 5:24; William Henry Harrison to Webster, December 1, 1840, PC, 2:90–91; *Journal of the Executive Proceedings of the Senate of the United States of America, 1837–1841*, March 5, 1841.

25. Remini, *The Man and His Time*, 513; Baxter, *One and Inseparable*, 299.

26. Alastair Watt, "The Case of Alexander McLeod," *Canadian Historical Review* 12, no. 2 (June 1931): 145–67; Kenneth R. Stevens, *Border Diplomacy: The Caroline and McLeod Affairs in Anglo-American-Canadian Relations, 1837–1842* (Tuscaloosa: University of Alabama Press, 1989), 71–89; Jones and Rakestraw, *Prologue to Manifest Destiny*, 46–48.

27. Thomas C. Hansard, ed., *Hansard's Parliamentary Debates*, 3d series, 356 vols., London, 1830–1891, 66:364–66; Henry Fox to Lord Palmerston, January 10, 1841, in The National Archives of the UK (TNA): Foreign Office (FO) 115/68; Lord Palmerston to Henry Fox, February 9, 1841, in Lord Palmerston's Letter-Books, Additional

Manuscripts, British Library, London; Lord Palmerston to Henry Fox, February 9, 1841, in TNA: FO 5/358; *The Times* quoted in Stevens, *Border Diplomacy*, 86; Jones and Rakestraw, *Prologue to Manifest Destiny*, 48–49.

28. Henry Fox to Webster, March 12, 1841, *DP*, 1:42; Jones and Rakestraw, *Prologue to Manifest Destiny*, 59; *Cong. Globe*, 27th Cong., 1st sess., 14, 42–46, 66–69, 82–83; See also, Stevens, *Border Diplomacy*, 115–20; 129. Jones and Rakestraw, *Prologue to Manifest Destiny*, 61.

29. Webster to Everett, July 24, 1841, and November 20, 1841, *DP*, 1:19–22. Webster informed Everett of his nomination on July 24 but did not follow with the details of the nomination votes until November 20, long after Everett had taken his post in London; Jones and Rakestraw, *Prologue to Manifest Destiny*, 61–62; Wilbur D. Jones, *The American Problem in British Diplomacy, 1841–1861* (Athens: University of Georgia Press, 1974), 1–16.

30. See Joshua Spencer to Webster, September 24, 1841, *DP*, 1:151–52. Spencer had written to Webster in late September confidant that the testimonies he had gathered would establish "strong and I think *impregnable*" proof of McLeod's innocence; the tension between Canada and New York appeared in the press on both sides of the border. See, for example, *The Catholic* (Hamilton), October 13, 1841, that discussed the threat of the Hunter's Lodges, reprinted an excerpt on the McCleod trial that indicated a pessimistic attitude toward peace on the frontier, and reprinted a pessimistic excerpt from the New York *Commercial Advertiser* (Utica).

31. Jones and Rakestraw, *Prologue to Manifest Destiny*, 68–69.

32. For details of the *Creole* affair, including graphic depictions of the rebellion itself, see documents on the *Creole* in US Congress, *Senate Docs.*, 27th Cong., 2nd sess., 1–46; Howard Jones, "The Peculiar Institution and National Honor; The Case of the *Creole* Slave Revolt," *Civil War History* 21 (March 1975): 28–50.

33. Hugh G. Soulsby, *The Right of Search and the Slave Trade in Anglo-America Relations, 1814–1862* (Baltimore: Johns Hopkins University Press, 1933), 46.

34. Jones and Rakestraw, *Prologue to Manifest Destiny*, 75–78.

35. Soulsby, *The Right of Search and the Slave Trade*, 90–91; For examples from Congress and the press, see ibid., 92–93.

36. Webster to Everett, January 29, 1842, *DP*, 1:179–80; Webster to Joseph Story, March 17, 1842, in Ibid., I:524–25; Everett to Lord Aberdeen, March 1, 1842, Department of State, Despatches, Great Britain, National Archives, Washington, DC; Jones and Rakestraw, *Prologue to Manifest Destiny*, 96.

37. Jones and Rakestraw, *Prologue to Manifest Destiny*, 98–100; See Fritz's report in *DP*, 1:185–92. An indication of the level of tension can be seen in Webster's dispatch of a secret agent, Fritz, to the Caribbean to gather intel about the British disposition there.

38. Jones and Rakestraw, *Prologue to Manifest Destiny*, 100–10.

39. Jones and Rakestraw, *Prologue to Manifest Destiny*, 101–2; See Richard Current, "Webster's Propaganda and the Ashburton Treaty," *Mississippi Valley Historical Review* 34, no. 2 (September 1947), 192. It should be noted that the propaganda campaign did not come without opposition. Both the Democratic Washington *Globe*

and the Whig *Courier* and the *Enquirer* (New York) decried the machinations of Webster and his agent Fog Smith.

40. Webster to Reuel Williams, February 18, 1842, *DP*, 1:518; Everett to Webster, December 31, 1841, ibid., 173–77.

41. Jones and Rakestraw, *Prologue to Manifest Destiny*, 102–4; Lady Ashburton to Webster, January 12, 1842, Van Tyne, *Letters*, 254.

42. Jones and Rakestraw, *Prologue to Manifest Destiny*, 106; Jared Sparks to Webster, February 15, 1842, *DP*, 1:514.

43. Herbert B. Adams, *The Life and Writings of Jared Sparks*, 2 vols. (Boston: Houghton, Mifflin, 1893), 2:393–418; Current, "Webster's Propaganda," 187–200.

44. For Palmerston's missed opportunity to acquire the Steuben map, see James Buchanan (British Consul) to Lord Palmerston, April 6; July 12, 1838, in TNA: FO 5/325; Dunbabin, "'Red Lines on Maps' Revisited," 42–43; Jones and Rakestraw, *Prologue to Manifest Destiny*, 108.

45. Everett to Webster, May 19, 1842, *DP*, 1:562–64; Webster to Everett, June 14, 1842, ibid., 580. Webster, certain that his application of the maps in hand would assure a compromise settlement, waved Everett off of his map search.

46. Jones and Rakestraw, *Prologue to Manifest Destiny*, 110–11; Peleg Sprague to Webster, February 17, 1842, *DP*, 1:517; Webster to Reuel Williams, February 18, 1842, ibid., 518–19; Webster's self-congratulatory "grand stroke" comment appears in Webster to Sparks, March 11, 1843, ibid., 786.

47. Jones and Rakestraw, *Prologue to Manifest Destiny*, 113; *Niles' National Register*, April 23, 1842, 115; Webster to John Fairfield and John Davis, April 11, 1842, *DP*, 1:534–37; Webster to Everett, April 25, 1842, ibid., 539–42; See Webster to Reuel Williams, May 7, 1842, ibid., 549. Webster knew that Maine would set the bar for compromise and Massachusetts would follow.

48. Sparks to Webster, May 19, 1842, *DP*, 1:564.

49. Jones and Rakestraw, *Prologue to Manifest Destiny*, 117; See Sparks to Webster, May 19, 1842, *DP*, 1:565. The money disclaimer was conveyed by Sparks in his May report; see Webster to Reuel Williams, May 14, 1842, ibid., 558. While Webster invited the participation of the states, he did caution against arriving at the table with rigid stipulations and rejected outright a request that the final treaty be submitted to Maine for acceptance or rejection. This, in the federal system, was simply not possible.

50. Baxter, *One and Inseparable*, 343–44.

51. Ashburton's son-in-law who had accompanied him to Washington panicked at the revised border's potential to derail the negotiation. Jones and Rakestraw, *Prologue to Manifest Destiny*, 117.

52. Jones and Rakestraw, *Prologue to Manifest Destiny*, 116–19.

Chapter Four

1. Ashburton to Webster, June 21, 1842, *DP*, 1:582–83.

2. Ashburton to Aberdeen, June 14, 1842, in Aberdeen Papers, Additional Manuscripts, British Library, London; Howard Jones and Donald A. Rakestraw, *Prologue to*

Manifest Destiny: Anglo-American Relations in the 1840s (Wilmington, DE: SR Books, 1997), 132.

3. Parliament, *Papers Relative to the Special Mission of Lord Ashburton to the United States of America in 1842* (London: T. R. Harrison, 1843), 7–8; Jones and Rakestraw, *Prologue to Manifest Destiny*, 123–24; Ashburton to Webster, June 21, 1842, DP, 1:586–87.

4. Maine Commissioners to Webster, June 29, 1842, ibid., 593–94; Webster to Ashburton, July 8, 1842, ibid., 605, 609.

5. Ashburton to Webster, July 1, 1842, William R. Manning, ed., *The Diplomatic Correspondence of the United States: Canadian Relations, 1784–1860*, 4 vols. (Washington, DC: Carnegie Endowment for International Peace, 1940), 3:144–45; Ashburton to Webster, July 1, 1842, DP, 1:604; it should be noted that Maine's contingent also contemplated conceding failure and returning to New England; Lyon G. Tyler, *The Letters and Times of the Tylers*, 3 vols. (Richmond, VA: Whittet and Shepperson, 1885), 2:218; Jones and Rakestraw, *Prologue to Manifest Destiny*, 125.

6. Jones and Rakestraw, *Prologue to Manifest Destiny*, 128; For Grattan's view of what transpired with the commissioners, especially Preble, see Thomas Colley Grattan, *Civilized America* (London: Bradbury and Evans, 1859), 1: 351–76, passim.

7. Webster to Ashburton, July 8, 1842, in *Special Mission of Ashburton*, 10–15; Ashburton to Aberdeen, July 13, 1842, in Ashburton Papers, TNA: FO 5/379; Webster to Maine Commissioners, July 15, 1842, W&S, 11:276–78; Jones and Rakestraw, *Prologue to Manifest Destiny*, 135.

8. Maine Commissioners to Webster, July 22, 1842, DP, 1:638–45; Jones and Rakestraw, *Prologue to Manifest Destiny*, 135–36; For congressional approval of the monetary award to the states, see *Cong. Globe*, 27th Cong., 3rd sess., 2; Relevant documents, including correspondence between Webster and Ashburton, appear in *Special Mission of Ashburton*, 2–30.

9. Article II of the treaty in Hunter Miller, ed., *Treaties and Other International Acts of the United States of America, 1776–1863*, 8 vols. (Washington, DC: United States Government Printing Office, 1931–1948), 4:365–66; Thomas LeDuc, "The Webster-Ashburton Treaty and the Minnesota Iron Ranges," *Journal of American History* 51, no. 3 (December 1964):476.

10. Ashburton to Webster, January 2, 1842, Van Tyne, *Letters*, 252–54; See also, Ashburton to Webster, January 2, 1842, DP, 1:486.

11. For details on the Cass proposal, see the pamphlet he floated at the time titled *An Examination of the Question Now in Discussion Between the American and British Governments, Concerning the Right of Search*, in *Sketch of the Life and Public Services of General Lewis Cass*, by William T. Young (Philadelphia: Butler and Company, 1853), 136–65. Jones and Rakestraw, *Prologue to Manifest Destiny*, 139.

12. In practice, "being British" might have less to do with citizenship than need and ethnicity; Webster to Ashburton, August 8, 1842, *Special Mission of Ashburton*, 59–63.

13. Everett to Webster, January 31, 1842, DP, 1:495; Ashburton to Webster, August 9, 1842, W&S, 11:328; Jones and Rakestraw, *Prologue to Manifest Destiny*, 292, fn 41.

14. Ashburton to Aberdeen, April 25, 1842, in TNA: FO 5:379; Everett saw no reason to avoid the Quintuple arrangement if, as Ashburton had intimated to him, the right of search would be strictly limited to the slave trade. See Everett to Webster, January 21, 1842, *DP*, 1:491–96. Ashburton's opinion on impressment is quoted ibid., 495; Webster to Captains (Charles) Bell and (John) Paine, April 30, 1842, *W&S*, 11:290–91; The report of Bell and Paine to Webster on May 10, 1842 ("Report of Naval Officers to the Government of the United States respecting Slave Trade") was enclosed in Ashburton to Aberdeen, May 12, 1842, *Correspondence between Great Britain and the United States Relative to the Treaty Lately Concluded at Washington, 1842–43* (London: T. R. Harrison, 1843), 5–9.

15. Miller, *Treaties*, 4:369; Jones and Rakestraw, *Prologue to Manifest Destiny*, 141–42.

16. Governor Tilghman Mayfield Tucker to Robert W. Roberts, Speaker of the House of Representatives, February 26, 1842, *DP*, 1:519–21; Anita Rupprecht, "'All We Have Done, We Have Done for Freedom': The *Creole* Slave-Ship Revolt (1841) and the Revolutionary Atlantic," *IRSH* 58 (2013), Special Issue, 271–72; Everett to Webster, January 31, 1842, *DP*, 1:495. Webster had known the Crown's legal position since the end of January when Everett informed him that the law officers had unanimously ruled that the Crown had no "power to deliver up the 19 slaves guilty of murder in the Creole." Quoted ibid.

17. The provisions under Jay's Treaty expired in 1807; Jones and Rakestraw, *Prologue to Manifest Destiny*, 93.

18. Ashburton to Webster, July 3, 1842, *DP*, 1:657; Webster to Ashburton, August 1, 1842, ibid., 665, 658–65.

19. Ashburton to Aberdeen, August 9, 1842, ibid., 680; Ashburton to Webster, August 6, 1842, ibid., 668; Jones and Rakestraw, *Prologue to Manifest Destiny*, 143. The owners of the *Creole* slaves would be compensated at $110,330 in 1853 via a claims commission; For all relevant exchanges between Webster and Ashburton, see "Correspondence Between Lord Ashburton and Mr. Webster, Respecting the Case of the Creole, etc." in *Special Mission of Ashburton*, 35–43.

20. Webster to Ashburton, July 27, 1842, *Special Mission of Ashburton*, 45.

21. Webster to Ashburton, July 27, 1842, ibid., 49.

22. Ashburton to Webster, July 28, 1842, ibid., 53–54.

23. Webster to Ashburton, August 6, 1842, ibid., 54–55.

24. "Bill to provide further Remedial Justice in the Courts of the United States," Daniel Webster to Lord Ashburton, August 29, 1842, ibid., 57; Relevant exchanges between Webster and Ashburton appear in "Correspondence Between Lord Ashburton and Mr. Webster, Respecting the Case of the Steam Boat 'Caroline,'" ibid., 45–58; For McLeod law, see *DP*, 1:705–9.

25. Donald A. Rakestraw, *For Honor or Destiny: The Anglo-American Crisis over the Oregon Territory* (New York: Peter Lang, 1995), 46; Waddy Thompson to Webster, April 29, 1842, *DP*, 1:420–21.

26. Rakestraw, *Honor or Destiny*, 46.

27. Peter A. Brinsmade to Webster, April 8, 1842, *DP*, 1:863; Rakestraw, *Honor or Destiny*, 50–51.

28. Ashburton to Aberdeen, June 29, 1842, Manning, *Diplomatic Correspondence of the United States*, 3:745fn; Rakestraw, *Honor or Destiny*, 51.

29. Anthony Clark Arend, "International Law and the Preemptive Use of Military Force," *Washington Quarterly* 26, no. 2 (Spring 2003):89–103; Kenneth R. Stevens, *Border Diplomacy: The Caroline and McLeod Affairs in Anglo-American-Canadian Relations, 1837–1842* (Tuscaloosa: University of Alabama Press, 1989) 166–68.

30. Lady Ashburton to Aberdeen, August 9, 1842, Aberdeen Papers, Additional Manuscripts, British Library, London; Dunbabin, "'Red Lines on Maps' Revisited," 49; Ashburton's ire was subdued also because he too had held secret maps provided by the New Brunswick officials on condition that he conceal them from the Americans.

31. For Benton's speech, see *Cong. Globe*, 27th Cong., 3rd Sess., Appendix, 1–30; Webster to Everett, December 29, 1842, DP, 1:871–72; Albert Gallatin, *A Memoir on the North-Eastern Boundary in Connexion with Mr. Jay's Map* (New York: New-York Historical Society, 1843), 67.

32. Baxter, *One and Inseparable*, 354–55. At Sparks's invitation, Webster contributed to an article the historian was writing in defense of the treaty for *North American Review*, which appeared in April. Ibid., 356–57.

33. Gallatin, *A Memoir on the North-Eastern Boundary*, 64.

34. Dunbabin, "Red Lines on Maps' Revisited," 54. Quote is attributed to the geologist George Featherstonhaugh, whom Aberdeen recruited to promote the treaty.

35. Dunbabin, "Red Lines on Maps' Revisited," 55.

36. Dunbabin, "Red Lines on Maps' Revisited," 55.

37. Hansard, *Parliamentary Debates*, March 21, 1843, 67:1193.

38. Hansard, *Parliamentary Debates*, March 21, 1843, 67:1246–50.

39. Webster to Everett, April 25, 1843, DP, 1:795–96.

40. Jones and Rakestraw, *Prologue to Manifest Destiny*, 130–32.

41. Webster was the only cabinet member to continue with Tyler after Harrison's death. Tyler's Democratic pedigree soon surfaced and made him unacceptable to the Whig Party that had nominated him.

42. Lamar had issued an invitation in 1840 and followed with a second at the time he mounted the expedition; R. Earl McClendon, "Daniel Webster and Mexican Relations: The Santa Fe Prisoners," *Southwestern Historical Quarterly* 36, no. 4 (April 1933):288–311.

43. Waddy Thompson to Webster, April 29, 1842, DP, 1:416–22; For the personal appeal for Crittenden's release, see letters from Webster to Waddy Thompson and George S. Curson, both dated February 7, 1843, in PC, 2:165–67.

44. James Chamberlain Pickett to Webster, September 6, 1842, DP, 1:453–54. In the first week of September, James Chamberlain Pickett sent word from the legation in Lima verifying the belief that the United States was at war with Mexico and that Mexico had ceded California to Britain. Jones, the report continued, was en route presumably to preempt the British move. See Gene A. Smith, "Thomas ap Catesby Jones and the First Implementation of the Monroe Doctrine," *Southern California Quarterly* 76 no. 2 (Summer 1994): 139–52.

45. Juan Nepomuceno Almonte to Webster, February 7, 1842, ibid., 461–62.

46. Juan Nepomuceno Almonte to Webster, February 7, 1842, ibid., 477–78.

47. Howard Jones, *Mutiny on the Amistad* (New York: Oxford University Press, 1987), 207.

48. Howard Jones, *Mutiny on the Amistad*, 152–53; Baxter, *One and Inseparable*, 454–55.

49. *DP*, 1:194–228. See exchanges between the Spanish minister to Washington Pedro Alcántara de Argaiz from May 29, 1841, to December 5, 1842, ibid. Washington Irving wrote from Madrid on December 5, 1842, that the Spanish had denied any linkage between claims owed and the *Amistad*. See Washington Irving to Webster, ibid., 226–29.

50. Aaron Vail to Webster, November 30, 1841, ibid., 364; John Tyler to Webster, December 16, 1841, ibid., 367; Webster to Robert Blair Campbell, January 14, 1843, ibid., 370; Webster to Washington Irving, March 14, 1843, ibid., 372.

51. "The 'Tyler Doctrine,'" ibid., 851–57; Webster to Timoteo Haalilio and William Richards, December 19, 1842, ibid., 870–71.

52. Richardson, *Messages*, 4:2064–65.

53. Peter Parker to Webster, January 30, 1841, *DP*, 1:885–89.

54. List of Articles for the Legation to China, ibid., 907–10.

55. Webster to Caleb Cushing, May 8, 1843, ibid., 923–25.

56. For a detailed examination of the critical first stages of US diplomacy with the Hawaiian Kingdom and China, see Kenneth E. Shewmaker, "Forging the 'Great Chain': Daniel Webster and the Origins of American Foreign Policy toward East Asia and the Pacific, 1841–1852," *Proceedings of the American Philosophical Society* 129 (September 1985): 225–59.

57. See *DP*, 1:796–802. Further, the extradition model established in the Webster-Ashburton Treaty prompted both France and Prussia to seek the same arrangement with the United States. Webster concluded a convention with France, signed by his successor the month after Webster's death. Complications delayed the Prussian version, however, and postponed success until his return to the State Department almost a decade later. See *DP*, 2:187–91; Webster to David Porter, February 2, 1842, ibid., 1:280–81.

Chapter Five

1. Quoted in Claude Moore Fuess, *Daniel Webster*, 2 vols. (Boston: Little, Brown, 1930), 2:133–34; Maurice Glen Baxter, *One and Inseparable: Daniel Webster and the Union* (Cambridge, MA: Harvard University Press, 1984), 368.

2. Quoted in Fuess, *Daniel Webster*, 2:138–39; Baxter, *One and Inseparable*, 369.

3. Donald A. Rakestraw, *For Honor or Destiny: The Anglo-American Crisis over the Oregon Territory* (New York: Peter Lang, 1995), 75–76.

4. Baxter, *One and Inseparable*, 371–72; Ward quoted in Robert Remini, *Daniel Webster: The Man and His Time* (New York: Norton, 1997), 601; for details of the an-

nuity, see David Sears to Webster, March 21, 1846, W&S, 16:445. While it was not novel for political figures to accept financial support, Webster's level of unabashed solicitation bordered on vulgar.

5. Upshur was killed at the end of February 1844 when a demonstration of naval ordinance on the battleship *Princeton* turned tragic as the cannon "peacemaker" exploded.

6. Pakenham to Lord Aberdeen, April 28, 1844, TNA: FO 5/404; Rakestraw, *For Honor or Destiny*, 80.

7. Webster to Robert Winthrop, April 28, 1844, *The Papers of Daniel Webster: Correspondence*, ed. Charles Wiltse, 7 vols. (Hanover, NH: Dartmouth, 1974), 6:46; Baxter, *One and Inseparable*, 375; *Cong. Globe*, 28th Cong., 2nd sess., 16–17, 19–20; Remini, *The Man and His Time*, 600.

8. Baxter, *One and Inseparable*, 373–76; *National Intelligencer*, March 16, 1844.

9. Baxter, *One and Inseparable*, 373; Allan L. Benson, *Daniel Webster* (New York: Cosmopolitan Book Corp., 1929), 292.

10. Baxter, *One and Inseparable*, 375–77; *Cong. Globe*, 29th Cong., 1st sess., 93.

11. Rakestraw, *For Honor or Destiny*, 74–80, 85.

12. Rakestraw, *For Honor or Destiny*, 87; Pakenham to Lord Aberdeen, December 29, 1844, in *British Documents on Foreign Policy: Reports from the Foreign Office Confidential Print*, eds. Kenneth Bourne and Cameron D. Watt, Part I, Series C, 6 vols. (Lanham, MD: University Publications of America, 1986), 2:152–54.

13. Rakestraw, *For Honor or Destiny*, 96; Edward Everett to James Buchanan, April 2, 1845, Department of State, Despatches, Great Britain, National Archives, Washington, DC, Aberdeen to Pakenham, April 6, 1845, TNA: FO 115/88; Hansard's Parliamentary Debates, LXXIX, 115–24.

14. Baxter, *One and Inseparable*, 379.

15. Peel to Lord Francis Egerton, January 6, 1846, in *Sir Robert Peel from His Private Papers*, ed. Charles Stuart Parker, 3 vols. (London: J. Murray, 1899), 3:324; Rakestraw, *For Honor or Destiny*, 126.

16. Speech in Faneuil Hall, November 7, 1845, W&S, 13:318; *National Intelligencer*, November 11, 1845; Baxter, *One and Inseparable*, 379; Webster to David Sears, January 17, 1846, Wiltse, *Papers: Correspondence*, 6:111–12.

17. Pakenham to Lord Aberdeen, November 13, 1845, TNA: FO 5/429; McLane to Polk, December 1, 1845, Polk Papers, Library of Congress, Washington, DC.

18. *Cong. Globe*, 29th Cong., 1st sess., 4–11.

19. Pakenham to Lord Aberdeen, July 29, 1845, TNA: FO 5/427; Rakestraw, *For Honor or Destiny*, 106.

20. *Cong. Globe*, 29th Cong., 1st sess., Appendix, 841–42, 63; W&S, 9:67.

21. Fuess, *Webster*, 2:157.

22. Ashburton to Webster, January 1846, C. H. Van Tyne, ed., *The Letters of Daniel Webster* (New York: Haskell House, 1969), 309; Rakestraw, *For Honor or Destiny*, 158; "The Oregon Question," *Quarterly Review* 154 (March 1846): 219–37.

23. The quote is from Pakenham to Aberdeen, February 8, 1846, TNA: FO 5/446; Congress was made aware of British actions in a document transfer from the president

that included a January dispatch from McLane to Buchanan. *Cong. Globe*, 29th Cong., 1st sess., 332–35.

24. Webster to Haven, February 2, 1846, *W&S*, 18:216; Webster to Everett, February 5, 1846, *Cong. Globe*, 29th Cong., 1st sess., 217; Fuess, *Webster*, 2:156–57.

25. Rakestraw, *For Honor or Destiny*, 158; Webster to Peter Harvey, May 1846, *W&S*, 16:453.

26. Rakestraw, *For Honor or Destiny*, 173; Fuess, *Webster*, 2:158.

27. Rakestraw, *For Honor or Destiny*, 161–62; Webster to F. Webster, May 20, 1846, *W&S*, 16:450.

28. Seward also confirmed this to a close friend of Webster's. See Seward to R. M. Blatchford, March 23, 1846, Van Tyne, *Letters*, 311–16; *W&S*, 14:294; Baxter, *One and Inseparable*, 382; Webster to F. Webster, May 20, 1846, *W&S*, 16:449.

29. Richard N. Current, *Daniel Webster and the Rise of National Conservatism* (Boston: Little, Brown, 1955; Prospect Heights, IL: Waveland Press, 1992), 139; Merrill D. Peterson, *The Great Triumvirate: Webster, Clay, and Calhoun* (New York: Oxford University Press, 1987), 391.

30. Webster to F. Webster, May 25, 1846, *W&S*, 16:450.

31. Webster to F. Webster, May 17, 31, 1846, *W&S*, 16:450–51. There are a number of pieces of Webster correspondence relevant to the Ingersoll matter in Van Tyne, *Letters*, 309–28. These include notes that Webster jotted down addressing each charge in turn, 319–23; for a detailed account of the Ingersoll attack on Webster, see Howard Jones, "The Attempt to Impeach Daniel Webster," *Capitol Studies* 3 (Fall 1975): 31–44.

32. Webster to F. Webster, January 27, 1846, Van Tyne, *Letters*, 307; Current, *Rise of National Conservatism*, 146–47.

33. *Cong. Globe*, 29th Cong., 1st sess., 1153–54; See Scott C. James and David A. Lake, "The Second Face of Hegemony: Britain's Repeal of the Corn Laws and the American Walker Tariff of 1846," *International Organization* 43, no. 1 (Winter 1989): 1–29.

34. Webster to Franklin Haven, May 28, Wiltse, *Papers: Correspondence*, 6:164; *Cong. Globe*, 29th Cong., 1st sess., 1014–16.

35. Quoted in Baxter, *One and Inseparable*, 396.

36. Baxter, *One and Inseparable*, 390–92.

37. *W&S*, 9:253; Fuess, *Webster*, 2:170.

38. Quoted in Fuess, *Webster*, 2:178.

39. Fuess, *Webster*, 2:183, 171; *W&S*, 10:3–33; Baxter, *One and Inseparable*, 402–3.

40. *W&S*, 10:34–44; *Cong. Globe*, 30th Cong., 1st sess., 1060–61, 1077–80; Baxter, *One and Inseparable*, 405.

41. Quoted in Irving H. Bartlett, *Daniel Webster* (New York: Norton, 1978), 223; Fuess, *Webster*, 2:184.

42. Webster to Blatchford, February 19, 1849, Wiltse, *Papers: Correspondence*, 6:315–17.

43. Quoted in Fuess, *Webster*, 2:194.

44. New Mexico, organized by the Mormons from Salt Lake, moved a bit slower and would not have an operational government until the following summer.

45. The meeting between Webster and Clay is described in Curtis, *The Life of Daniel Webster*, 2:397; *Cong. Globe*, 31st Cong., 1st sess., 244–52; Baxter, *One and Inseparable*, 409–10.

46. Webster to F. Webster, February 24, 1850, *W&S*, 16:534.

47. *W&S*, 10:57–99, exchange with Calhoun, 76–77; Baxter, *One and Inseparable*, 413; *The Great Speeches and Orations of Daniel Webster*, Edwin Whipple, ed. (Boston: Little, Brown, 1879), 607, 612; Bartlett, *Daniel Webster*, 246–51.

48. "Speech of the 7th of March, 1850," in Whipple, *Speeches and Orations*, 604, 622; Baxter, *One and Inseparable*, 419; Robert Winthrop felt that the speech "knocked the Nashville Convention into a cocked hat." Quoted in Fuess, *Webster*, 2:233.

49. Bartlett, *Daniel Webster*, 244, 249; *W&S*, 10:97; Whipple, *Speeches and Orations*, 623.

50. Quoted in Bartlett, *Daniel Webster*, 268.

51. Webster to Mr. Harvey, March 28, 1850, *W&S*, 18:363; Bartlett, *Daniel Webster*, 251; *W&S*, 13:387.

52. *W&S*, 10:161; Bartlett, *Daniel Webster*, 251–52.

53. Remini, *The Man and His Time*, 691–93.

54. Remini, *The Man and His Time*, 688–89, 693; Webster to Peter Harvey, September 10, 1850, Wiltse, *Papers: Correspondence*, 7:143.

Chapter Six

1. Claude Moore Fuess, *Daniel Webster*, 2 vols. (Boston: Little, Brown, 1930), 2:248; It is not surprising that Webster's foes in Congress would find troubling his pressing for the final indemnity from the Treaty of Guadalupe Hidalgo. After all, his Boston friends, including the agent for Baring Brothers, were tasked with the distribution of funds. See *Cong. Globe*, 31st Cong., 2nd sess., 686–704 and correspondence from a number of supporters calling the charges slanderous in George Ticknor Curtis, *Life of Daniel Webster*, 2 vols. (New York: D. Appleton and Company, 1870), 2:492–97; In February, Massachusetts congressman George Ashmun defended Webster in the House and expressed confidence that all "generous-hearted men of all parties" would join him in "repelling the attacks." *Cong. Globe*, 31st Cong., 2nd sess., 687.

2. Webster to Richard Blatchford, May 4, 1851, *PC*, 2:441; Quoted in Kenneth E. Shewmaker, "Daniel Webster and the Politics of Foreign Policy, 1850–1852," *Journal of American History* 63, no. 2 (September 1976): 304.

3. Webster to George Ticknor, August 15, 1850, *W&S*, 16:562; Maurice Glen Baxter, *One and Inseparable: Daniel Webster and the Union* (Cambridge, MA: Harvard University Press, 1984), 461.

4. Fuess, *Daniel Webster*, 2:249–50.

5. James D. Richardson, ed., *A Compilation of the Messages and Papers of the Presidents*, 20 vols. (Washington, DC: Bureau of National Literature, 1917), 6:2550;

Fuess, *Daniel Webster*, 2:250; Baxter, *One and Inseparable*, 464; Hülsemann to Webster, September 30, 1850, DP, 2:45.

6. Emerson's comment appears in Ralph Waldo Emerson, "Address to Citizens of Concord, 3 May, 1851," *The Complete Works*, 12 vols. (New York and Boston: Houghton, Mifflin, 1904), 11:201; Bartlett attributes a similar quote to Emerson in "Daniel Webster as a Symbolic Hero," *New England Quarterly* XLV (December 1972): 487.

7. Hülsemann to Webster, September 30, 1850, DP, 2:44–45.

8. Webster to Fillmore, January 16, 1851, W&S, 16:585.

9. Fuess, *Daniel Webster*, 2:251; Baxter, *One and Inseparable*, 465.

10. Italicized emphasis appears in the original. Webster to Ticknor, January 16, 1851, W&S, 16:586; Webster to Hülsemann, December 21, 1850, DP, 2:50.

11. Webster to Hülsemann, December 21, 1850, ibid., 56.

12. Webster to Hülsemann, December 21, 1850, ibid., 53–54.

13. Webster to Everett, October 20, 1850, ibid., 47; Robert Remini, *Daniel Webster: The Man and His Time* (New York: Norton, 1997), 699; Webster to Hülsemann, December 21, 1850, DP, 2:54.

14. Curtis, *The Life of Daniel Webster*, 2:558; Robert Remini, *The Man and His Time* (New York: Norton, 1997), 698.

15. Webster to Hülsemann, December 21, 1850, DP, 2:58–60; Hülsemann to Webster, March 11, 1851, W&S, 12:179.

16. Baxter, *One and Inseparable*, 467; What would over time evolve into the notion of American exceptionalism appeared in Tocqueville's *Democracy in America*, ed. J. P. Mayer (New York, Perennial Classics, 2000), 455; Samuel Finley Breeze Morse to Webster, January 20, 1851, DP, 2:64.

17. Webster to George P. Marsh, February 28, 1851, W&S, 12:265; For an example of the American interest in Kossuth see, J. W. Oliver, "Louis Kossuth's Appeal to the Middle West—1852," *The Mississippi Valley Historical Review* 14 (March 1928):481–95.

18. Speech delivered to the Pennsylvania House of Representatives, April 1, 1851, W&S, 13:401–4.

19. Webster to Franklin Haven, December 23, 1851, ibid., 18:497; Webster to Richard Blatchford, December 30, 1851, ibid., 501–2.

20. Address to Kossuth Banquet, January 7, 1852, DP, 2:97–105; W&S, 13:452–62; See also Remini, *The Man and His Time*, 702–3; *National Intelligencer* (Washington, DC), January 8, 1852.

21. F. Webster to Webster, November 28, 1851, *The Papers of Daniel Webster Correspondence*, ed. Charles Wiltse, 7 vols. (Hanover, NH: Dartmouth, 1974), 7:289–90; Quoted in Remini, *The Man and His Time*, 730.

22. Hülsemann to Webster, April 29, 1852, DP, 2:118.

23. Remini, *The Man and His Time*, 704.

24. Webster to Fillmore, January 7, 1852, PC, 2:503; Webster to Richard Blatchford, January 11, 1852, DP, 2:106; Remini, *The Man and His Time*, 704.

25. Quoted in Clyde Augustus Duniway, "Daniel Webster: Secretary of State," in *The American Secretaries of State and Their Diplomacy*, ed. Samuel Flagg Bemis, 20 vols. (New York: Cooper Square Publishers, 1963), 6:93.

26. Quoted in *DP*, 2:11.

27. *Cong. Globe*, 31st Cong., 1st sess., 1032–34.

28. Fuess, *Daniel Webster*, 2:258; Webster to Richard Blatchford, April 30, 1851, *W&S*, 18:437.

29. Webster to Angel Calderón de la Barca, November 13, 1851, *DP*, 2: 398; Duniway, "Webster: Secretary of State," 105–6; Fuess, *Daniel Webster*, 2:259.

30. *W&S*, 12:183; Duniway, "Webster: Secretary of State," 107.

31. Duniway, "Webster: Secretary of State," 107. See Curtis, *The Life of Daniel Webster*, 2:553–57.

32. Duniway, "Webster: Secretary of State," 95; Webster to Fillmore, February 3, 1851, *W&S*, 18:416–17; Fuess, *Daniel Webster*, 2:260.

33. Webster to Lawrence, December 3, 1851, *W&S*, 14:450; Webster to Lawrence, December 29, 1851, ibid., 16:634.

34. Quoted in "Daniel Webster and the Western Hemisphere," *DP*, 2:313. Webster's decision to accept military pressure on an American state by Europeans strayed from the intent of the Monroe Doctrine. See Dexter Perkins, *The Monroe Doctrine 1826–1867* (Baltimore: Johns Hopkins University Press, 1933), 266–67.

35. Palmer called for compensation for Japanese ill treatment of American sailors, a commitment to grant American whalers unimpeded access to Japanese waters, provide for coaling stations, and sign a commercial treaty or face a US naval blockade. See Aaron Haight Palmer, *Documents and Facts Illustrating the Origin of the Mission to Japan, Authorized by the Government of the United States, May 10, 1851; And Which Finally Resulted in Treaty Concluded by Commodore M.C. Perry, U.S. Navy, With the Japanese Commissioners at Kanagawa Bay of Yedo, on the 31st March 1854* (Washington: Henry Polkinhorn, 1857), 11–13; *DP*, 2:254; Palmer, *Mission to Japan*, 20; Glynn to Fillmore, June 10, 1851, *DP*, 2:292–97; "Daniel Webster and the Pacific and East Asia," ibid., 246, 253; Webster to John H. Aulick, June 10, 1851, ibid., 289–90; Glynn to Fillmore, June 10, 1851, ibid., 293–94.

36. In 1837 the American ship *Morrison* and in 1845 the *Manhattan* out of New York both had unsuccessfully attempted to use the return of Japanese sailors as an opening to commerce with the Empire. See "Daniel Webster and the Pacific and East Asia," ibid., 252–53; Remini, *The Man and His Time*, 711; Webster to William Alexander Graham, May 9, 1851, *DP*, 2:288. Webster to William Alexander Graham, May 9, 1851, *DP*, 2:290–91.

37. Webster to William Alexander Graham, May 9, 1851, *DP*, 2:290–91.

38. Fillmore to Webster, January 12, 1852, ibid., 298; Webster to Matthew Perry, March 16, 1852, ibid., 299; Webster to George Folsom, June 14, 1852, ibid., 302.

39. "Daniel Webster and the Pacific and East Asia," ibid., 258; See Shewmaker, "Forging the 'Great Chain,'" 238–59.

40. "Daniel Webster and the Pacific and East Asia," *DP*, 2:250–51.

41. Shewmaker, "Forging the 'Great Chain,'" 243–44.
42. Webster to David Porter, February 2, 1842, *DP*, 1:280–81.
43. Webster to George Perkins Marsh, April 29, 1852, ibid., *DP*, 2:205–6.
44. Webster to George Perkins Marsh, April 29, 1852, *DP*, 2: 208.
45. Baxter, *One and Inseparable*, 468; *DP*, 2:508.
46. Quoted in "Daniel Webster and the Western Hemisphere," *DP*, 2:511.
47. "Daniel Webster and the Western Hemisphere," *DP*, 2:512. See Remini, *The Man and His Time*, 516–18.
48. "Daniel Webster and the Western Hemisphere," *DP*, 2:518. See also J. Fred Rippy, "Diplomacy of the United States and Mexico Regarding the Isthmus of Tehuantepec, 1848–1860," *The Mississippi Valley Historical Review*, 6, no. 4 (March 1920): 503–31.
49. Remini, *The Man and His Time*, 751; Webster to Jewett, June 5, 1852, *DP*, 2:737.
50. *DP*, 2:713; Webster's instructions to his Marshfield hands often included the proper mix of guano. See, for example, Webster to Porter Wright, November 13, 1851, *PC*, 2:486.
51. Webster to Robinson, September 25, 1850, *DP*, 2:726, 715; Richardson, *Messages and Papers*, 5:83.
52. "Daniel Webster's Final Days," *DP*, 2:719; Filmore to Webster, July 8, 1852, ibid., 743; Webster to Fillmore, July 13, 1852, ibid., 744; Remini, *The Man and His Time*, 752.
53. Webster to Hiram Ketchum, August 21, 1852, *DP*, 2:760.
54. Webster to Juan Ygnacio de Osma, August 21, 1852, ibid., 761–68.
55. John Randolph Clay to Webster, June 24, 1852, ibid., 739–42.
56. Webster to John Randolph Clay, August 30, 1852, ibid., 772–73.
57. Fillmore to Webster, September 19, 1852, ibid., 775–77; Webster to Fillmore, September 15, 1852, ibid., 774.
58. Charles Mynn Conrad to John Randolph Clay, September 21, 1852, ibid., 777–79; Everett to Joaquin José de Osma, November 16, 1852, ibid., 787.
59. For details on Webster's mishandling of the Lobos Island affair, see Kenneth E. Shewmaker, "'Untaught Diplomacy': Daniel Webster and the Lobos Islands Controversy," *Diplomatic History* I (Fall 1977): 321–40.
60. Miller, ed., *Treaties*, 2:658–59; "Daniel Webster's Final Days," *DP*, 2:673; For an exhaustive treatment of the fisheries dispute, see Kenneth E. Shewmaker, "'Hook and Line, Bob and Sinker': Daniel Webster and the Fisheries Dispute of 1852," *Diplomatic History* 68, no. 2 (April 1985): 113–29.
61. Quoted in Wilbur Devereux Jones, *The American Problem in British Diplomacy, 1841–1861* (Athens: University of Georgia Press, 1974), 109.
62. Webster to Crampton, July 17, 1852, *W&S*, 18:39; Webster to Crampton, July 17, 1852, enclosed in Webster to Fillmore, same date, *DP*, 2:688; Fuess, *Daniel Webster*, 2:262.
63. Remini, *The Man and His Times*, 746; Webster's letter appeared in the Boston *Courier*, July 19, 1852.

64. Four days after Webster's Seventh of March speech in the Clay compromise debates of 1850, Seward declared that Congress must yield the disposition of slavery to a "higher law than the Constitution." *Cong. Globe*, 31st Cong., 1st sess., 265; For congressional reaction to Webster's letter, see *Cong. Globe*, 32nd Cong., 1st sess., 1890–97; "Daniel Webster's Final Days," *DP*, 2:677.

65. Curtis, *The Life of Daniel Webster*, 2:645–46.

66. Webster to Fillmore, July 25, 1852, *DP*, 2:696–97; Webster had telegrammed State Department secretary William Hunter from New Hampshire requesting that the president dispatch a naval vessel to the area "to give notice." See Webster to Hunter, July 19, 1852, ibid., 688.

67. Lord Malmesbury to Crampton, August 10, 1852, ibid., 706–11; Lord Malmesbury to Abbott Lawrence, August 13, 1852, ibid., 711.

68. Webster to F. Webster, August 10, 1852, Van Tyne, *Letters*, 536; Webster to Richard Blatchford, August 24, 1852, *DP*, 2:712.

69. Webster to Fillmore, October 18, Wiltse, *Paper: Correspondence*, 7:364–65.

70. Quoted in Bartlett, *Daniel Webster*, 292.

Epilogue

1. Quoted in Kenneth E. Shewmaker, ed., *Daniel Webster: "The Completest Man"* (Hanover, NH: University Press of New England, 1990), xix.

2. Webster to Sergio T. de Macedo, May 7, 1851, *DP*, 2:659.

3. Irving H. Bartlett, *Daniel Webster* (New York: Norton, 1978), 264.

4. Charles Sumner, *The Works of Charles Sumner* (Boston: Lee and Shepard, 1874), 1:314–15.

5. Webster to Everett, January 29, 1843, *W&S*, 11:271.

6. Howard Jones, "The Diplomatist," in Shewmaker, *"The Completest Man,"* 224.

Bibliographical Essay

Daniel Webster has generated a small library of work from his own pen, that of his contemporaries, and over a century of biographers and Webster scholars. Harold D. Moser has drawn all of this together in his masterful work, *Daniel Webster: A Bibilography* (Westport, CT: Praeger, 2005), providing an exhaustive compilation of annotated titles from archival materials to scholarly articles. Few veins of primary sources are richer than Webster's; and thanks to the dedication of Webster scholars and his beloved Dartmouth College, that vein has not only been mined, but its lode has been made available in a variety of media from microfilm, to print, and finally digital facsimile. Fletcher Webster's two volumes of his father's letters, *The Private Correspondence of Daniel Webster* (Boston, 1857), provide candid insight into Webster's approach to life and work. Daniel Webster's former student, then colleague, Edward Everett, edited one of the earliest collections of Webster papers in his six-volume *The Works of Daniel Webster* (Boston, 1851). *The Life of Daniel Webster* (New York, 1870), a two-volume biography by Webster contemporary George Ticknor Curtis, contains entire passages from Webster documents and is a valuable resource for all aspects of Webster's life. In the early twentieth century, C.H. Van Tyne edited *The Letters of Daniel Webster* (New York, 1902), providing an important collection of Webster correspondence. The following year, James W. McIntyre published an exhaustive eighteen-volume collection of Webster materials in his National Edition of Daniel Webster, *Writings and Speeches* (Boston, 1903). All of the above sources have been digitized and are available online.

No one has made Webster's documents and papers more accessible than Kenneth E. Shewmaker and Charles M. Wiltse. The latter was chief editor of the multi-volume collections of *The Papers of Daniel Webster: Correspondence* (Hanover, 1974-86) and *The Papers of Daniel Webster: Speeches and Formal Writings* (Hanover, 1986-88). Shewmaker's two volume collection, *The Papers of Daniel Webster: Diplomatic Papers* (Hanover, 1983-1987) is essential for all studies of Webster's foreign policy. For Webster's legal career, Andrew J. King and Alfred S. Konefsky have edited several volumes of *The Papers of Daniel Webster: Legal Papers* (Hanover, 1982-1989). An excellent source for Webster's speeches remains Edwin P. Whipple, *The Great Speeches and Orations of Daniel Webster* (Boston, 1879). Lyon G. Tyler's three-volume collection, *The Letters and Times of the Tylers* (Richmond and Williamsburg, 1884-96) and Frank Severance's two-volume, *Millard Fillmore Papers* (Buffalo, 1907) provide additional sources for the two presidents in whose cabinet Webster served.

There are a number of excellent biographies of Webster, the earliest of which is Samuel P. Lyman, *Life and Memorials of Daniel Webster* (New York, 1858). The most recent is Robert Remini's, *Daniel Webster: The Man and His Times* (New York, 1997). Remini provides the most comprehensive study of Webster to date and is essential to following Webster's life and development into an iconic figure in American history. Maurice G. Baxter's *One and Inseparable: Daniel Webster and the Union* (Cambridge, 1984) remains an excellent scholarly treatment that gives considerable attention to Webster's foreign policy; Irving H. Bartlett, *Daniel Webster* (New York, 1978) brings Webster's personality to life, adding color and dimension to Black Dan while Richard Current's *Daniel Webster and the Rise of National Conservatism* (Boston, 1955) provides an essential and concise treatment of Webster the politician. Claude Fuess's two-volume *Daniel Webster* (Boston, 1930) remains a good treatment of Webster that offers unique contours in a comprehensive examination of Webster's life and career.

Daniel Webster served in Congress during the administrations of ten presidents and on the cabinets of three. Of these, Andrew Jackson, William Henry Harrison, John Tyler, James K. Polk, and Millard Fillmore merit particular attention. For Jackson, Arthur Schlesinger, Jr.'s *The Age of Jackson* (Boston, 1945); Robert Remini's *Andrew Jackson* (New York, 1969); and H.W. Brands' *Andrew Jackson: His Life and Times* (New York, 2005) are useful. Edward P. Crapol's *John Tyler: The Accidental President* (Chapel Hill, 2006) offers a balanced appraisal of the Tyler presidency. An additional source for Tyler that also addresses Harrison is Norma Lois Peterson's *The Presidencies of William Henry Harrison and John Tyler* (Lawrence, 1989). Paul

Bergeron's concise treatment in *The Presidency of James K. Polk* (Lawrence, 1987) contains coverage of important foreign policy questions that concerned Webster between his two terms at State. My own work, *For Honor or Destiny: The Anglo-American Crisis over the Oregon Territory* (New York, 1995), provides detailed coverage of the dispute over the Pacific Northwest that involved Webster. Robert J. Rayback's *Millard Fillmore: Biography of a President* (Buffalo, 1959) remains a reliable source for the thirteenth president. Elbert B. Smith's contribution to the University of Kansas presidential series, *The Presidencies of Zachary Taylor and Millard Fillmore* (Lawrence, 1988), is a concise and thoughtful account of the administration of Taylor and Fillmore. A more recent study by Paul Finkelman, *Millard Fillmore: The American Presidents Series: The 13th President, 1850-1853* (New York, 2011), is also helpful.

For the study of Webster the diplomatist, two historians merit particular attention. No scholar has devoted more time and effort to Webster's foreign policy than Kenneth E. Shewmaker. In addition to his editing of Webster's diplomatic papers, he has produced a number of articles addressing Webster's diplomacy. Among those most helpful are, "Daniel Webster and the Politics of Foreign Policy, 1850-1852," *Journal of American History* 63 (September 1976): 303-15; "'Untaught Diplomacy'": Daniel Webster and the Lobos Islands Controversy," *Diplomatic History*, 1 (October 1977): 321-40; "Daniel Webster and the Oregon Question," *Pacific Historical Review*, 51 (May 1982):195-201; "Hook and Line, and Bob and Sinker: Daniel Webster and the Fisheries Dispute of 1852." *Diplomatic History* 9 (Spring 1985): 113-29; "Forging the 'Great Chain': Daniel Webster and the Origins of American Foreign Policy toward East Asia and the Pacific, 1841-1852," *Proceedings of the American Philosophical Society*, 129 (September 1985): 225-259; "'Congress Can Only Declare War' and 'the President Is Commander in Chief': Daniel Webster and the War Power," *Diplomatic History* 12 (Fall 1988): 383-410; "'This unblessed war': Daniel Webster's opposition to the War of 1812," *Historical New Hampshire*, 53 (Spring-Summer 1998): 21-45; and, a collection of essays with selected documentary evidence, *Daniel Webster: "The Completest Man."* (1990). Likewise, Howard Jones has spent decades developing Webster's diplomatic record. The most essential Jones works are "The Peculiar Institution and National Honor: The Case of the *Creole* Slave Revolt," *Civil War History* 21 (March 1975): 28-50; "The Attempt to Impeach Daniel Webster," *Capitol Studies*, 3 (Fall 1975):31-44; "Anglophobia and the Aroostook War," New England Quarterly 48 (December 1975): 519-39; "The *Caroline* Affair," *Historian* 38 (May 1976): 485-502; "Daniel Webster: The Diplomatist," in *Daniel Webster: "The Completest Man,"* ed.

Kenneth E. Shewmaker (Hanover, 1990):203-96; and his books *To the Webster-Ashburton Treaty* (Chapel Hill, 1977), *Mutiny on the Amistad: The Saga of a Slave Revolt and Its Impact on American Abolition, Law, and Diplomacy* (New York, 1987), and with Donald A. Rakestraw, *Prologue to Manifest Destiny: Anglo-American Relations in the 1840s* (Wilmington, 1997).

Among other works useful for the study of Webster's diplomacy are: J. W. Oliver, "Louis Kossuth's Appeal to the Middle West – 1852," *The Mississippi Valley Historical. Review* 14 (March 1928):481-495; Alastair Watt, "The Case of Alexander McLeod," *The Canadian Historical Review* 12 (June 1931): 145-67; Earl R. McClendon, "Daniel Webster and Mexican Relations: The Santa Fe Prisoners," *Southwestern Historical Quarterly* 36 (April 1933): 288-311; Hugh G. Soulsby, *The Right of Search and the Slave Trade in Anglo-American Relations, 1814-1862* (Baltimore, 1933); Ralph S. Kuykendall, *The Hawaiian Kingdom, 1778 – 1854: Foundation and Transformation* (Honolulu, 1938-67); Harold Whitman Bradley, *The American Frontier in Hawaii* (Stanford, 1942); Richard Current, "Webster's Propaganda and the Ashburton Treaty," *The Mississippi Valley Historical Review* 34 (September 1947): 187-200; Chester A. Bain, "Commodore Matthew Perry, Humphrey Marshall, and the Taiping Rebellion," *Far Eastern Quarterly* (May 1951): 258-70; Frederick Merk, "The Oregon Question in the Webster-Ashburton Negotiations," *Mississippi Valley Historical Review* 43 (December 1956): 379-404; Wilbur D. Jones, *Lord Aberdeen and the Americas* (Athens, 1958) and *The American Problem in British Diplomacy, 1841-1861* (Athens, 1974); Clyde Augustus Duniway, "Daniel Webster: Secretary of State," in *The American Secretaries of State and their Diplomacy*, ed. Samuel Flagg Bemis (New York, 1963): 3-64, 77-113; Thomas LeDuc, "The Webster-Ashburton Treaty and the Minnesota Iron Ranges," *The Journal of American History* 51 (December 1964):476-81; Betty Fladeland, *Men and Brothers: Anglo-American Antislavery Cooperation* (Urbana, 1972); Donald S. Spencer, *Louis Kossuth and Young America: A Study of Sectionalism and Foreign Policy, 1848-1852* (Columbia, 1977); Merrill D. Peterson, *The Great Triumvirate: Webster, Clay, and Calhoun* (New York, 1987); J. Chris Arndt, "Maine in the Northeastern Boundary Controversy: States' Rights in Antebellum New England," *The New England Quarterly* 62 (June 1989):205-23; Kenneth R. Stevens, *Border Diplomacy: The Caroline and McLeod Affairs in Anglo-American-Canadian Relations, 1837-1842* (Tuscaloosa, 1989); Paul A. Varg, *Edward Everett: The Intellectual in the Turmoil of Politics* (Selinsgrove, 1992); Tom Chaffin, *Fatal Glory: Narciso López and the First Clandestine U.S. War against Cuba* (Baton Rouge, 1996); Timothy D. Johnson, *Winfield Scott: The Quest for Military Glory* (Knoxville, 1998); Francis M. Carroll, "Kings and Crises: Arbitrating the Canadian-American

Boundary Dispute in the Belgium Crisis of 1830-1831," *The New England Quarterly* 73 (June 2000): 179-201 and *A Good and Wise Measure: The Search for the Canadian-American Boundary, 1783-1842* (Toronto, 2001); David M. Pletcher, *The Diplomacy of Involvement: American Economic Expansion across the Pacific, 1784-1900* (Columbia, 2001); Robert A. May, *Manifest Destiny's Underworld: Filibustering in Antebellum America* (Chapel Hill, 2002); Anthony Clark Arend, "International Law and the Preemptive Use of Military Force," *The Washington Quarterly* 26 (Spring 2003): 89-103; Kaufman, Scott, and John A. Soares, Jr. "'Sagacious Beyond Praise'? Winfield Scott and Anglo-American-Canadian Border Diplomacy, 1837-1860,"*Diplomatic History* 30 (January 2006): 57-82; Macabe Keliher, "Anglo-American Rivalry and the Origins of U.S. China Policy," *Diplomatic History* (April 2007): 227-57; John P.D. Dunbabin, "'Red Lines on Maps' Revisited: The Role of Maps in Negotiating and Defending the 1842 Webster-Ashburton Treaty," *Imago Mundi: The International Journal for the History of Cartography* 63 (January 2011):39-61; Arthur T. Downey, *The Creole Affair: The Slave Rebellion That Led the U.S. and Great Britain to the Brink of War* (Lanham, 2014).

Additional collections from which useful material may be drawn for studies of Webster's foreign policy are Herbert B. Adams, *The Life and Writings of Jared Sparks: Comprising Selections from His Journal and Correspondence* (Boston, 1893); John C. Dent, *The Story of the Upper Canadian Rebellion: Largely Derived from Original Sources and Documents* (Toronto, 1885); Great Britain, *British and Foreign State Papers*; Thomas C. Hansard, ed., *Hansard's Parliamentary Debates* (London, 1830-1891); William R. Manning, ed., *Diplomatic Correspondence of the United States. Canadian Relations, 1784-1860* (Millwood, 1940-45); *American State Papers, Foreign Relations* (Washington, 1832-1859); *Annals of Congress, Register of Debates*, and *Congressional Globe*; General Records of the Department of State, National Archives, College Park, MD; James K. Polk Papers, Library of Congress; the Lord Aberdeen Papers and Sir Robert Peel Papers at the British Library; and the Lord Ashburton Papers, Baring Brothers Papers, and Foreign Office files at the British National Archives at Kew Gardens, UK.

A figure as large as Webster generated considerable press. Examples of newspapers useful to understanding the public's perception of and influence on Webster as well as the diplomatic issues he faced are the *Advertiser* and the *Courier* (Boston); *Advertiser* (Portland); *Age* (Augusta); *Democratic Review*; *Morning Chronicle* (London); *Morning Herald* (London); *National Intelligencer* (Washington, DC); *Niles [National] Register*; *North American Review*; *Patriot* (Boston); *Punch* (London); *Royal Gazette* (New Brunswick); *Times* (London); and *Whig* (Bangor).

Index

abolitionism, 65, 81, 95, 105, 115, 118, 122
Aberdeen, Lord: on *Creole* Affair, 84; in the Foreign Office, 63, 111; on impressment, 81; on joint–squadron compromise, 82; on Northeastern Boundary Dispute, 67–69, 71, 76–78, 91–92, 148–52; on Oregon Question, 87–88, 106–9; on Quintuple Treaty, 64; on Tariff of 1842, 113
Adams, John, 19
Adams, John Quincy: and Adams–Onís Treaty (1819), 20; and *Amistad*, 95; character of, 112; and Cherokee Nation, 43; and conflict with Jacksonians, 156; and elections of 1824, 29; and noncolonization principle, 159; and presidency, 30–34, 49; as secretary of state, 19–20, 26–27, 49
Adams–Onís Treaty (1819), 19–21, 29, 162, 170n40
Agricola (ship), 67
Allen, Charles, 105
Allen, William, 108

Alligator (ship), 22
American and Foreign Agency of New York, 138
American Anti–Slavery Society, 103
American System, 28, 157, 171–72n11
Amin Bey, 131
Amistad (ship), 95–96, 182n49
Andover, Massachusetts, 101–2
Anglo–American relations: 4–7, 46–86, 88–92, 97, 100, 105–11, 135–37, 148–52, 158–59. *See also* Britain; foreign relations: and Britain
Anti–Masons, 36
Aroostook Valley, 48, 53–54, 58, 71
Aroostook War, 53, 66, 158
Ashburton, Lady, 68–69, 89
Ashburton, Lord (Alexander Barring): and *Caroline* Affair, 85–86; and *Creole* Affair, 82–84; as diplomat, 56, 67–69; on impressment, 81–82, 180n14; and Northeastern Boundary Dispute, 69, 72–81, 89–91, 108–9, 111–12, 163, 181n30; and Oregon Question, 86–88; on slave trade, 82, 179–80n14; and

197

Webster–Ashburton Treaty, 88–93, 158–59, 163, 182n57
Attucks, Crispus, 157
Aulick, John H., 138–39
Austria: and Hungarian Revolution of 1848, 126–34; and Quintuple Treaty, 64. See also foreign relations: and Austria

Bahamas, 64–65, 83–84
Bank of the United States, 45, 57, 162. See also National Bank
Bank War, 36–37, 40. See also National Bank
Barca, Calderon de la, 135
Baring Brothers, 41, 56–57, 67–68, 163
Baring, Alexander, See also Ashburton, Lord
Bartlett, Ichabod, 28
Bates, Joshua, 59
Battle of San Jacinto, 42
Bay Islands, 136
Bay of Fundy, 148
Belize, 136
Bell, Peter H., 123–24
Benjamin, Judah P., 142–43
Benton, Thomas Hart, 40–41, 62, 72, 89
Berkeley Plantation, 59
Berlin decree, 9
Berrien, John McPherson, 86
Biddle, Nicholas, 40
Bingham, William, 68
Blake, George, 22–23
Blatchford, Richard Milford, 118, 126, 133, 152
Bliss, Alexander, 20–22
Boscawen, New Hampshire, 5, 12
Boston, 4, 10, 15–30 passim., 34, 53, 56, 58, 73, 111, 122, 130, 149–50, 162
Brinsmade, Peter, 87
Britain: on Canadian–American fishing dispute, 148–52; and *Caroline* Affair, 50–53, 85–86, 88; and Central America, 136–37; and Clayton–Bulwer Treaty, 136; and *Creole* Affair, 65, 83–84, 88; and Emancipation Act, 65; and impressment, 8, 64, 79, 81–82, 158; and international trade, 5–7, 55, 57–58, 106–7, 168n11, 173n29; and Jay's Treaty (1794), 4, 20, 83; and McLeod Affair, 60, 62–63; and Northeastern Boundary Dispute, 47–49, 53–55, 60, 65–67, 69–74, 76–80, 88–92, 99; and Orders in Council (OIC), 5–7; and Oregon Question, 86–88, 100, 107–11; and Quintuple Treaty, 64; and Webster–Ashburton Treaty, 69–93
British Colonial Office, 62
British Museum, 91
British Orders in Council (OIC), 5–7, 9, 11
Brooks, Peter Chardon, 20–21
Brougham, Henry, 56
Brownville, Texas, 144
Buchanan, James, 107–8
Buckingham Palace, 56
Buffalo, New York, 50–51
Bull, John, 65, 108
Bulwer, Henry, 91, 136–37, 149, 164
Bunker Hill address: first (1825), 30; second (1843), 101, 164
Butler, Andrew, 150

Calhoun, John C.: on California statehood, 119–20; and Committee on Foreign Relations, 10–12, 37; as congressman, 10–12, 15; and death of, 120; and "Great Triumvirate", ix, 10, 119, 168n20; and Hawaiian independence, 98; and Mexican Cession, 117; and National Bank, 15; on Northeastern Boundary Dispute, 90; and Oregon Question,

Index ~ 199

105–8; as secretary of state, 98, 103, 105–8, 117, 119–20; as senator, 37, 39, 90; on tariffs, 37, 39; on Texas annexation, 103, 120, on War of 1812, 10–12
California: annexation of, 116–17, 138, 142; and Compromise of 1850, 119–20; and gold rush, 118; and Mexican–American War, 94, 181n44; and statehood, 118–20
Campbell, Robert Blain, 96–97
Canada: and Canadian–American fishing dispute, 148–52; and *Caroline* Affair, 85–86; and McLeod Affair, 51–53, 60, 62–63, 163, 176n26, 177n30; and Northeastern Boundary Dispute, 12–14, 47–49, 53–55, 60, 65–67, 69–74, 76–80, 88–92, 99; and trade reciprocity agreement, 149, 164
Caroline Affair, 50–53, 60, 62–63, 79, 84–86, 88, 158–59
Caroline Doctrine: 88, 159
Carson, Samuel P., 42
Carvajal, José Maria Jesus, 144
Cass, Lewis, 81, 102, 106, 118, 132
Cherokee Nation, 43–44
Cherokee National Council, 43
Chesapeake, USS, 5, 168n13
Choate, Rufus, 102–3, 125
Christian Mirror (Portland), 66–67
Churchill, Winston, 159
Clay, Henry: on Adams–Onís Treaty, 29; and his American System, 28, 171–72n11; on California statehood, 119, 164; on Cherokee Nation, 43–44, and Compromise of 1850, 119–20; and compromise tariff, 39–40; and elections of 1832, 37; and elections of 1844, 102, 105; as "The Great Compromiser," 119–20; and the "Great Triumvirate," ix, 10, 119, 168n20; on National Bank, 36–37; on protectionism, 28; as secretary of state, 30, 33, 36–37, 39–40, 43–44, 46, 60; as speaker of the house, 10, 13, 15, 25, 28–29; on Specie Circular, 46; on tariffs, 28
Clay, John Randolph, 146–47
Clayton, John, 117–18, 126–29, 134–37, 142, 145
Clayton–Bulwer Treaty, 136, 164
Colbrooke, William, 73–74
Columbia River, 21, 86–87, 105–6
Committee on Foreign Relations: House, 10, 27; Senate, 54, 108
Compromise of 1850, 119–27, 164
Concord, New Hampshire, 2, 5, 34
Connecticut River, 48, 76
Conrad, Charles M., 147
Conscience Whigs, 104–5, 122
Convention of 1818, 148–9
Convention of Kanagawa, 139
Corn Laws (British), 106, 113–14
Costa Rica, 137, 164
Cotton Whigs, 104, 115, 122, 156
Courier (Boston), 177n39
Court of St. James's, 29, 37, 98, 130, 158
Crampton, John Fiennes, 137, 149–52
Crawford, William, 29
Creole Affair, 63–65, 79, 81–84, 88, 158, 180 (nn16, 19)
Crittenden, George, 94
Crittenden, John, 94, 135
Cuba: and American commerce, 32, 96; and *Amistad*, 95–96; and annexation, 105, 134–37; and Panama Congress of 1826, 159; and Spain, 32, 96, 134–37
Curtis, Edward, 153
Cushing, Caleb, 98–100, 159, 164

Daily Times (New York), 165
d'Anville, Jean–Baptiste Bourguignon, 69

Dartmouth College, 3–4, 17, 161–62
Davies, John, 71
Davis, John, 42, 111
Democratic party, 40–41, 45, 58, 67, 92, 102–3, 113–14
Deshima, 138–39
Dickens, Charles, 56
Dickinson, Daniel, 117
Disraeli, Benjamin, 56
Dominican Republic, 137
Douglas, Stephen, 117, 124
Drew, Andrew, 50
Durfree, Amos, 50–52

Eastern Argus (Portland), 66–67
Elms Farm, 2, 58, 146, 149
Embargo Act (1807), 5–6, 161
Emerson, Ralph Waldo, 101, 122, 127, 155
Enquirer (New York), 177n39
Enquirer (Richmond), 67
Erskine Agreement, 6–8, 168n15
Erskine, David, 6–8
Evening Post (New York), 103
Everett, Edward: and Webster, 43, 58, 89, 128–29, 153; on *Creole* Affair, 64–65, 83, 180n16; as diplomat, 59, 63–65, 67, 71, 81–83, 92, 98, 105–6, 163; on equal protection, 142; on Greek War of Independence, 26–27, 171n4; on Hülsemann response, 128; on impressment, 81–82; on Northeastern Boundary Dispute, 67, 71, 92, 152, 178n45; on Oregon Question, 105–6, 109; on Quintuple Treaty, 64, 82, 179–80n14; as secretary of state, 136, 142, 147, 152; on slavery, 122
expansionism, 88, 93, 95–96, 102–4, 116–17, 124, 157
extradition, 65, 83, 88, 163, 165, 182n57

Fairfield, John, 72–73
Faneuil Hall, 18, 39, 102, 104–5, 107, 115, 127, 133, 155
Federalist party, 4–7, 10–13, 15, 25, 33, 156, 169n32, 171n11
Ferdinand VII (king of Spain), 3
filibustering, 134–35, 144, 159, 165
Fillmore, Millard: on Hungarian Revolution of 1848, 130–31, 133; on Central America, 135–37; on Compromise of 1850, 124, 127–28; on Crampton letter, 149–52; on equal protection, 141; on filibustering, 135; on Garray grant, 143–44; on Japan, 138; on Jonas King Affair, 141; on Lobos Affair, 145–47; and presidency, 122–52, 164; as vice president, 118
First Church in Plymouth, 19
First Seminole War, 19–20, 58, 60, 170n40
Fish River, 66
Fletcher, Grace, 5, 12, 15, 17, 33–35
Florida, 3, 19–21, 58, 60, 104
Foot, Samuel, 35
Force Bill (1833), 39
Foreign Office, 51, 63, 69, 71, 76, 82, 91, 111
foreign relations: and Austria, 126–34; and Britain, 4–7, 46–86, 88–92, 105–11, 135–37, 148–52, 158–59; and Central America, 30–33, 136–37, 164–65; and China, 98–99, 159; and France, 1–12, 22–23, 41, 64, 67, 95, 135–36, 140–41; and Greece, 25–28, 141–42, 162; and Japan, 138–40, 159; and Mexico, 30–32, 42–43, 86–87, 93–94, 109, 111–12, 114–16, 142–44, 160; and Netherlands, 138–39; and Peru, 144–47; and Spain, 96, 134–36
Foreign Relations Committee. *See* Committee on Foreign Relations

Forsyth, John, 51, 54, 96, 98
Fort Schlosser, 50, 84
Fox, Henry, 51–54, 62, 67, 84–85
France: and April decree, 11–12; and Cuba, 135–37; and extradition, 83, 182n57; and Hawaii, 140–41; and Napoleonic Wars, 3, 5–9; and Quintuple Treaty, 64; and slave trade, 22–23
Franklin, Benjamin, 69. *See also* red-line (Franklin) map
free trade, 33, 107, 113–14
Fryeburg, Maine, 3–4
fugitive slave law, 119, 122, 127, 157

Gallatin, Albert, 90
Garray grant, 142–43
Garray, José de, 142
George III (king of Great Britain and Ireland), 91
George's Island, 69
Ghent, 14–15, 33, 48–49, 162, 174–75n2
Gibbons v. Ogden, 17–18, 156, 162
Gladstone, William, 56
Globe (Washington), 90, 177n39
Glynn, James, 138
Goldsborough, Robert, 43–44
Gore, Christopher, 4, 10, 17, 20, 156, 161
Gorham, Benjamin, 25
Granville, Lord, 137
Grattan, Thomas, 73, 77–78
Great Triumvirate, ix, 10, 44, 119, 168n20
Greek War of Independence, 25–28, 162, 171n4
Greytown, 136–37
Griswold, George, 125
Grundy, Felix, 11
guano, 144–47, 165, 188n50. *See also* Lobos Islands

Hague court, 49, 73, 139
Haiti, 137
Halifax, 74
Hamilton, James, 74
Hargous, Louis, 142–43
Hargous, Peter, 142–43
Harrison, William Henry: and Berkeley Plantation, 59; and death of, 60, 163; and elections of 1836, 41–42, 45; and elections of 1840, 58–59; and presidency, 53, 59–60, 62, 98; and Webster appointment, 59, 102, 158, 163
Hartford Convention, 15, 18, 35, 41, 157, 169n32
Havana, Cuba, 95–96
Haven, Franklin, 114
Hawaii (Sandwich Islands): annexation of, 140–41, 163; and Christian missions, 97; and France, 97, 140–41, 159; and independence, 97–98, 159; and Kamehameha III, 97, 140–41; and trade with China, 97; and Tyler Doctrine, 137, 140, 159, 163; and US diplomacy with, 97–98, 140–41, 159, 163
Hayne, Robert Y., ix, 35–37, 39, 155, 162
Henderson, James Pinkney, 57
Herald (New York), 50, 133
Hermosa, 83
Hispaniola, 137, 159
Honduras, 136
Hone, Philip, 118
Hudson's Bay Company, 105
Hülsemann Letter, 127–30, 132–34, 164
Hülsemann, Chevalier J. G., 127–30, 132–34
Hungarian Revolution of 1848, 126–34
Hunter, William, 128, 147
Hunters' Lodge, 62

impressment, 8, 64, 79, 81–82, 88, 158, 180n14
independent treasury, 45–46
Independence Day addresses: first (1800), 3; second (1806), 5; third (1812), 8
Indian Removal Act, 43–44
Ingersoll, Charles J., 103, 112–14. *See also* McDuffie–Ingersoll joint resolution
Insurance Company of North America, 21
Irving, Washington, 59, 96
Isthmus of Tehuantepec, 142–43

Jackson, Andrew: and elections of 1824, 29; and elections of 1828, 34; and elections of 1832, 36; and elections of 1836, 40, 43, 45; and Florida incursion (First Seminole War), 19–20, 58, 60, 170n40; and Force Bill (1833), 39; and France, 41; and Indian Removal Act, 43–44; and Northeastern Boundary Dispute, 49; and nullification dispute, 37, 39; and opposition to National Bank, 36–37, 40, 45, 172n27; and presidency, 34, 36–37, 39–45, 49, 55; and South Carolina, 37, 39–40, and Specie Circular, 45; and tariff compromise, 39; and Texas independence, 43; and War of 1812, 15, 162
Jackson, Isaac, 59
Jacksonians, 31, 34, 59, 156
Jaudon, Samuel, 55–57
Jay map, 90
Jay, John, 90. *See also* Jay map; Jay's Treaty (1794)
Jay's Treat (1794), 4, 20, 83, 180n17
Jefferson map, 89
Jeffersonianism, 4
Jewett, James C., 144–48, 165
joint–squadron compromise, 82

Jones, Thomas ap Catesby, 94
Juan de Fuca Strait, 87

Kamehameha III (king of Hawaii), 97, 140–41
Kendall, George Wilkins, 93
Ketchum, Hiram, 56, 146
King George map, 91–92
King, Jonas, 141–42
King, Rufus, 10, 18
Kingdom of the Two Sicilies, 41
Kossuth, Louis, 126–28, 131–34, 165

La Jeune Eugenie (ship), 22, 95, 158
Lafayette, Marquis de, 30
Lake Champlain, 48, 69
Lake Huron, 69, 79
Lake of the Woods, 48–49, 79
Lake Superior, 69, 79
Lamar, Mirabeau, 93
Lawrence, Abbott, 130, 137, 152
Leopard, HMS, 5
LeRoy, Caroline, 35
Letcher, Robert, 142–44
Lewiston, New York, 52
Library of Congress, 89
Lima, 145–47
Liverpool, 56
Lobos Islands, 144–48, 153, 165
López, Narciso, 134–35, 165
Louisiana Territory, 20, 67
Louis Philippe (king of France), 57
Luriottis, Andreas, 26–27

Mackenzie, William Lyon, 50
MacLauchlan, James, 53
Macon's Bill No. 2, 7–9
Madawaska River, 66
Madison, James: and embargo, 12–13; and Enlistment Bill, 12–13; and Erskine Agreement, 6–7; and Macon's Bill No. 2, 7–9; and presidency, 6–15; and Rockingham

Memorial, 8; and War of 1812, 7–15, 114
Maine: and Aroostook War, 53–54; and Northeastern Boundary Dispute, 48–49, 53–55, 65–74, 76–78, 89, 92, 112, 117, 124, 148, 158, 175n3, 178 (nn47, 49), 179n5; and statehood, 18. *See also* Northeastern Boundary Dispute
Malmesbury, Lord, 152
Manifest Destiny, 116, 134, 140, 157
Mann, A. Dudley, 126–30
Maria Amalia (queen of France),
Marquesas Islands, 97
Marsh, George Perkins, 141–42
Marshall Court, 17, 156–57, 162
Marshall, John, *See* Marshall Court
Marshfield, Massachusetts, 101, 131, 143, 145, 147–50, 152, 165
Mason, Jeremiah, 10, 12
Massachusetts: and constitution, 18–19, 21; and Maine, 18, 49; Massachusetts State House, 18; Massachusetts Volunteers, 117–18; and Northeastern Boundary Dispute, 49, 67, 71–73, 78, 92, 112, 178n47; and nullification, 39; and slavery, 116, 127; and War of 1812, 48; Webster as senator of, 33, 35–36, 162–63; and Whig state convention (1847), 115; Whigs, 115, 127;
McCulloch v. Maryland, 17, 156, 162, 172n27
McDuffie, George, 31, 103. *See also* McDuffie–Ingersoll joint resolution
McDuffie–Ingersoll joint resolution, 103, 105
McGregor, James, 109
McIntire, Rufus, 53
McKean, John, 45
McLane, Louis, 31–33, 107, 109–11
McLeod, Alexander: McLeod Affair, 49, 51–53, 60, 62–63, 84, 86, 88, 112, 150, 158–59, 160, 163, 177n30; McLeod Law, 86
Mediator (ship), 58
Melbourne, Lord, 63
Mercury (Quebec), 51
Merrimack Valley, 2
Mersey River, 56
Mesabi range, 79
Mexican Cession, 115–19
Mexican–American War, 109, 111–12, 114–18, 142
Mexico: and Cuba, 32; and filibustering, 144; and Garray grant, 142–44; and isthmus of Tehuantepec, 142–44, 165; and Mexican–American War, 109, 111, 114–15, 164, 181n44; and New Mexico, 93; and San Francisco, 86; and Texas annexation, 42–43, 93, 104, 111; and Treaty of Guadalupe Hidalgo, 116, 125, 164; and US western expansion, 93, 109; and Webster–Ashburton Treaty, 93. *See also* Mexican–American War; foreign relations: and Mexico
Mier prisoners, 94
Milan decree, 9
Miles, William, 146–48, 165
Mills, Elijah, 33
Mississippi, 32, 43, 83
Missouri Compromise, 18, 117
Mitchell map, 47–48, 69, 71, 89, 90–91
Monroe Doctrine, 26, 96, 137, 159, 162
Monroe, James: and "Era of Good Feelings," 33; and First Seminole War, 20; and Greek War of Independence, 26; and *La Jeune Eugenie*, 22; and Monroe Doctrine, 26; and presidency, 17, 20, 22, 26; as secretary of state, 10, 12, 14; and slave trade, 22; and War of 1812, 10, 12, 14.

Monterey, California, 94
Morell, Benjamin, 146
Morse, Samuel F. B., 130–31
Mosquito Coast, 136
Mulligan, John, 71

Napoleonic Wars, 3, 5–11, 13–14, 20, 41, 161, 165, 168n11
Napoleon Bonaparte, 5–7, 11, 13–14, 20, 168n11. *See also* Napoleonic Wars
Nashville Convention, 119, 121
National Bank, 15, 36–37, 40, 45–46, 172n27. *See also* Bank of the United States; Bank War
National Hotel, 132
National Intelligencer (Washington), 132, 149
National Republican party, 156
Navy Island, 50–51
Netherlands, 138–39
Neutrality Act (1818), 50
New Brunswick, 48–49, 53–54, 66, 73–74, 76–78, 148, 158. *See also* Northeastern Boundary Dispute
New Echota Treaty, 43
New Hampshire: Federalists, 4; Old Whigs, 4; Republicans, 4; as Webster's birthplace, ix, 1–2, 4–6, 8, 12, 56, 59, 149, 161; Webster as congressman of, 15–16
New London, Connecticut, 4
New Mexico: and Compromise of 1850, 119–20, 123–24; and statehood, 119, 185n44; and Texas, 93–94, 119–20, 123–24; and Treaty of Guadalupe Hidalgo, 116. *See also* Compromise of 1850; Treaty of Guadalupe Hidalgo
New Orleans, Louisiana: and Battle of New Orleans, 14–15, 162; and *Creole* Affair, 65; and Cuba, 135; and *Picayune*, 93; Tehuantepec Company, 142

New York: and *Caroline* Affair, 51; and Compromise of 1850, 127; and *Gibbons v. Ogden*, 17; and Kossuth visit, 131; and McLeod Affair, 51–52, 60, 62–63, 112, 163; and Northeastern Boundary Dispute, 73; and Patriot War, 49–50; and War of 1812, 48
New York Historical Society, 89–90
New Zealand, 97
Niagara River, 50–51
Nicaragua, 136–37, 165
Niles' National Register (Baltimore), 72
Non–Intercourse Act (1809), 6–9, 13, 168n15
non–intervention policy, 27, 128, 131, 133–34, 157
North American Review (Boston), 26
Northeastern Boundary Dispute: and *Caroline* Affair, 50–53, 60, 62–63, 79, 84–86, 88, 158–59; and compromise proposals, 47–49, 53–55, 60, 65–67, 69–74, 76–80, 88–92, 99; and d'Anville maps, 69, 91; and Jay map, 90; and Jefferson map, 89; and King George map, 91–92; and Mitchell map, 47–48, 69, 71, 89, 90–91;and red–line (Franklin) map, 69, 71, 89–92; and Spark's map, 69–73, 76, 89–92; and Steuben map, 72; and trade agreement, 152
Northwest Ordinance of 1787, 18
no–transfer policy, 136
Nova Scotia, 48
Nueces River, 111, 116

Olympic Peninsula, 87
Onís, Don Luis de, 19–20. *See also* Adams–Onís Treaty (1819)
Opium War, 98
Ordinance of 1787, 18, 121
Oregon Question, ix, 79, 86–88, 100, 102, 105–11, 117, 138

Oregon Trail, 105
Oregon Treaty, 111, 114, 164
Osma, Juan Ygnacio de, 146–47
Oswald, Richard, 90–91
Ottoman Empire, 141

Pacific Northwest, 102, 106
Pakenham, Richard, 101, 103, 105–11
Palmer, Aaron Haight, 138
Palmerston, Lord, 56, 58, 62–64, 71, 91–92, 111, 137
Panama Congress of 1826, 30–33, 159, 162
Panama Resolution, 30–33
Panic of 1837, 45
Paris peace commission, 69, 71, 89–92, 148
Parker, Peter, 98
Peel, Robert, 56, 63–64, 67, 69, 81, 91–92, 105–6, 108–9
Peking, 98–99
Perry, Matthew Calbraith, 139–40, 152, 159, 165
Peru, 144–47, 165
Phillips Academy in Exeter, 2
Philomela, 144
Pinckney's Treaty of 1795, 19, 96
Pizarro, Francisco, 146
Poinsett, Joel, 27–28, 55
Polk, James Knox: and Cuba, 134; and elections of 1844, 102; and expansionism, 102; and inaugural address, 106; and Mexican–American War, 111, 114–15, 117; and Oregon Question, 106–9; and presidency, 105–6; and Tariff of 1842, 113
Portsmouth, Virginia, 5, 8, 12–17
Preble, William Pitt, 49, 73, 77–78
protectionism, 18, 28, 33–34, 113, 156–57
Prussia, 5, 27, 64, 83, 163, 165, 182n57
Puget Sound, 87, 138
Punch Brook Mill, 2

Quarterly Review (London), 109
Quebec, 48, 74
Quintuple Treaty, 64, 82, 179–80n14

Randolph, John, 28–29
red–line (Franklin) map, 69, 71, 89–92
Remedial Justice Act, 63, 159
right of search, 79, 81, 179–80n14
Rio Grande, 111
Robinson, Solon, 145
Rockingham County, New Hampshire, 8
Rockingham Memorial, 8–10, 156, 161
Rocky Mountain, 48, 79
Ross, John, 43
Rouses Point, 48, 69, 76, 78
Royal Agricultural Society, 56–57, 163
Royal Navy, 79, 81. *See also* impressment
Russell, Lord John, 62, 109
Russell, Jonathan, 10–11
Rutland, Duke of, 57

Salisbury, New Hampshire, 1–4, 27, 161
San Diego, 102, 116, 138
San Francisco, 86–88, 138
St. Croix River, 48
St. George's Island, 69, 79
St. John River, 49, 69, 76
St. John Valley, 54, 74
St. Lawrence River, 74
San Juan de Nicaragua River, 136
San Juan del Norte, 136–37
Sandwich Islands. *See* Hawaii
Santa Anna, Antonio Lopez de, 42
Santa Fe, 93, 123
Sargent, Nathan, 126
Savannah, Georgia, 116
Scott, Walter, 83
Scott, Winfield, x, 44, 51, 54, 62, 65–66
Sears, David, 107
Seminoles, 19–20. *See also* First Seminole War

Senate Finance Committee, 41
Seventh of March speech, 120–24, 155, 158
Severance, Luther, 140–41, 164
Seward, William, 60, 62–63, 150, 188n64
Seymour, Sir George, 106
Shelburne, Lord, 71
Short Street School, 26
Sims, Thomas, 157
Sino–American relations, 98–99, 159
slavery: and *Amistad*, 95–96; and Compromise of 1850, 127; and *Creole* Affair, 63–65, 81–83; and expansionism, 42, 93, 103–4, 115–22, 127, 174n44; and Mexican Cession, 115–19; opinions on, 42, 104, 120–22, 157; and Texas, 42, 103–4, 174n44; Webster on, 18, 23, 42, 95, 104, 120–22, 157–58
slave trade, 21–23, 63–64, 79, 81–84, 88, 95, 119, 157–58, 179–80n14
Slidell, John, 111
Smith, Albert, 71–72
Smith, Francis O. J. ("Fog"), 66–67, 72
Smith, Sarah, 153
Soulé, Pierre, 150
South Carolina: and Ordinance of Nullification, 37, 39; and threat of secession, 37, 39–40, 128
Spain: and *Amistad*, 96; and Cuba, 32, 134–36; and First Seminole War, 19–20; and Floridas, 3; and Haiti, 134; and Pinckney's Treaty of 1795, 19–20. *See also* foreign relations: and Spain
Sparks map, 69–73, 76, 89–92. *See also* Sparks, Jared
Sparks, Jared, 69–73, 76, 91–92, 113. *See also* Sparks map
Specie Circular, 45–46
Spencer, Joshua, 62, 112, 177n30
Spencer, Lord, 57

Sprague, Peleg, 71–72
State Paper Office, 71, 91
Steuben, Friedrich von, 71. *See also* Steuben map
Steuben map, 72. *See also* Steuben, Friedrich von
Stevenson, Andrew, 63–64
Stockton, Robert, 22–23
Story, Joseph, 22–23, 31, 33–35, 84, 95
Stuart, Moses, 101–2
Stubbs, Edward, 112–13
Sumner, Charles, ix, 157
Sutter's Mill, 116, 118
Swann House, 101
Supreme Court, US, 17, 62, 83, 95, 104, 120, 155–56. *See also* Marshall Court

Taney, Roger, 40
Tappan, Arthur, 103
Tappan, Benjamin, 103
Tappan, Lewis, 103
tariff, 15, 18–19, 28, 33–39, 102, 107, 113–14, 157
Tariff of 1842, 113–14
Taylor, Zachary: and California statehood, 118–19; and death of, 122, 164; and elections of 1848, 116; and Hungarian Revolution of 1848, 126–29; and Mexican–American War, 111; and presidency, 118–19, 126–29, 164
Tehuantepec Treaty, 144, 164–65
Texas: and annexation, 42–43, 93, 100–105, 111, 120–21, 164, 174n44; and Compromise of 1850, 119–20, 123–24; and New Mexico, 93–94, 119–20, 123–24; Republic of, 43, 57; and slavery, 42, 103–4, 174n44
Thompson, Thomas, 2–4
Thompson, Waddy, 86–87, 93–94, 96
Three–Million Bill, 115–16
Ticknor, George, 1, 19, 128, 153

Times (London), 62, 109
Tirado, José Manuel, 145
Trail of Tears, 44
trans–isthmian railroad, 142
Treaty of Guadalupe Hidalgo, 116–18, 125, 142–44, 164, 185n1
Treaty of Nanking, 98, 163
Treaty of Paris (1783), 47–48, 92, 148
Treaty of Wanghia, 99, 159
Tripartite proposal: and Oregon Question, 87; and Cuba,136–37
Trist, Nicholas, 116–18, 142
Trustees of Dartmouth College v. William H. Woodward, 17, 156
Tyler Doctrine, 97–98, 100, 137–40, 159, 163–64
Tyler, John: and China, 98–99; and *Creole* Affair, 65, 84; and Cuba, 96; and elections of 1844, 99–100, 105; on expansionism, 93; and Hawaii, 97; and Mexican–American War, 94; and Northeastern Boundary Dispute, 66; and political party affiliation, 99; and presidency, 60, 64–66, 75, 77, 84–85, 93–105, 163; and Quintuple Treaty, 64–65; on slavery, 65; and Texas annexation, 100, 103, 105; and Tyler Doctrine, 97–98, 100, 137–40, 159, 163–64; and Webster–Ashburton Treaty, 75, 77, 84–85; and Webster's impeachment hearing, 113; and Webster's resignation, 99–100

US Navy, 137, 140, 145
University College, Oxford, 57
Upshur, Abel, 103, 183n5

Vail, Aaron, 96
Valley Forge, 104
Van Buren, Martin: and *Caroline* Affair, 51; and Court of St. James's, 37; and elections of 1836, 45; and elections of 1840, 58–59; and elections of 1844, 102; and independent treasury, 45–46; and McLeod Affair, 52–53; and Neutrality Act (1818), 50; and Northeastern Boundary Dispute, 50–55; and Panic of 1837, 45; and presidency, 43, 45; on tariffs, 34; and Webster, 55, 173n29
Van Rensselaer, Henry K., 50
Vancouver Island, 105, 108
Vergennes, Comte de, 69
Vermillion range, 79
Versailles, 57
Victoria (Oregon Territory), 105
Victoria (queen of the United Kingdom), 56, 67

Walker Tariff, 113–14
Walker, Robert, 113–114
War of 1812, 7–15, 35, 48–49, 148, 156, 162
Ward, Thomas Wren, 41, 56, 102
Warspite (ship), 72
Washington Benevolent Society, 8
Washington Treaty (1842). *See* Webster–Ashburton Treaty
Webster, Abigail, 1, 4
Webster, Daniel: 20th century influence, 159; on Bank War, ix, 15, 36–37; birth and childhood of, 2–3; as "Black Dan," 112, 155; and campaign for presidency, 40–42, 45, 116, 132–33, 156; as chair of Judiciary Committee, 25; as congressman, 10, 13–15, 22, 25–33; as constitutional scholar, 19, 23, 31–32, 36–37, 39, 54–55, 105, 117, 122, 140, 156; and death of, 153; as diplomat, 66, 75–100, 127–153, 158–60; and education of, 2–3; essays and pamphlets by, 3, 6; on expansionism, 93, 116, 157; and family, 1–5, 12, 15–17, 33–35,

117–18, 169n25; as a Federalist, 33; and foreign policy, x, 23, 27; on free trade, 28; and "Great Triumvirate," ix, 10, 44, 119, 168n20; on Hungarian Revolution of 1848, 128; and impeachment hearing, 113; on independent treasury, 45; on Indian Removal Act, 43–44; and legal practice of, 4–5, 19–23, 28–29, 41, 156, 160; on Macon's Bill No. 2, 8–9; on Mexican–American War, 115; and nationalism, 3, 17, 92, 156–57; and Northeastern Boundary Dispute, 69, 71–74, 90–92; as orator, x, 3, 5, 18–19, 27, 30, 32, 35–36, 54, 56–57, 101–2, 107, 114–15, 120, 122, 130, 132, 155–56, 160; and personal finances, 29, 46, 55–57, 59, 102–3, 112, 125, 157; and political opponents, 92–93, 112–13, 125; on protectionism, 18–19, 28, 33–34, 39, 113, 156–57; and "second reply to Hayne," 35–36, 162; as secretary of state, x, 53–54, 59–60, 62, 64, 66, 73–100, 122–153, 158; as senator, 33–37, 39–40, 42–46, 102–22; on slavery, 18, 23, 42, 95, 104, 120–22, 157; on slave trade, 158; on Specie Circular, 45–46; and Supreme Court, 17; on tariffs, 28, 33–37, 39; and teaching career, 3–4; on Texas annexation, 104–5; and trip to Europe, 46, 56–57; on War of 1812, 7–15

Webster, Ebenezer, 1–4
Webster, Edward, 117–18
Webster, Fletcher, 12, 30, 59, 118, 164, 169n25
Webster, Grace (daughter), 12, 16, 169n25
Webster, Grace (wife), 5, 12, 15, 17, 33–35
Webster, Julia, 102, 118, 153
Webster–Ashburton Treaty, 69–93, 100, 158–59, 163, 182n57
Wellington, Duke of, 56
westward expansion, 87–88, 93, 157
Wheaton, Henry, 41, 173n37
Whig party, 40–42, 45, 58–60, 101–5, 107, 115–17, 122, 127, 156, 181n41
White, Hugh Lawson, 45
Willamette Valley, 105
William I (king of the Netherlands), 49, 71
Williams, Reuel, 72
Wilmot Proviso, 115–16, 121
Wilmot, David, 115–16
Wood, Samuel, 2

Yancey, William Lowndes, 112
Yulee, David Levy, 134–35

About the Author

Donald A. Rakestraw is university college professor of history at Winthrop University and professor emeritus at Georgia Southern University. Among his numerous publications on nineteenth-century American history and US foreign relations are *For Honor or Destiny: The Anglo-American Crisis over the Oregon Territory* and *Prologue to Manifest Destiny: Anglo-American Relations in the 1840s* (with Howard Jones). He has delivered countless lectures on Anglo-American relations and the history of US foreign relations in both the United States and the United Kingdom.

CPSIA information can be obtained
at www.ICGtesting.com
Printed in the USA
LVHW052025060519
616799LV00009B/130/P